John Warwick Montgomery

**Fighting the Good Fight:
A Life in Defense of the Faith**

Christliche Philosophie heute – Christian Philosophy Today – Quomodo Philosophia Christianorum Hodie Estimatur

Volume 17

Vol. 1: John Warwick Montgomery. Tractatus Logico-Theologicus.
Vol. 2: John W. Montgomery. Hat die Weltgeschichte einen Sinn? Geschichtsphilosophien auf dem Prüfstand.
Vol. 3: John W. Montgomery. Jésus: La raison rejoint l'histoire.
Vol. 4: Horst Waldemar Beck. Marken dieses Äons: Wissenschaftskritische und theologische Diagnosen.
Vol. 5: Ross Clifford. John Warwick Montgomery's Legal Apologetic: An Apologetic for All Seasons.
Vol. 6: Thomas K. Johnson. Natural Law Ethics: An Evangelical Proposal.
Vol. 7: Lydia Jaeger. Wissenschaft ohne Gott? Zum Verhältnis zwischen christlichem Glauben und Wissenschaft.
Vol. 8: Herman Bavinck. Christliche Weltanschauung. hrsg. von Thomas K. Johnson und Ron Kubsch.
Vol. 9: John W. Montgomery. La Mort de Dieu: Exposé et critique du plus récent mouvement théologique en Amérique: Réimpression de l'édition 1971.
Vol. 10: David Andersen. Martin Luther – The Problem of Faith and Reason: A Reexamination in Light of the Epistemological and Christological Issues.
Vol. 11: Wim Rietkerk. In dubio: Handbuch für Zweifler.
Vol. 12: Patrick Werder: Wenig niedriger als Gott: Der Mensch als Person von der Antike bis zur Gegenwart.
Vol. 13: John Warwick Montgomery: Christ As Centre and Circumference: Essays Theological, Cultural and Polemic.
Vol. 14: Lydia Jaeger. Als Mensch in Gottes Welt: Im Licht der Schöpfung leben.
Vol. 15: Frederik Herzberg. Theo-Logik: Über den Beitrag des Jansenismus zur formalen Methode in Theologie und Religionsphilosophie.
Vol. 16: Hanniel Strebel. Eine Theologie des Lernens: Systematisch-theologische Beiträge aus dem Werk von Herman Bavinck.
Vol. 17: John Warwick Montgomery. Fighting the Good Fight – A Life in Defense of the Faith.
Vol. 18: Henry Hock Guan Teh. Principles of the Law of Evidence and Rationality Applied in the Johannine Christology: An Argument for the Legal Evidential Apologetics.
Vol. 19: John Warwick Montgomery. Defending the Gospel in Legal Style – Essays on Legal Apologetics & the Justification of Classical Christian Faith.
Vo. 20: S. Ross Hickling. An Evidentiary Analysis of Doctor Richard Carrier's Objections to the Resurrection of Jesus Christ.
Vol. 21: John Warwick Montgomery. Tractatus Logico-Theologicus. (French Edition / Édition française.)
Vol. 22: John Warwick Montgomery. Theology: Good, Bad, and Mysterious – A Theological and Apologetical Potpourri.

John Warwick Montgomery

Fighting the Good Fight:
A Life in Defense of the Faith

WIPF & STOCK · Eugene, Oregon

Wipf and Stock Publishers
199 W 8th Ave, Suite 3
Eugene, OR 97401

Fighting the Good Fight, 3rd and Enlarged Edition
A Life in Defense of the Faith
By Montgomery, John Warwick
Copyright © 2020 Verlag für Kultur und Wissenschaft
Culture and Science Publ. All rights reserved.
Softcover ISBN-13: 978-1-7252-8967-3
Publication date 10/23/2020
Previously published by Verlag für Kultur und Wissenschaft
Culture and Science Publ., 2020

For Kurt and Debra Winrich
without whose consistent support the life here
recorded would have had immensely less impact

Contents

Introduction 13

Chapter 1
Name and Lineage 17

Chapter 2
Childhood Recollections (1931–1948) 22

Chapter 3
Cornell University and Conversion (1948–1952) 29

Chapter 4
Far-West, Mid-West, and Canada (1952–1963) 37

Chapter 5
First Encounter with France; Trinity
Evangelical Divinity School (1963–1974) 47

Chapter 6
Seminars, Debates and Tours 61

Chapter 7
The Jealous Mistress of the Law:
Washington, D.C.; Life Among the Charismatics:
Southern California (1974–1980) 71

Chapter 8
Legal Eagling and the Simon
Greenleaf School of Law (1980–1987) 79

Chapter 9
Annus Horribilis and New Beginnings (1988–1991) 88

Chapter 10
Merrie Olde Englande (1991–1996) 102

Chapter 11
La Belle France (1997–) 114

Chapter 12
Present and Future 134

APPENDICES

1. Likes and Dislikes 148
2. Le Comte de St Germain de Montgommery 153
3. Autobiographical Letter by John Warwick Montgomery,
   the Author's Great Grandfather 155
4. Biographical Article on
   Maurice Warwick Montgomery,
   the Author's Father 167
5. John Warwick Montgomery's
   Maternal Grandmother, Flora Wellman Watrous 169
6. John Warwick Montgomery
   as a callow youth 174
7. Teaching New Testament Greek at the
   Revd Dr Don Deffner's University Lutheran
   Chapel, Berkeley, California (18 April 1954) 175
8. Preaching Assignments During
   a Year at the Hamma Divinity School 176
9. James Lutzweiler, Archivist,
   on John Warwick Montgomery 177
10. Professor Don Morgenson
    on John Warwick Montgomery 182
11. The Paris Latin Quarter During
    the "Days of May," 1968 184
12. Flyers for the "Defending the Biblical
    Gospel" and "Practical Christian Living" Seminars 185

13. Tour Brochures 189
14. Israel Photos: One with Halvor
    Ronning, the Others with a Camel 194
15. Typical Activities at the Simon
    Greenleaf School of Law 196
16. Letter of the Revd Pomeroy Moore
    on the Simon Greenleaf Crisis 202
17. Cross-Examinations in the
    Central Lutheran Church Case 203
18. The Old School House, Lidlington, Bedfordshire 218
19. The Bessarabian Church Case at the
    European Court of Human Rights 219
20. Appointment as Emeritus Professor,
    University of Bedfordshire 235
21. International Academy of Apologetics,
    Evangelism and Human Rights, Strasbourg, France 236
22. Jean-Marie Montgomery's Fathers' Day Poem, 2009 238
23. So You Think Becoming a Barrister is Difficult? 239
24. Preaching at the Christmas Service,
    2010, at the Marseilles Cathedral 245
25. Congratulations: John Warwick Montgomery's
    Contributions to Religious Freedom Advocacy 246
26. Poetical Contribution to *Enchantons la Vie* 249
27. Photo Album 251
Index of Names and Places 281

"He who lives more lives than one, more deaths than one must die"
—Oscar Wilde, *The Ballad of Reading Gaol*

"Living well is the best revenge"
—George Herbert, 1593-1633
(English clergyman & metaphysical poet)

"We know that all things work together for good to them that love God, to them who are called according to his purpose. ... What shall we then say to these things? If God be for us, who can be against us? He that spared not his own Son, but delivered him up for us all, how shall be not with him also freely give us all things?"
—Romans 8: 28-32

Introduction

Autobiography is a dangerous business. There is the overarching temptation to self-justification ("*now* I'll have the last word!").[1] There is also the opportunity to reveal the worst about others. I was much impressed by a dinner table comment of Dr Harold Lindsell, sometime editor of *Christianity Today* magazine (we had weekly dinners together on the night Harold taught at my Simon Greenleaf School of Law); said he, "I'll never write my autobiography: I know too much dirt on my fellow evangelicals." And so, sadly, he didn't leave us with an account of his many-faceted life.

The book to follow makes no pretence of avoiding these errors. I have postponed writing it for a very long time—the chief reason being that though I love to discuss issues, I am uncomfortable discussing myself. It has always been a source of embarrassment for me when, in a question-and-answer session following one of my public lectures, the questioner says: "Now tell us about yourself—how you have accomplished so much." What has finally pushed me to get down to my autobiography is the magnificent Festschrift recently published in my honour and edited by Drs Dembski and Schirrmacher.[2] If they (and the numerous contributors to that volume) went to such trouble in my behalf, I myself can hardly refuse to say a little something about my life and career.

And if the result seems too much what lawyers call "self-serving," let me go on record at the very outset. Whatever good has come about is to be attributed, not to me but to the God of all grace: *soli gloria Deo*—the phrase with which so many writers during the centu-

---

[1] I think immediately of presuppositionalist and evangelical philosopher Gordon Clark, whose last work (published posthumously) was titled, *Clark Speaks from the Grave*. This gave Clark the opportunity to stick it to the present author for his evidentialist approach to defending the faith. But Dr Clark was a gentleman in every sense (even taking his last book into account)—a far cry from such presuppositionalists as Greg Bahnsen (properly and thoroughly refuted by Gary Habermas in the Festschrift cited in the following footnote).

[2] *Tough-Minded Christianity: Honoring the Legacy of John Warwick Montgomery,* ed. William Dembski and Thomas Schirrmacher (Nashville, TN: B&H, 2008).

ries preceding the modern secular era began or ended their books.³ Or, putting it more eloquently, in the words of the Third Article of Martin Luther's *Shorter Catechism*:

> "I believe that I cannot of my own understanding and strength believe in or come to Jesus Christ my Lord, but that the Holy Ghost has called me by the Gospel, and illuminated me with His gifts, and sanctified and preserved me in the true faith, just as He calls, gathers together, illuminates, sanctifies, and preserves in Jesus Christ all Christendom throughout the earth in the one true faith; in which Christendom He daily bestows abundantly on me and all believers forgiveness of sins; and on the last day He will awaken me and all the dead, and will give to me and all that believe in Christ eternal life. This is most certainly true."

It should be noted at the very outset that this autobiography, though containing a fair number of scholarly and semi-scholarly notes, is not the result of my researches in the John Warwick Montgomery Archives, previously located at Syracuse University and now permanently residing at Southeastern Baptist Theological Seminary (owing to the good offices of its distinguished former archivist, James Lutzweiler). The footnotes in the present book are due to my love of and penchant for footnotes as such.⁴ I leave it to future biographers to plumb the depths of the Archive collection, correcting, if necessary, any *lapsus memoriae* contained in what I have written here on the basis of my recollections and the materials easily accessible in my personal library at our home in France.

Finally, I trust that the frequent mention in this book of famous (or notorious) people with whom I have had contact will not be considered *de trop*. One recalls the story of the inveterate name-dropper to whom a friend finally declared, in desperation, "You cannot seem to open your mouth without telling about some important person

---

³ We shall have more to say of this in our final chapter.
⁴ Cf. Anthony Grafton, *The Footnote: A Curious History* (London: Faber and Faber, 2003).

you've just been with." To which the name-dropper replied: "It's funny you should say that. At Buckingham Palace last week, that's exactly what the Queen said to me."

JWM

Easter: The Festival of the Resurrection
Anno Domini 2015

Chapter 1

NAME AND LINEAGE

There is the story (originally told to me by my mother) of the fellow with the name *André Poubelle*—in French, "garbage can." In France, unlike the situation in Anglo-Saxon common-law countries, one can only change one's name by court action. After much procedural difficulty, the right was granted. Result: the gentleman became *Sébastien* Poubelle.

Contrary to the implication of this story (doubtless more appropriate in a vaudeville performance at the Players' Theatre in London than to an autobiography), the surname has an importance today not carried by the first or Christian name. True, this can go too far: the legal philosopher Alan Gewirth rightly criticises one who thinks that because he is named "Wordsworth Donisthorpe" he has rights per se which others do not have.[1] We do not go to that length, but we do see special value in the Montgomery connection.

The earliest of the celebrated Montgomerys was Comte Roger de Montgommery (11th century), companion in arms to William the Conqueror.[2] William granted him extensive lands in recognition of his having sustained the Norman holdings in France during the first phase of the Conquest. From England and Wales, the Montgomerys

---

[1] See my critiques of Neo-Kantian human rights theories in my *Tractatus Logico-Theologicus* and *Christ Our Advocate*. For bibliographical information on my publications cited throughout the present work, see the comprehensive bibliography of my works by Will Moore included in the Festschrift edited by Dembski and Schirrmacher (noted in the Introduction, *supra*).

[2] The Montgomerys, as Norman nobility, came from Viking stock (thus my standard comment that whereas others collect stamps as a hobby, we Montgomerys engage in raping and pillaging). The standard history of the family is that by a Swedish count, B. G. de Montgomery: *Origin and History of the Montgomerys* (Edinburgh: William Blackwood, 1948). In a series of programmes on the Normans, presented by Professor Robert Bartlett on BBC 2 (August, 2010), great stress was placed on the following Norman characteristics: the warrior spirit, energy, controlling leadership, impatience, goal-oriented commitment, vision, Christian piety combined with intimidation and ruthlessness, aesthetic refinement (the Norman abbeys). I leave it to the reader to decide if these qualities have been genetically passed on to the author.

17

Chapter 1

established themselves in Scotland, and at the time of the Plantation of Ulster (early 17th century), many settled in County Antrim and County Down. This was true of the branch of the family of which Sir Bernard Montgomery of Alamein was the most famous 20th century representative.[3]

It was also true of John Warwick Montgomery's family.[4] From the little townland of Ballywoodock near Ballymena, County Antrim, my great grandfather, for whom I was named, immigrated to America during one of the dreadful mid-19th century Irish potato famines.[5] He sailed on the Brooksby, a 500 tonner built in 1843, which made regular sailings from Glasgow to New York. John's vessel departed for New York on Friday, 5 April 1850, but had to return to port and finally sailed on Tuesday, 9 April. On 14 May it was waiting off New York and docked on 16 May.[6] John is mentioned in the passenger records for the vessel maintained by the American immigration authorities. He settled in Warsaw, New York,[7] married another Irish immigrant (Rose Ann—or Anna—Crawford) on 9 February 1860,

---

[3] We are personally acquainted with those celebrated Montgomerys. Indeed, Lady Montgomery (the wife of Sir Bernard's son) recommended my wife Lanalee for membership in the (U.K.) Overseas Women's Club.

[4] The second Christian name ("Warwick"), given to the male members of our family, comes from the Antrim-county Warwick family with which the Montgomerys intermarried. On a visit to the area, I discovered that the present-day Montgomerys are tall and thin, whilst the Warwicks are short and stocky; clearly the Montgomery genes have predominated. It is also worth noting that, even though the Warwicks, like the Montgomerys, probably came to Northern Ireland from Scotland, they are totally unrelated to the obnoxious crocodile Warwick in André Hodeir and Tomi Ungerer's children's book, *Warwick's 3 Bottles* (New York: Grove Press, 1966 [also in German and French translation]).

[5] For the genealogical chart of the family, see the royal grant of arms to the present author as recorded at the College of Arms, London.

[6] These data were obtained from *Lloyds List* and *Lloyds Register of Shipping*; I consulted the records at the London Guildhall Library.

[7] He is listed, age 23, in the 17 August 1850 Warsaw census as living in a boarding house. The standard history of Warsaw is: Andrew W. Young, *History of the Town of Warsaw, New York, from Its First Settlement to the Present Time* (Buffalo, New York: Sage, 1869). No one knows why the town was named "Warsaw" (it was not due to Polish immigration or influence, though we certainly would not mind if it were!).

and practiced the trade of selling and repairing shoes.[8] He would never again see his parents or other Northern Irish relations in this life.

His son, my paternal grandfather James Franklin Montgomery established a lumber, coal and animal feed business in Warsaw, and my father (Maurice Warwick Montgomery) and uncle (James Montgomery) later divided and ran those businesses. I was born in Warsaw in the midst of the Great Depression (1931). In 1991, I returned to my roots in the United Kingdom.

Warsaw is a small town, the County seat of Wyoming County. It is located roughly the same distance (some 40 miles) from both Buffalo and Rochester. My family avoided Buffalo like the plague, owing to its industrialisation: one thinks of the "dark Satanic mills" in William Blake's poem, *Jerusalem*; and it is a clear case of temporal judgment that Prometheus Press, the atheistic/free thought publication house, should be located there. When my mother took me to the big city for shopping, it was always Rochester—where, incidentally, my second wife and professional harpist Lanalee de Kant would receive her training at the University of Rochester's Eastman School of Music. The winters in Warsaw were very severe in the 1930's: I remember our having to clear the snow in order even to open the front door of the house, and as a child I recall being able to make snow houses big enough to sit in by tunneling in the snow drifts. Warsaw lies in a valley between two steep hills, and lorries coming down the east hill were often unaware of the severe gradient, and would regularly smash into a particular house at the bottom of the hill. The owner

---

[8] The present author's great grandfather was a strong Christian believer, his faith deriving from his solid Presbyterian background in Northern Ireland. The surviving handwritten autobiographical account of his life is photographically reproduced in the Appendix, *infra*, together with his obituary notices and two touching handwritten documents by his sister Ann Jane who predeceased him and is mentioned in his autobiographical narrative. The history of the church in which my great grandfather grew up in County Antrim was written by one of my relatives, Francis J. Montgomery: *A Short History of Second Donegore Presbyterian Church, 1788–1988* (privately published by the church in 1988); it is a very scholarly piece of work. Francis and his sister May assisted me greatly in genealogical research on the members of our family who did not emigrate but remained in Ulster. Montgomery & Murdock Hardware in Ballymena is owned by Northern Irish members of our family.

finally erected a reinforced concrete wall in front of his house so that the trucks would glance off it (and presumably crash into someone else's house farther along the street).

In recognition of the Northern Irish connections of the family, I have been granted arms by the Queen through the office of the Norroy and Ulster King of Arms of the Royal College of Arms. I also hold the feudal lordship of Morris's, once possessed by the father of Lord Chancellor and scientific philosopher Francis Bacon; the barony of Kiltartan in Ireland (made famous by poet Lady Gregory); and I am Comte de Saint-Germain de Montgommery, on the basis of land holdings in the Norman French territory from which Comte Roger de Montgomery came to England at the time of the Conquest. A few words about these titles should not be out of place.

Baron of Kiltartan

The Barony of Kiltartan, County Galway, Ireland, was granted to me by Francis Arthur John French, 7th Baron de Freyne of Coolavin, County Roscommon, in the Peerage of the United Kingdom. Lord de Frayne's ancestor, like my ancestor Comte Roger de Montgomery, attended William the Conqueror; de Frayne is said to have descended from Rollo, first Duke of Normandy, who married Gisla, daughter of Charles the Simple, King of France, in 912. To correspond with the subdivision of the English shires into Honors or Baronies, Irish counties were granted out to the Anglo-Norman nobility in cantreds ("territories") or precincts, later designated, as in England, Honors of Baronies. This was true of Kiltartan, which lies in the south of the County of Galway, bordering Galway Bay in the west and County Clare in the south.

Lord of Morris's

This manor, situated in the Suffolk parish of Great Waldingfield, was held at the time of the Domesday survey by Richard, Earl of Gislebert, i. e., de Clare. After various private ownerships in the medieval period, by 1474 the manor had returned to the Crown. During the 16th century the Lordship again passed through several hands, the most distinguished of which were those of Sir Francis Bacon's father Sir Nicholas Bacon; in 1559, Sir Nicholas was made Lord Keeper of the

Great Seal, becoming, in effect, the Lord Chancellor of England. He was, like myself, a convinced Protestant. The Bacons sold Morris's to one Ambrose Kedington in 1764; Kedington's father Roger was a preacher and defender of orthodox Christianity (cf. his 1753 tract, *On the Folly of Heathenism*). Like myself, he was an apologist; unlike myself, he ended his life in a state of insanity! The Lordship remained in the Kedington family until 1830, with a subsequent clear chain of title to my present ownership of it.

Comte de St Germain de Montgommery

The title was researched by Burke's Peerage and verified by the Conseil Français d'Héraldique—my arms being recorded in the *Armorial du IIIème Millénaire*, Fascicule No. 28, Planche No. 134. I thus became the present-day recipient of the title first held by William the Conqueror's companion-in-arms Roger de Montgomery. Two Normandy villages retain the Montgomery name: Ste Foi de Montgommery and St Germain de Montgommery. I have transferred ownership of my Norman land in the region to my son, Jean-Marie, who will one day inherit the title.[9]

*****

A word of laudation for the Montgomery heritage is a fitting conclusion to this chapter:

> Nous voici arrivés à l'une des familles les plus rudement guerrières du moyen âge. La chevalerie née avec Roland, morte avec Bayard, n'a pas de représentans plus illustres. En France, en Angleterre, en Palestine, partout où il se remue quelque chose de considerable, on retrouve un Montgommery. ... La branche de cette famille subsistante en Angleterre se signala toujours par ce caractère d'entreprise, de courtoisie et de brillante valeur particulier à toute sa race. ...[10]

---

[9] A French news article pertaining to the title, with photograph of the family, appears in the Appendix, *infra*.
[10] L'Abbé d'Ormancey de Fréjacques, *Illustrations de la noblesse européenne* (Paris, 1848), pp. 57, 75 (art. "Montgommery").

Chapter 2

CHILDHOOD RECOLLECTIONS (1931–1948)

What one remembers from early childhood is always fragmentary. The following items will thus necessarily have a kind of stream-of-consciousness quality about them (though, hopefully, not with the dark ambiguities present in James Joyce's *Ulysses*).

Pneumonia as a baby left its mark: severe asthma. (Interestingly, my adopted son Jean-Marie also suffered as a child from asthma.) In my case, the asthma entailed an allergic reaction to animal odours. Since my father was the owner of Warsaw's retail animal feed mill, I turned out to be allergic to my father—*not* in the Freudian sense, I hasten to add.[1] Our house on West Court Street was necessarily impregnated with animal smells, so the decision was made that I should live across town, on Brooklyn Street, with my maternal grandmother, Flora Wellman Watrous. She deserves considerable attention here.

My grandmother had married Fred Rodell Smith, an insurance salesman; he died, tragically young, run over by an automobile.[2] (This was not a common demise, considering the small number of autos on the roads in those days, but no less tragic.) The one offspring of that marriage was my mother, Harriette Genevieve.[3] Much later,

---

[1] The detailed biographical entry for my father in John Theodore Horton, Edward T. Williams, and Harry S. Douglass, *History of Northwestern New York* (3 vols.; New York: Lewis Historical Publishing Co., 1947), III, 456-57, is reproduced as an Appendix, *infra*. My father had intended to go into medicine and spent a semester at Cornell, two years at the University of Buffalo, and a summer session at Alfred University, but he never completed his premedical studies (transcripts in the Montgomery archives). When he retired, he sold the feed mill; then, on May 3, 1979, it burned to the ground, seemingly through arson. I believe that my father had wished that I continue the family business, but that was obviously impossible, considering my history of asthma—and my own academic inclinations.

[2] Their wedding photograph is included in the Appendix, *infra*, together with the August 4, 1921, newspaper article from the *Wyoming County Times* concerning Fred Rodell Smith's accidental death.

[3] Apparently, the first college graduate in our immediate family; she received her

my grandmother married again, but it was not a happy experience. I vaguely remember Guy Watrous—bald as the proverbial billiard ball and unable to cope with the presence of a small child (me). He died a few years later and my grandmother, though sought after by a fine and eligible gentleman, had had enough: she never married again.

Flora was a member of the small, fundamentalist Baptist church on Main Street. I remember being taken to a few Sunday evening services there—which frightened me half to death. The preacher would name sinners from the pulpit, and I was always expecting to be the next one caught out. When my mother married, she began attending my father's church, where I was baptised as an infant. That church had been Presbyterian until it entered into a very early local ecumenical union (prior to the days of grand denominational unions) with the local Congregational church, forming the "United Church of Warsaw." Those two churches had relatively little doctrinal rigour prior to the union; after it, there was zero—if any—historic Christianity left. My mother was certainly a believer; as for my father, I am not really sure. He was a third-degree master Mason, but this never seemed to be more than a social connection for him. He was a morally upstanding man in every respect, but I could never get him to discuss religion. Toward the time of his death, he was present at lectures I gave, but I could not make out to what extent he agreed or disagreed with them. It is clear that he would have wished me to be more of an outdoor type, but the asthma finished that off. My younger (and only) sister Mary lived at home, and my father's relationship with her was understandably much stronger than his with me.

When my grandmother's first husband was suddenly run over by a car, she herself took over his insurance agency—with great success. With only a normal school certificate, she had been a teacher in a one-room school —1st to 8th grade—but she possessed a very strong personality (it was said that she controlled and disciplined 8th grade

---

Bachelor of Arts degree from Cornell University in 1923 (her college transcript is preserved in the Montgomery Archives). It was therefore natural that I should myself attend Cornell. My mother also obtained an elementary and secondary school teaching certificate, as well as a certificate in special education for the teaching of mentally handicapped children; she taught briefly in the Warsaw Central Schools prior to her marriage.

Chapter 2

boys bigger than she was).[4] So effective was her salesmanship that when she grew too old to continue and attempted to resign, the Penn Mutual Life Insurance Company refused to accept her resignation: they said that her work had been so stellar that she would continue to represent the company in Wyoming County as long as she lived.

Flora's driving became a local legend. My mother had taught her to drive in the days when no driving licences were necessary. The story is that at a first attempt she drove right through the back of her garage, and my mother (following the approach of pilots involved in crash landings) insisted that she get right back into her car and try again. I remember a wondrous Minstrel Show (*confound* the politically-correct who brought about their end!), in which one of the End Men remarked, "Ah saw Mis Watrous come down the East Hill, go right through the red light, and up the West Hill." Interlocutor: "Wasn't she caught by the police?" End Man: "Sure was. The policeman, he said, 'Don't you know what it meant when I raised my hand as you went by likity-split?' Mis Watrous, she answered: 'Young man, I didn't teach school all those years for nothing. If you want to go to the bathroom, you go right ahead!'" Flora made it a habit to drive the wrong way on a particular one-way Warsaw street; everyone knew this, and simply got out of her way.

My grandmother was a real taskmaster. When I came home from school, there was no nonsense: the homework had to be done fully and correctly. From her I learned the need to set goals and achieve them. More important, I got into Bible reading; her respect for every word of it certainly impacted my thinking. I wasn't saved through her Baptist church (to say nothing of the United Church!), but seeds were planted which eventually bore fruit.

The asthma kept me from my mother and father's house except for occasional Sunday dinners—and it was not uncommon for me to return to grandmother's house wheezing and coughing. In March, 1937 (I was five years old), my mother and my paternal grandparents took me to Florida for a complete climate change.[5] I remember

---

[4] See in the Appendix, a photograph of her as a young teacher in her classroom, together with a photograph of her with my mother.

[5] My father had to stay in Warsaw to take care of business. In the Montgomery archives there are twelve letters he wrote to my mother whilst she was in Florida.

travelling in an old Hupmobile, singing, with the adults, "The Blue Ridge Mountains of Virginia," as we drove through that State. In Florida, we stayed at the Soreno Hotel in St Petersburg—it belonged to friends of my parents (the Lunds) and I played in the sand on the beach with their son Jacky.[6] I recall a day trip in a tourist boat, and seeing a local boy of about my age, dressed poorly and working on the boat, and feeling strange that we were so different.

Back home I was always into projects. I built a very involved pasteboard castle, with secret passageways and hidden doors. I loved Latin, and when a history project required a history of Rome, I did it all in Latin on a scroll. I was a cub scout, then a boy scout, and attained Eagle rank with silver palm.

I also loved listening to the radio (this was, of course, prior to television). After school, I would follow the late afternoon serials (*The Shadow*, etc.). I responded regularly to the "free offers" presented, and on one occasion, at Sunday dinner, my father, knowing this, read out loud the word "free" from a ketchup bottle label; I grabbed it right away, and found the words "free from artificial flavours."

On Sunday nights, when my grandmother went to the evening service at the Baptist Church, I would listen to Edgar Bergen and Charlie McCarthy (and even had a Charlie of my own, but never mastered the ventriloquist's art), Jack Benny, Fred Allen, George Burns and Gracie Allen, Fibber McGee & Molly, and The Great Gildersleeve.

She kept these letters the rest of her life; they came into my hands after her death.

[6] "In 1923 construction began on Soren Lund's 'Million Dollar' Mediterranean Revival hotel. Prominent features were its clay tiled roof, rough textured stucco, baroque-type arched entrance and sqraffito decorations. It encompassed the north half of the 100 block of Beach Drive. Noted region architect Geoffrey Lloyd Preacher designed the Hotel. The Soreno, named for Lund's only son [Jacky's father, Soreno Lund], was finished, and the majority of its rooms leased prior to the opening of the 1924 tourist season. Its completion established a new elegance on the downtown waterfront. The Soreno was the first of ten grand hotels built between 1923 and 1926, which defined St Petersburg as a winter tourist destination, and was the climax of the Florida land boom in the 1920s. The unusual addition of a seventh floor was completed in 1929, bringing the total number of rooms to 300. Lund's lifelong experience and reputation in the hotel industry kept the hotel full throughout his ownership. During World War II, the Soreno was occupied by servicemen, then operated as a winter season hotel until it was closed in 1984. It was demolished in 1992"—*Florida Historical Marker F-422*. Years later, I met Jacky (John) Lund again briefly; he, too, had by then become a Christian believer.

Chapter 2

One Sunday night, whilst listening and making model fighter planes, I decided on more realistic dogfights and lit paper streamers with matches. A wastepaper basket caught fire, melting the linoleum floor under it, the flames reaching and scorching the ceiling. In a panic, I phoned my parents at home; my father arrived at grandma's house, cleaned up the mess, and gave me a memorable thrashing. That was only exceeded when one of my toy rockets, filled with homemade gunpowder, plowed into our Jewish neighbour's house and had to be removed with carpenter's tools. Result: I was grounded from going to the movies for six months, thereby losing the glorious opportunity of seeing (for 10 cents a performance) the cowboy films of my favourites: Roy Rogers and Hopalong Cassidy.

Though Warsaw and Wyoming County were not known for fine cuisine (that should come as no surprise), I remember fondly the times when our family drove to the Glen Iris Inn at Letchworth State Park in Castile. This was my first contact with fine dining and was a harbinger of things to come when much later Europe beckoned.

During the summers, I would have much preferred to stay home and devote myself to personal interests, but my parents had other ideas. I was enrolled in swimming class in the local public pool and eventually (during high school) obtained a lifeguard certificate—later, after my conversion, serving as a lifeguard. (With nothing to do most of the time in the lifeguard's chair, I memorised Scripture verses using the Navigators' system; fortunately, no one drowned whilst that was going on.)

High school friends included Jimmy Farnholtz, boisterous play with whom resulted in my falling out of a second-storey barn window, producing a torn foot ligament and months in bed; Albin McWilliams, who as an adult became a newspaper man on a county paper and sadly died young; Norman Wheeler, an evangelical believer who later, after my conversion, teamed up with me to give free New Testaments to all the children in my swimming class at the Warsaw public pool—something that today the ACLU would doubtless have tried to suppress. During the two-hour lunch break between the swimming classes and my lifeguard duties, I taught myself touch-typing.

Childhood Recollections (1931–1948)

One summer my parents sent me off to summer camp. This was Camp Cory, a YMCA camp on Keuka Lake, one of the Finger Lakes in Upstate New York.[7] One of my tent mates had a severe asthma attack, and I used my inhaler on him. As a result, at the final campfire, when the parents came to retrieve their offspring, I was named Honour Camper of the season.[8] My father, who was not an emotionally demonstrable individual, was visibly impressed.

In high school, contact sports were of no interest to me at all (I did enjoy swimming and tennis, but they were not in the curriculum). A friend of mine and I would play outfield—he centre and I left field. We would then move toward each other, sit down in the grass and play cards. The inevitable happened: we were caught and severely punished by the principal—who had a habit of pounding an erring pupil's head against his office wall. My algebra teacher, on one occasion, hit me over the head with her umbrella as compensation for a truly stupid answer. None of this did me any harm, and perhaps some good.

As suggested above, I was much fascinated by rocketry. I read avidly on the subject: the American Rocket Society's edition of Robert Goddard's seminal papers and the books of Willy Ley, who, with Wernher von Braun, did so much to raise American awareness of the value of conquering space. On a school trip to Washington, D.C., I visited Ley at his home and requested escape velocity calculations so that I could make a miniature rocket capable on a small scale of paralleling the trajectories of the full-size ones. Ley was very gracious to a high school amateur and sent me the calculations I needed. I still have the copy of his *Rockets and Space Travel* that he autographed to me on 22 February 1947.

I also learned piano and took correspondence courses in harmony and dance band arranging. I became a member of the local chapter of the S.P.E.B.S.Q.S.A., which—as everyone should know—stands for the Society for the Preservation and Encouragement of Barbershop Quartet Singing in America. I played piano in the high school dance

---

[7] URL: http://www.campcory.org/general_info_history.asp
[8] The year was 1944, and a communication from the present executive director of Camp Cory informs me that the *Sons of Cory* shield of that year, with my name inscribed, is still hanging in the Camp Dining Hall.

Chapter 2

band and did some arrangements for them. I even had the idea of going into music, but my paternal grandmother, Bessie Rector Montgomery (never a tactful woman) convinced me—quite correctly—that my talents lay elsewhere.[9]

The Warsaw High School principal's daughter, Louise Ball, was in my class and was a very smart girl. Who would be valedictorian—she or I? I managed to beat her out, and therefore delivered the major student address at graduation (she, as salutatorian, gave a lesser one). The lights failed briefly in the middle of my address, but I went on anyway, and this much impressed the audience—more so than my rather ordinary remarks ("the future is before us," etc.).[10]

Two images remain strongly fixed in my mind from early childhood. The first, an illustration from a Dick-and-Jane style book for young readers: it showed a beautiful garden scene with children playing under a canopy of green, leafy trees, illuminated by shafts of descending sunlight. Simone Weil speaks of "intimations of Christianity among the ancient Greeks." Was this "intimations of heaven for a child not yet in personal fellowship with Jesus Christ"? The second image derived from one of my cub- or boy-scout manuals; it was a drawing of a fledgling warrier on his knees, keeping vigil in a chapel, on the eve of his being knighted. If there is one motif which has characterised my lifestyle it has been that of the Quest: the need to set goals and achieve them. This, of course, is not a virtue per se; like faith, its moral value depends entirely on its being directed to valid objects. And that takes us—without further delay—to my conversion.

---

[9] In her will, she left something to my sister Mary, but never even mentioned me.
[10] My MS address (title: "The True Purpose of Education") has been preserved in the Montgomery Archives. Read it and weep.

Chapter 3

CORNELL UNIVERSITY AND CONVERSION (1948–1952)

As noted in the previous chapter, my mother was a Cornellian—and she was privileged to study under such greats as literary scholar Lane Cooper. (Father never obtained a college degree; there is an unsubstantiated story that he left college—or was told to leave—after having punched a gym instructor's lights out.)[1] I entered Cornell as a naïve frosh in September, 1948, majoring in philosophy and the classics (Greek and Latin).

The first semester was a terror. I dropped a sociology course early in the term, disgusted by the instructor who was in the habit of making suggestive remarks to the girls in the front seats, reducing them to embarrassment and tears; also, the content in the course, if converted into hair, would not have made a wig for a grape (one of my favorite expressions). My first Greek course was overwhelming, not in the least helped by the presence of a Jewish senior, a physics major, who decided to learn classical Greek as a lark, and who effortlessly obtained the highest marks—whilst I was burning the midnight oil to stuff the grammar into my recalcitrant noggin. I chose to take astronomy that same term to satisfy my science requirement—requiring late night labs at the observatory when my Greek class met early the following mornings. By the end of the semester, I told my parents that they should expect me to flunk out and return in disgrace to Warsaw. This, however, did not occur; I ended up with a very high average—which was maintained fairly consistently throughout my college career, leading to Phi Beta Kappa in my senior year and graduation with distinction in philosophy.[2]

---

[1] According to his obituary, Maurice Warwick Montgomery was valedictorian of his Warsaw High School class of 1920. A yellowing Alfred University (Alfred, N.Y.) transcript indicates that he attended summer school there in 1923, taking a Physics course and receiving a grade of B. He was particularly proud in later life of serving as a councilman and Town of Warsaw supervisor.

[2] For the record, I was also elected to the Phi Kappa Phi scholastic honorary society

29

Chapter 3

Early in that first term, I met an engineering student by the name of Herman John Eckelmann—surely one of the most eventful acquaintanceships of my entire life. Freshmen students such as I were housed in the "temporary," Quonset hut dormitories built for soldier-students returning from the Second World War, but still in use years later. Upper classmen could move into the gorgeous, gothic dormitories which graced the historic Cornell campus. Eckelmann, however, chose to stay in Quonset hell. Why? As an evangelical Christian and a personal witness *par excellence,* he wanted to be the agent in the conversion of young freshmen and sophomore "intellectuals." I was thus ideal grist for his mill.

My objections were legion—but so were the apologetics volumes with which his room was stuffed. The books which had the most impact were those with the most substantial content: Wilbur Smith's *Therefore Stand,* E. J. Carnell's *Introduction to Christian Apologetics,* and C. S. Lewis's *Miracles* and broadcast talks (later published as *Mere Christianity*). Thank goodness I didn't encounter the kind of pabulum-level devotional literature which makes up a large percentage of the books foisted on the evangelical public today by "Bible bookstores"; and thank goodness the day of the TV evangelist had not arrived (with friends like that, the potential convert needs few enemies).

By the spring semester, I was (to paraphrase C. S. Lewis' words) dragged kicking and screaming into the Kingdom by the sheer weight of the evidence for the truth of the faith. The day following Christ's entry into the centre of my consciousness, even the leaves on the trees seemed to glow with a new splendour. Later I would read Luther's comment, when talking about the Real Presence of the Lord in the Eucharist, that "Christ is present in the leaf of every tree"—a truth entirely backed up by Colossians 1:12–17.

I joined the Cornell chapter of Inter-Varsity Christian Fellowship and attended its worship services. Heaven's portals literally opened—especially through the wonderful evangelical hymns in the

---

at Cornell, and later, at the University of California at Berkeley, to the library science honorary society, Beta Phi Mu. Since vanity compels members of such societies to display their keys on their watch chains, there exists the following definition of a super-salesman: someone who can sell a double-breasted suit to a Phi Beta Kappa.

IVCF hymnbook.[3] This book preceded the "I'm so happy," subjective, feely, overhead-projector school of today, so I had the privilege of being introduced to many of the greatest melodies and lyrics of classical Christian hymnody—hymns focusing on what God in Christ has objectively done for us when we were entirely incapable of saving ourselves: "Great is Thy Faithfulness," "Guide me, O Thou great Jehovah," "Lord, Thy Word Abideth," "Praise, my soul, the King of heaven," "To God be the glory," etc., etc.

Some years later, I would attend Inter-Varsity's Campus-in-the-Woods summer conference in Canada, and sit under such evangelical luminaries as William Childs Robinson (who had the misfortune to have as his son James M. Robinson, the post-Bultmannian author of *The New Quest of the Historical Jesus*), J. F. Strombeck *(So Great Salvation; Disciplined by Grace)*, and Ruth Paxson *(Life on the Highest Plane)*.

At the end of my freshman year, I returned to Warsaw for the summer. Two interesting events occurred. First, I spent an afternoon with the pastor of the United Church of Warsaw, of which I was a member. I showed him a chart I had made of the plan of salvation, from Genesis to Revelation, and I asked him why he had never, in my recollection, preached a single sermon on the death of Christ for the sins of the world. He replied, "But which atonement theory are you talking about?" Said I (not having reached a suitable level of sanctification): "You know—or should know—damned well! The one clearly set out—if anything is set out—in the Holy Scriptures. I might as well have grown up in darkest Africa for all the gospel I ever heard in your church."

That summer I spent a week at a Presbyterian church camp and witnessed as best I could to those who, like me, had had the misfortune to grow up in a liberal church—roughly equivalent to the Rotary Club (but less fun). One girl at the camp appeared to undergo conversion. But later, in correspondence with me, she said that she had read a copy of notorious liberal Harry Emerson Fosdick's *Modern Use of the Bible,* and she now realised that I had been presenting a

---

[3] *Hymns*, ed. Paul Beckwith (Chicago: Inter-Varsity Christian Fellowship, 1947).

naïve fundamentalism and so she had "given up blood religion." The very last thing I would like is to stand in the shoes of liberal clergy on the Day of Judgment.[4]

Fellow members of the Cornell IVCF chapter included Armand Nicholi, who would later become a Harvard psychiatrist, and Irving Hoffman, who spent his life with the North Africa Mission preparing evangelistic literature for the conversion of Muslims. At Cornell, Irv was my best friend—though we had cultural differences. I enjoyed good food (or what, in Ithaca, New York, could pass for good food).

Irv regarded eating as a poor use of time, when there was so much to be done in preaching the gospel; he said that he regarded eating as a train pulling up briefly to a water tower where the nutriment would be poured in and the train could start up again. I called him a "Unitarian of the Second Person" (one with no doctrine of creation—the Unitarian sect being "Unitarians of the First Person," having no doctrine of redemption). But we remained best of friends.

The Cornell Inter-Varsity chapter regularly sponsored guest lecturers as a means of campus evangelism. I remember a talk given by the great Donald Grey Barnhouse of Philadelphia's historic Tenth Presbyterian Church. In the discussion following, a snotty student, in an attempt to make a fool of Barnhouse, posed the ironic question: "So you actually think that heaven is a certain number of miles from here?" Barnhouse: "Exactly." (To be sure, this answer did not take into account a multidimensional universe, but it made the fundamental point that Christian faith is a matter of solid factuality, not poetical metaphor.)

All the evangelical guest lecturers, however, did not come up to Barnhouse's level. Recently, Neal Jordan, a fellow Cornellian of that era, wrote to me as follows: "You worked so hard to get prominent

---

[4] The girl's letters are preserved with my notes in the John Warwick Montgomery archives at Southeastern Baptist Theological Seminary. –And here's a gigantic kudo to Mrs Beth Dietz, Fellow (as is her husband James) of the International Academy of Apologetics, Evangelism and Human Rights, for having engaged with me in the herculean labour of preparing those archival materials for transmittal to Southeastern!

Not so incidentally, I once made the mistake of attending a service at Fosdick's Riverside Church in New York City. The text was an article from *The New York Times*. It was Fosdick—a Northern Baptist—who once preached an Easter sermon on "The Peril of Worshiping Jesus" (5/3 *Church Monthly* [January, 1931], 43-48).

speakers for the Sunday afternoon meetings. I remember your being irate when Jack Wyrtzen declined with the comment that he thought '... the intellectual approach to the Gospel was bunk.' And, with regard to a few that did accept, I remember you observing wryly that it was 'tough to deplete the treasury to pay their expenses and then to have to sit in the front row and pray that they would shut up.'"

My freshman grade average turned out (amazingly!) to be high enough to place me in an Honours Reading Programme in which a small number of students met at faculty homes for "Great Books" discussions on a regular basis. Through this programme I read such important works as John Henry Newman's *Idea of a University* (my first encounter with a Christian understanding of what an education should be), Samuel Butler's *The Way of All Flesh* and James Joyce's *Portrait of the Artist As a Young Man* (where the 19th century shift to secularism was so effectively presented and advocated), Norman Douglas's *South Wind,* etc.

Among the homes in which these discussions took place was that of my logic professor Max Black, author of a most detailed *Commentary on Wittgenstein's Tractatus*. Black was not an easy man; behind his back he could be characterised as "Black Max." But he was said to be one of only a dozen who understood Russell and Whitehead's *Principia Mathematica* when it first appeared. As a freshman, I received a 98% grade in Black's classic logic course, and, thinking myself a logical whiz, in my junior year enrolled in Black's course in modern/existential logic. After a few weeks I realised that I was understanding about as much as if the lectures were in Swahili; I dropped the course before it could be credited against me.

Other faculty members with whom I studied at Cornell included Carl Stephenson, the great medieval historian; Mario Einaudi, professor of government and son of the first president of the Republic of Italy; Edwin A. Burtt, author of *The Metaphysical Foundations of Modern Science*; and Harry Caplan, pedagogue extraordinaire, who had his Latin students memorise and recite lines from Horace's *Odes*. Caplan and Stephenson drove doctoral students to distraction: at a prearranged signal, one of them would say to the exhausted candidate at the end of the oral final, "Just one more question, Mr X: 'Why did Rome fall?'" Caplan was a lay Jew par excellence; I tried once to witness to him, and he quickly, but kindly, cut me off: "As a

33

Jew, I shall never become Christian." Anomalously, his scholarly specialty was medieval rhetoric—the domain of Christian preachers.[5] Burtt, after giving up creedal Christianity, became a Quaker—which demonstrated far more integrity than that possessed by those Presbyterian and Baptist religious liberals (e. g., Fosdick) who stayed in Christian denominations in defiance of the historic theology of those churches.

At the end of my freshman year, I was elected to Watermargin's Telluride House—the only "academic" fraternity at Cornell. This was a boon to my parents, for room and board were provided *gratis* at the palatial house maintained by the organisation. The year was not, however, a happy one for me. The members were aggressively pagan and did everything to uproot my Christian faith—without success, owing to my realisation (1) that their arguments did not hold water ("Watermargin"—heh!), and (2) the alternative to Christian belief was a meaningless universe, devoid of any reason for living, even at their subsidised rates). I recall one Sunday afternoon, listening to the whole of Händel's *Messiah* in the lounge, and thinking, *Here's reality; they haven't got a clue.* I resigned and subjected my parents to higher university costs my junior and senior years.

The secular atmosphere at Cornell got to me at intervals during my freshman and sophomore years and I seriously considered transferring to Wheaton College. I attended the Wheaton summer session in 1951, between my junior and senior years. But I was sickened by the students who had pledged not to drink or go to the movies and then did so anyway. (I didn't think that the Bible prohibited either of those activities, but if I was going to promise not to do something, I was honour-bound to keep my word.) I heard more dirty jokes that summer than I had heard during my three years in a secular university. In a fit of sanctification, I went to the Sword of the Lord Bookstore in the town, looking for "deeper life" publications. Mrs John R. Rice (it was, unbelievably, she—bosomy and domineering), who

---

[5] Harry Caplan, *Of Eloquence: Studies in Ancient and Mediaeval Rhetoric*, ed. Anne King and Helen North (Ithaca, NY: Cornell University Press, 1970); Luitpold Wallach (ed.), *The Classical Tradition: Literary and Historical Studies in Honor of Harry Caplan* (Ithaca, NY: Cornell University Press, 1966). For my contact with Cornell philosophy professor—and Wittgenstein's student and friend—Norman Malcolm, see the Preface to my *Tractatus Logico-Theologicus*.

said, "We don't have that kind of thing. John R. says that if believers would spend their time preaching the gospel, they wouldn't have time to read such pablum." That was just the advice I needed—and I returned to Cornell for my final college year.

That year I lived off campus. One of my roommates was Jim Christ, a pre-seminary student and Lutheran. He later spent his career in the semi-liberal United Lutheran Church (which finally entered into the ELCA—the Evangelical Lutheran Church in America—now in pulpit and altar fellowship with the American Episcopal Church, which has at least one lesbian bishop and has effectively split apart the world Anglican communion). But in those days, a liberal Lutheran was like a conservative Methodist. A couple of months before graduation, we went to a fair and I won a duck. We covered the floor of our room with paper and the duck lived with us. When my parents came for my graduation, the duck was packed with my other belongings and taken home. Some months later, I learned that my parents had eaten my duck.

During my senior year, a new ecumenical Religious Centre was built on campus. Its chapel had a revolving altar so that the chapel could accommodate all faiths (a cross on one side, a star of David on another side, and a puff of smoke on a third side—or something like it—to take care of all the mystical belief systems). I wrote a letter that was published in the campus newspaper, *The Cornell Daily Sun,* in which I recommended motorising the altar, like a Tibetan prayer wheel, so as to blend at high speed all these mutually contradictory religious ideas and arrive at a more meritorious result. The letter was taken seriously by some of the religious liberals but scandalised a number of campus leaders. Non-believers on campus were impressed by the fact that the letter pointed up the impossibility of mutually contradictory religious ideas all being true. The result was several weeks of religious excitement on campus and a great opportunity for solid Christian witness.

I searched Ithaca for a church. My studies in New Testament Greek had given me the opportunity to check the major confessional writings of Christendom against the biblical text. I compared, at the points of conflict, the Roman Catholic *Canons and Decrees of the Council of Trent,* the Lutheran *Book of Concord,* the Anglican *Thirty-Nine Articles,* the Calvinist-Reformed *Westminster Confession,* etc. To my amazement, it seemed that in every case of differences of approach, the Lutheran theology was exactly on target scripturally. Near the campus, there were only two churches maintaining a solid view of the Scriptures: a Baptist church (where the pastor put his arms around you at the door) and a Lutheran church (where the pastor mercifully did not). I started attending that Lutheran church—though with zero liturgical background. When the congregation stood up, I was sitting down; when the congregation sat down, I was standing up. But eventually I got the hang of it, and found it a wonderful sacramental support in the rigours and temptations of university life.

The present book is autobiography, not theology. However, I cannot resist mentioning the major reasons for my going Lutheran. First, whilst most church bodies stress peripheral issues, as their names often suggest (Presbyterian and Episcopal = forms of church government), the Lutheran churches have focused on what is surely central in Scripture, namely the Word, both living (Christ) and written (the Bible). No church has been, literally, more *gospel-centred* throughout its history. Secondly, Lutherans retain in liturgy and church practice whatever is historic, save if it contradicts Holy Writ—giving Lutheran worship the benefit of Christian experience across the ages. But, unlike Roman Catholicism and Eastern Orthodoxy, Lutheranism judges tradition by the clear teaching of Scripture, and refuses (unlike Anglicanism) to elevate reason or tradition to the level of the Bible in the determination of doctrine. Moreover, Lutheranism insists that the accepted creedal statements of the church (collected in the *Book of Concord*) be accepted *quia* (*because* they conform to Scripture), not *quatenus* (*insofar as* they conform to biblical teaching)—thus maintaining doctrinal rigour without compromise. But having given this short *apologia pro confessione sua*, I must immediately add that I am in no way condoning the *sociological* atmosphere so often associated with Lutheranism—the Germanic authoritarianism and the Scandinavian stuffiness.[6]

---

[6] Cf. the novels of Garrison Keillor—and his book, *Life among the Lutherans* (Minneapolis: Augsburg Fortress, 2009).

Chapter 4

FAR-WEST, MID-WEST, AND CANADA (1952–1963)

After graduation, I married Joyce Ann Bailer, whom I had dated my senior year in high school. After my conversion at Cornell, I had witnessed to her and she became a believer. The marriage ultimately turned out to be a grave mistake, but being young and immature at the time one knew no better.

We settled in California for my graduate studies. I looked forward to an academic career and decided on the broadest of all fields: librarianship. After obtaining the graduate Bachelor of Library Science degree at the University of California at Berkeley, I was one of the few chosen for a Library of Congress internship; but this programme was suddenly cancelled owing to a cut in Library of Congress appropriations. I therefore obtained a position in the General Reference Department at UC Berkeley. The annual salary was $6,000 and entirely sufficient at the time.

One of the (minor) reasons for my success at Cornell was that I did not own a car—and I did not in fact obtain a driver's licence until just before graduation. This meant that I was still a fledgling driver in California. Indeed, I was mortified to receive my first moving violation for driving too *slowly* on the Pasadena freeway.

Whilst whiling away the time at the University's General Reference Desk, I broke the simple substitution code used by Sinclair Lewis for his diary—and then found that it had already been broken. But interest in cryptography remained and years later this was useful in computer activities. The very first research question asked me by a library user—and this after a year of detailed study of reference sources in all known fields, based on C M. Winchell's *Guide to Reference Books:* "Where is the men's room?" I consoled myself by studying for the M.A., and my thesis, *A Seventeenth- Century View of European Libraries,* was subsequently published by the University of California Press. I dedicated it to my dear new friend, the Lutheran

Chapter 4

campus pastor, Don Deffner.[1] At his University Lutheran Chapel (supported by the Lutheran Church-Missouri Synod), I developed a technique for the accelerated teaching of New Testament Greek to laymen who wanted to read the biblical text in the original language.[2]

Joyce and I were already having trouble, and she left me, returning to the East; there she obtained an annulment of the marriage and enrolled in the Cornell Nursing School in New York City. I believed that our marriage should be maintained[3] and Don Deffner helped me financially to spend the next summer at Columbia University, where I obtained certification as a medical librarian and persuaded Joyce to remarry and return to California with me.

Though librarianship was fascinating as an academic field, and would be tremendously valuable in my subsequent graduate work and scholarly research and writing, the practice was insufficiently stimulating. I enrolled at Pacific Lutheran Theological Seminary and there completed the first year of pastoral studies. My cronies were Ed Moeckel (who had enrolled after a successful business career, and who was to die young) and Bob Ove (whose pastoral career would span a half century and who is one of the contributors to my Festschrift). But keeping the wolf from the door whilst carrying on a full-time seminary programme was exceedingly difficult—especially since a library job involved many clock hours per week. I therefore sought and obtained a New Testament Greek instructorship at the Hamma Divinity School of Wittenberg University in Springfield, Ohio.

The small number of teaching hours and the fact that I knew my Greek already and therefore did not need much preparation time coordinated far better with a full-time seminary class schedule. Also,

---

[1] Later, a regular visiting professor at Concordia Theological Seminary, Ft. Wayne, Indiana. He died from skin cancer a decade ago.

[2] A photo of one of these classes, showing the very thin (emaciated?) professor, appears in the Appendix below.

[3] The pastor of the United Church of Warsaw, who had married us, supported Joyce's seeking and obtaining the annulment. I wrote him from California, finally resigning from membership in the United Church and the Presbyterian denomination—an inevitable move in any event because of the theological liberalism of the pastor and of the denomination. (Letter in the John Warwick Montgomery archives at Southeastern Baptist Theological Seminary.)

Ohio, Indiana, and Kentucky were replete with little Lutheran and other denominational churches too poor to have full-time clergy, so the seminarians had almost unlimited preaching opportunities (valuable as experience but also in terms of income).[4] I bought my first new car: a Renault Dauphine, which, on one early Sunday preaching assignment, I managed to turn on its side whilst rounding a sharp corner. The car was so light that I pushed it upright again and went on to preach two services! On another occasion I preached at a Unitarian church and gave the congregation a tremendous dose of Trinitarian theology; at the church door, everyone said that that was what they always believed. (Apparently, they had no idea what a Unitarian was supposed not to believe. They simply went along with the Bible.)

I spent three years at Hamma—two finishing the Bachelor of Divinity degree (now designated, with typical American grade inflation, as the M.Div. degree), and one year for the Master of Sacred Theology with a thesis offering for the first time a translation from the Latin of a work on biblical sacrifice by one of Luther's own students (published as *Chytraeus on Sacrifice*).

One of the summers between academic years at Hamma, I returned to the University of California at Berkeley to complete my M.A., the thesis (mentioned above) being on a thrilling subject, 17th-century European libraries. Amazingly, this thesis was published in a monographic series by the University of California Press, and I have joked for years that every time a copy is sold, the publishers send me a telegram: they are so delighted. My only companion during that summer was my cat Putty, who should herself have received a degree for going through the experience—travelling halfway across the country, both ways, by automobile, and keeping quiet whilst I ground out the thesis.[5]

Professors at Hamma included, *inter alia,* church historian W. D. Allbeck, author of *Studies in the Lutheran Confessions*[6] the dogmatician T. A. Kantonen and the New Testament scholar E. E. Flack. Kan-

---

[4] A list of my preaching assignments for one of these years is given in an Appendix, *infra.*

[5] Putty, who at an advanced age died falling out of our 6th floor (7th by American designation) apartment window in Strasbourg, France, will be mentioned again *infra,* in this book's concluding chapter. Cats, sadly, do *not* have nine lives …

[6] Allbeck's little volume, *Theology at Wittenberg 1845–1945,* introduction by E. E.

tonen had finished his doctorate at Boston University as a flaming liberal, but had then needed pastoral experience before becoming a seminary professor; he found that his liberal views were hopeless in the parish and this forced a total rethinking of his theology. As he wryly put it, "I wanted to become famous. But to become famous in theology, you need to be original. I suddenly realised that since the faith had been around for two thousand years, anything original I developed in Christian dogmatics would necessarily turn out to be heresy. So here I am: not famous but faithful."[7]

E. E. Flack was not only a careful scholar,[8] but at the same time a truly memorable character. He treated us, his seminarians, as "his boys," advising the married men, for example, not to have sex on Saturday night before preaching on Sunday. His anecdotes were so extensive and classic that a little book of them was eventually published. Here is an example of his stories:

> A guest preacher in a large church in Cleveland was accosted by a man at the door following the sermon: "Your sermon was lousy," the man exclaimed. The local pastor, embarrassed by this outburst of criticism of his guest speaker, said to the preacher: "Oh, don't pay any attention to that man. He is a moron. He only repeats what everybody else is saying."[9]

Flack (Springfield, OH: Wittenberg Press, 1945) contains interesting information on the institution and its faculty members, many of whom were still teaching when I was a student and an instructor there.

[7] Kantonen's publications included *Resurgence of the Gospel, The Christian Hope, Theology of Evangelism,* and *A Theology for Christian Stewardship.* The Foreword to the latter work gives an idea as to his developed theological perspective: "My primary source has been the New Testament. ... And if I have leaned heavily on Luther in the interpretation of the living message of the gospel, it is not in the interest of denominationalism (Lutherans indeed have no monopoly on Luther!), but because I know no better guide to the heart of the gospel."

[8] He was Old Testament editor for the *Twentieth Century Encyclopedia of Religious Knowledge,* ed. L. A. Loetscher (this was the 2-vol., 1955 supplement to *The New Schaff-Herzog Encyclopedia of Religious Knowledge*).

[9] Elmer E. Flack, *Leaves from the Dean's Joke Book* (Lima, OH: C.S.S. Publishing Co., 1971), no. 95.

When I was offered the opportunity to join the Federated Theological Faculty of the University of Chicago as Head Librarian of the Divinity School, Flack strongly encouraged me to take the position. Said he: "You can make the impact I myself have never been able to make here at a small seminary in a small university." But his impact on several generations of theology students was far greater than he realised.

So it was off to Chicago—the south side, just north of the Esplanade, dividing the very rough Black area from the University. We lived in a tolerable, if somewhat run-down, apartment building. One of our neighbours was held up on the street in broad daylight; another had her apartment rifled. Whilst serving as Divinity School librarian, I completed the course work and the qualifying examinations for the Ph.D.—but in the Graduate Library School, not in the Federated Theological Faculty. True, there were Lutheran scholars such as Jaroslav Pelikan, but, in general, the Federated Faculty was a theological catastrophe.

Examples: I had master's level students complaining that in the card catalogue the biblical books were arranged in canonical order (they wanted them alphabetical, since they had no idea where in the Bible a given book was placed). And when I tried to explain to one student how to use a concordance to the Bible, he said, "Only a fundamentalist would use a thing like that." I immediately called an acquaintance in the University's literature department and informed him that, according to people in the Divinity School, the Shakespeare specialist was surely a fundamentalist, since he was always using a concordance to Shakespeare's plays. Later, I would do an article titled "Bibliographical Bigotry" for *Christianity Today* magazine,[10] in which I contrasted the liberal Divinity School library, which had practically no evangelical scholarship represented in it when I arrived as Librarian, with the library of the Trinity Evangelical Divinity School, which had both evangelical materials *and the prominent liberal publications*.

---

[10] Included in my book, *Suicide of Christian Theology*.

As Librarian of the University of Chicago Divinity School, I delivered major papers at national meetings of the American Theological Library Association[11] and prepared the first printed catalogue of serial publications in the Protestant theological libraries of the Chicago area.[12] But there was very little opportunity to teach: I gave one course in Theological Bibliography, but that was all.

So when a call went out for a chairman of the History Department at Waterloo Lutheran University in Canada, I applied and received the appointment. The next three years were Canadian years—and at the time of the Cuban Missile Crisis. The Canadians were generally against U. S. opposition to Castro, and I occasionally had to remind them that the range of the missiles included Toronto as well as New York City.

The twin cities of Kitchener and Waterloo are about sixty miles due west of Toronto. Waterloo was thus a quiet place, and the University was a good experience—except for a powerful and continual smell from the local beer processing plant, the consequence of much German settlement. (Indeed, Kitchener had been patriotically—and pragmatically—renamed for the English military hero at the time of the First World War; its earlier name had been "Berlin"!)

At Waterloo Lutheran, I taught the required Western history survey course, American history, and philosophy of history. My approach in all these courses was to avoid the dull, fact-after-fact lecturing so characteristic of the professional historian, and instead to push the students in the direction of the history of ideas and the theological foundations of historical study. Inevitably, my history courses took on an apologetic thrust. One of my students was Ronald Sider, a Mennonite, who later would become well known for his efforts in behalf of evangelical social action. Sadly, Sider never felt comfortable with the doctrine of the inerrancy of the Scriptures, but he held

---

[11] At the Sixtieth Annual Conference of the ATLA, held in Chicago, 21–24 June 2006, archivist James Lutzweiler gave to the Special Collections interest group a presentation on the bibliographical aspects of my career; it was extracted from his longer contribution to the Festschrift for me edited by William Dembski and Thomas Schirrmacher. So insightful (and hilarious) is this extract that it has been included below in the Appendix.

[12] *A Union List of Serial Publications in Chicago-area Protestant Theological Libraries* (Chicago: University of Chicago Divinity and Philosophy Library, 1960).

firmly to the historicity of the events of our Lord's life. Another student was David Craig, who would later devote his life to missionary work in Nigeria, Switzerland, and Quebec; a recent book on Craig's career stresses the deep impact my instruction had upon him.[13]

Waterloo Lutheran was supposed to be among the most conservative academic institutions in the LCA, but I discovered that its theological seminary, on the same campus, did not have a single faculty member who believed in an inerrant Bible. Unlike those who had grown up in relatively closed Lutheran circles, I had seen the effects of theological liberalism. Finding "errors" in the Bible was like the proverbial camel: let him into the tent and soon he will be sitting on your dining room table. I became less and less enchanted with the church body in which I had been ordained.

Winters were long, cold, and dull in Kitchener-Waterloo. In the winter of 1963, I read in the paper of a lecture on religion given at the University of British Columbia by Avrum Stroll, a professor of philosophy on that faculty.[14] Stroll had said that the story of Jesus in the New Testament was of little or no historical value. I called in a reporter for the local paper and commented that this was a "village idiot's view of Christianity." Reporters like that sort of comment, and my remark crossed Canada to the west coast. I was therefore invited to debate Stroll on the subject at UBC. The result was the publication of my argument, first in a series of articles in the old *His* magazine of the Inter-Varsity Christian Fellowship, afterwards in book form (Inter-Varsity Press; then Campus Crusade's Here's Life Publishers; then Bethany Fellowship), and recently expanded as *History, Law and Christianity* (Canadian Institute for Law, Theology, and Public Policy).[15]

---

[13] Jason Zuidema, *The Life and Thought of David Craig (1937–2001): Canadian Presbyterian Missionary* (Toronto: Clements Publishing, 2008). The book is also available in French from the same publisher.

[14] Stroll later moved to the University of California at San Diego. He is a respected historian of philosophy, having, *inter alia,* contributed heavily to *The Columbia History of Western Philosophy,* ed. Richard H. Popkin (New York: Columbia University Press, 1999).

[15] The original title is also available in German, French, Spanish, and Chinese editions. My publications issued by the Canadian Institute for Law, Theology and Public Policy are now obtainable from New Reformation Press (www.newreformationpress.com OR www.1517legacy.com).

Chapter 4

At one point in the debate, I summed up by saying that one could theoretically reject the New Testament picture of Christ, but to do so one would first have to reject virtually one's entire knowledge of the classical, Greco-Roman world—since the New Testament documents are far better attested historiographically than are the documents on which classical historians rely for their secular data. Upon which Stroll said, "Then I shall give up my knowledge of the classical world." At that point, the chairman of the Classics Department jumped up and cried, "Good Lord, Avrum: *not that!*" It was painfully obvious that Stroll would do no such thing. But it was also clear how much he wanted to avoid Jesus Christ.

Those who sponsored my presence at UBC asked me if I would contact C. S. Lewis to see if he would come to the University to provide follow-up lectures. I sent him what I had presented and received a letter saying that his health did not permit his doing this, and that my lectures "did me good and I shall constantly find them useful." He went on to say that he didn't think they "could be bettered." This was a wonderful testimonial. Lewis' letter to me was dated 29 August 1963 and he was to die less than three months later—on the same day President Kennedy was assassinated (22 November 1963). I therefore never met Lewis face-to-face, but we had also corresponded previously, when I had sent him my essay, written during my Chicago doctoral programme, on "The Chronicles of Narnia and the Adolescent Reader").[16]

During my third year of teaching, I applied for and won a Canada Council Senior Research Fellowship—a grant making possible a year of graduate study abroad. Having finished my Chicago Ph.D. dissertation during my first two years at Waterloo,[17] I wanted to obtain a

---

[16] These letters from Lewis are reproduced in my books, *History and Christianity* and *Myth, Allegory and Gospel*. They also appear in the definitive edition of Lewis' correspondence, edited by Walter Hooper and published by Oxford University Press. I recently (2009) delivered a guest lecture at the Oxford C. S. Lewis Society, and Walter Hooper graciously attended and was much pleased with the presentation. Hooper and I are members of the Athenaeum Club in London and try to sit together at the annual Members' Christmas Lunch.

[17] "The Libraries of France at the Ascendancy of Mazarin" (University of Chicago, 1962), v, 327 p. (microform). The dissertation is—finally—to appear in print as a published book, due to the good offices of the Verlag fuer Kultur und Wissenschaft.

theological doctorate as well. I had been taking summer courses at the Chicago Lutheran Theological Seminary, then in the suburb of Maywood, Illinois; these were excellent, owing to the guest professors, such as the great English hymnologist Erik Routley and the theologians George Forell and Yale's George Lindbeck.[18] I discussed the question of where to take a Th.D. with President Stoughton of Wittenberg. Said he: "One never rises above the level of one's doctorates. Chicago Lutheran will never have the reputation of a great European university." So I started researching the European possibilities.

I definitely did not want to go to a German university; the German faculties of theology had been the baneful source of most of the critical views of the Bible that, in my view, had undermined so much of American academic theology, transforming parish life into little more than the equivalent of social clubs. I found that the most distinguished French-speaking Lutheran faculty of theology in the world was to be found at the University of Strasbourg. So I applied and was accepted as a doctoral student.

Having studied only academic French, I drove to Toronto once a week for a crash programme in speaking the language. Providentially, my Berlitz instructor was willing to modify the standard pedagogical routine to discuss theology with me, preparing me for the eventual public oral thesis examination on which the entire degree depended.

When the academic year 1962–1963 ended, we sailed for France, stopping first in Paris to pick up a glorious Citroën ID-21 "break" (station wagon), with hydraulic suspension and *strapontins* (jump seats that folded into the floor in the back). This was the beginning of a lifelong love affair with the Citroën car company—whose innovations and style have surpassed all others. From Paris we crossed the country to Strasbourg, on the Rhine river and the French border with Germany.

The final event in Waterloo had been a faculty send-off party at which my friend and colleague Don Morgenson, who taught psychology, presented a six-stanza minor epic poem in my honour. The theme, interestingly, was that of a crusading knight, "Sir John War-

---

[18] Dr Forell kindly contributed an essay to my Festschrift. He was one of the most dynamic lecturers with whom I have ever had the privilege of studying.

Chapter 4

wick of Gomery," going forth "for conquests in Gaul" —to do battle for academic and theological truth—"with "Squire Luther right at his side." I had suggested nothing to Don as to a theme for his poem. But, good psychologist that he was, his literary endeavour was right on the mark.[19]

---

[19] For (a slightly edited version of) this deathless epic, see the Appendix, *infra*. Dr Donald Morgenson spent his entire academic career at WLU; he is now Emeritus Professor of Psychology there.

Chapter 5

FIRST ENCOUNTER WITH FRANCE; TRINITY EVANGELICAL DIVINITY SCHOOL (1963-1974)

I shall not go into detail as to the academic experience at the University of Strasbourg, since that was the subject of my influential *Christianity Today* article, "On Taking a European Theological Doctorate."[1] However, it might be well to clarify the nature of the doctorate I obtained. Today, with the 2008 restoration of a single Strasbourg University (for several decades after I took the doctorate, there were three universities in Strasbourg: an arts, a social sciences/law, and a science university), there is but a single doctorate available, which requires considerable residential study. In my day (academic year 1963-1964), in the single University of Strasbourg, there were three doctorates: the state doctorate *(doctorat d'Etat)*, which alone qualified for a French university post, such posts being limited to French citizens, a "university" doctorate *(doctorat d'Université)*, on the same level, but primarily for foreign students who had reached the level of the French candidate after passing his/her qualifying examinations and successfully defending the equivalent of an American master's thesis), and the "third cycle" doctorate *(doctorat de 3ème cycle)*, which was a stepping stone toward the *doctorat d'état,* but could be taken by non-French students.[2] I obtained the *doctorat d'Université,* which required the public defence of a publishable dissertation, but no course work as such (though I regularly attended lectures in the Faculty of Protestant Theology—such as those of Lutheran scholar of Calvin, François Wendel, who went to Italy after the Easter holiday, and never turned up for the rest of that academic year!).

I worked very intensively on my dissertation. The subject was a 17th century Lutheran pastor, theologian, and littérateur—Johann Valentin Andreae—whose career had centred at Tuebingen and in

---

[1] Included in my book, *The Suicide of Christian Theology.*
[2] Faculté de Théologie Protestante, Université de Strasbourg, *Livret-guide de l'étudiant* (1960), especially pp. 39–40.

Black Forest towns across the Rhine river from Strasbourg. I travelled to all the locations of his ministry and worked extensively in the archive collections in Germany where his letters and manuscripts survived. When the smoke cleared, I had prepared a definitive three-volume work which was later published in two-volumes in the prestigious Nijhoff academic series, the International Archives of the History of Ideas, edited by Paul Dibon of the Sorbonne. I asked Professor Dibon whether it should be done in French or in English; he told me that if published in French, the number of copies sold would be a third of the number were the book to be published in English. So, the book was done in English, and a French summary published in the *Revue d'histoire et de théologie religieuses* (the journal of the University of Strasbourg's Faculty of Protestant Theology). Years later, I was invited to lecture at a conference in Amsterdam on the subject of my dissertation; this gave me a further opportunity to stick it to occultists who are still trying to turn Andreae into one of the founders of Rosicrucianism.[3]

My dissertation was being prepared for publication right at the time of the "Days of May," 1968—that heady time of mini-revolution in France, when general strikes took place and President de Gaulle, smarter than the revolutionaries, kept quiet at a French military base across the Rhine until the French people became terrified at the potential anarchy, and then returned to Paris in a stronger position than before. (The French for centuries have swung from autocracy on the right—the Old Régime—to political chaos on the left—the Revolution—and back again—Napoleon.) In Paris, I needed to meet with Paul Dibon at the Sorbonne. The Latin quarter was a mess: student barricades in the streets, the revolutionaries throwing paving stones at the police, who, in turn, were using tear gas.[4] I was walking down a narrow, medieval street, when—coming toward me—was a short, thin student revolutionary selling an anarchist newspaper. "How much?" I asked. "One franc," he replied. (This was in pre-euro

---

[3] My essay, titled "The World-view of Johann Valentin Andreae," was published in the book of symposium essays: *Das Erbe des Christian Rosenkreuz*, ed. F. A. Janssen (Amsterdam: In de Pelikaan, 1988), pp. 152-69.

[4] A typical photo of the time is included in the Appendix, *infra*.

days.) Noting that he was much smaller than I, I grabbed the newspaper and continued on my way. "Where's my franc?" he yelled. "My friend," I said, "I have just given you an important lesson in anarchy."

The theology represented at the Faculty of Protestant Theology during my student days there was generally of the neo-orthodox variety—rather Barthian, but more along the lines of Oscar Cullmann. My major professor was François Wendel, a church historian with both legal and theological training; he was Lutheran but his specialty (oddly enough) was the life and thought of John Calvin. The most radical teacher was probably New Testament scholar Etienne Trocmé, at that time a *maître de conference* (assistant professor), but who would much later become president of the university and try (unsuccessfully, thank goodness) to add a Muslim theological faculty to the University. Trocmé, whom I knew well, had no real confidence in the New Testament narrative of the life of Christ, but, inconsistently, was a pious member of a local Lutheran church.

After my time at Strasbourg, Marc Lienhard, a solid, confessional Lutheran, assumed the chair of historical theology, and Gabriel Vahanian (formerly of Syracuse University and death-of-God notoriety) joined the faculty. I once attended a Vahanian lecture, which entirely gave the lie to the notion of French rationality—*l'esprit cartésien*. Vahanian tried to deep-six the dissertation of David Cullen, one of my very fine students whom I had encouraged to go to Strasbourg for his graduate studies. Learning this, I invited another faculty member to a very fine lunch and got him to have Vahanian removed from Cullen's dissertation committee; Cullen then received his theological doctorate with no further fuss.

Today, in line with the inevitable entropic drift of liberal theology, the Protestant Theological Faculty is in the hands of such ciphers as J.-F. Collange, who promoted the recent (2008) entry of the Church of the Augsburg Confession of the Alsace and the Lorraine (Lutheran) and the Reformed Protestant Church of the Alsace and the Lorraine (Calvinist) into an umbrella organisation, the Union of the Protestant Churches of the Alsace and the Lorraine—an ecumenical arrangement which has effectively cancelled out the distinctives to which generations of Strasbourg and other confessional Lutherans committed themselves.[5]

Living in Europe was an epiphany. I revelled in the history, the culture, the lifestyle that left very largely aside the superficialities of money, sport, and success so characteristic of the western hemisphere. We did the tourist thing whenever possible—Italy and Spain, to be sure, but particularly those locations vital to the history of the Reformation (Germany, Switzerland, England, Scotland). Some visits were to places off the beaten track, for example, the little town of Zutphen in the Netherlands, where an amazing medieval chained library can still be seen. I had to go there, for that library had been referenced in my University of California master's thesis, *A Seventeenth-Century View of European Libraries*. As always, I plumbed the depths of the second-hand and antiquarian book stores, adding to a considerable personal library begun at Cornell and steadily augmented ever since. I visited thinkers in the history of ideas for whom I had great respect (for example, Heinrich Bornkamm at Heidelberg, brother of the infamous post-Bultmannian Günther Bornkamm) and those with whom I strongly disagreed (e.g., Voltaire scholar and bibliographer Theodore Besterman in Geneva).

The city of Strasbourg was a particularly wonderful location. The city had begun as a Roman military encampment, as did many of the great cities—Mainz, Cologne, etc.—along the Rhine river. In the Middle Ages, this "crossroads" city (that is what the word "Strasbourg" signifies) was a Free City of the Holy Roman Empire, meaning that it was not under the immediate political control of the Emperor and therefore had more freedom to develop commercially and culturally. It was one of the first cities to become Protestant in the 16th century. The first generation of the Reform in Strasbourg, under Calvin and more especially Bucer, waffled between Lutheranism and Calvinism, but the second generation became solidly Lutheran. Indeed, at ten o'clock in the evening, the chimes of the Cathedral still mark

---

[5] On Strasbourg University's Faculty of Protestant Theology, see Marc Lienhard (ed.), *La Faculté de Théologie Protestante de Strasbourg hier & aujourd'hui 1538-1988* (Strasbourg: Editions Oberlin, 1988).

the time when, in the 17th century, the non-Lutherans had to exit through the city gates so as not to remain in the city proper! (Those were the days!)

After the Thirty Years War and the weakening of the Holy Roman Empire, the Alsace, and later the city of Strasbourg itself, became part of France, remaining such until France's defeat in the Franco-Prussian war (1870–1871). From then until Germany lost the First World War, the city was subjected to the heavy Prussian boot, having been absorbed into the Second Reich; citizens wept with joy in the streets at the return of the Alsace to France in 1918. Same scenario during the Hitler years: totalitarian German control, with even a concentration camp in the Vosges mountains. Eventually, after murderous fighting, the Allies, by way of Maréchal Leclerc's Second Armoured Division and American forces, drove the Germans back across the Rhine. After the Second World War, Strasbourg became the seat of the Parliament of Europe and the European Court of Human Rights (where I would eventually win some four major cases defending religious liberty). Today, the city combines the modern with the historic: the Petite France section is like jumping into a time machine, the buildings being 15th, 16th, or 17th century.[6]

As the academic year at the University of Strasbourg drew to a close, I discovered that the then president of Waterloo Lutheran University, one Villaume, had gone back on his promise to continue the use of my textbook on the philosophy of history, *The Shape of the Past*, while I was on my year's leave-of-absence.[7] I was deeply incensed, phoned the man, and resigned my professorship and department headship—and this without any other position in the offing.

Having realised that I had made a very dangerous move, I phoned Carl F. H. Henry, who had thought very highly of my papers delivered at such theological conferences as the annual meetings of the

---

[6] One of the best historical treatments of Strasbourg is the composite work *Histoire de Strasbourg des origines à nos jours,* under the direction of Georges Livet and Francis Rapp (4 vols.; Strasbourg: Editions des Dernières Nouvelles, 1980-1982). My personal library contains an impressive collection of materials, some quite rare, on the history of the Alsace in general and Strasbourg in particular.

[7] A few years later, Waterloo Lutheran University secularised, becoming Wilfred Laurier University. The initials (WLU) thus remained the same—presumably to save money by minimising changes to the University logo?

(then very young) Evangelical Theological Society. Henry told me that Kenneth Kantzer had just been given the green light by his church body, the Evangelical Free Church, to create a really great theological seminary on the campus of Trinity College in Deerfield, Illinois, in the north Chicago suburbs. Henry said that they were looking for a librarian. I said that I would certainly consider Trinity—but only if I were given a teaching appointment.

The upshot was that I was offered the chairmanship of the Department of Church History, and this was soon combined with a Philosophy of Religion chair and the teaching of the required first-year apologetics course. Among the variety of elective courses I taught was one on the European Renaissance, in which I argued that only the Christian believer has the motivation and the resources, by way of the biblical doctrines of creation and redemption, to become a genuinely Renaissance person (the root of the French term, not accidentally, is *renaître*—"to be born again"). One of my students, David Stott Gordon, attributes his career choice and philosophy of life to what he learned in that course.[8]

Another change occurred at that point: my denominational affiliation. I wanted a Lutheran connection that would consistently maintain the classic Lutheran (and scriptural) conviction that the Bible is entirely reliable: inerrant as God had initially revealed it; this position was certainly not any longer being held by the officials or the seminary teachers of the Lutheran Church in America. At the same time, my experiences in the LCA had not been unattractive, and I did not want to offend my former teachers and fellow pastors by creating a public fuss. Perhaps the faculty members at Hamma/Wittenberg did not like "inerrancy" terminology, but they always treated the Scriptures as if they were factually true and they never criticised the Bible from the pulpit.[9] I therefore decided that the ideal time to make

---

[8] See his essay in the Festschrift for me, edited by William Dembski and Thomas Schirrmacher.

[9] It was definitely *not* the case that the systematic theology of the Flack years was "essentially neo-orthodox in orientation, and its biblical instruction featuring a judicious use of historical-critical methodology": Donald L. Huber, *Educating Lutheran Pastors in Ohio 1830-1980* ("Studies in American Religion," 33; Lewiston, NY: Edwin Mellen Press, 1989), p. 220. Huber is really describing his own position—and that of the Trinity Lutheran Seminary, which absorbed the Hamma Divinity School in 1978.

the denominational change from LCA to Lutheran Church-Missouri Synod would be at the point of my move from France (and Canada) to the U.S.

I entered into correspondence with the Revd Dr Jacob Preus, then chairman of the Synod's Colloquy Committee (which set the requirements for clergy of other denominations who wished to become clergy in the Missouri Synod). Preus was concerned to strengthen the conservative element in the denomination, particularly in light of the fact that some professors who saw no problem with the so-called "higher" biblical criticism had begun to surface at the Synod's schools. He offered me the opportunity to satisfy the Synod's colloquy requirements by teaching a course in theological bibliography at the Concordia Seminary in St Louis the summer of our return from France. I jumped at the chance—especially since we were nearly broke, and had had to borrow money from our Canadian bank to survive the last few months of the academic year.[10]

The summer in St Louis was an experience. I was there all alone and the heat was almost unbearable. I spent what little free time I had building my kit model of *Le France*—the glorious vessel on which we returned to the States and which now has been broken up, thus ending an era of French transatlantic sea travel—but only after our adopted son, daughter-in-law, and the Montgomerys were on its final Mediterranean voyage!). In my theological bibliography course, I pointed out the necessity of holding to the classic theological (and consistently Reformation) view of an inerrant Bible, and I criticised specifically certain profs at the Seminary who were deviating from that position.

The result was that one day I was called on the carpet by the then dean, Alfred von Rohr Sauer—a bombastic German, as the name suggests. He informed me that, as a visiting professor, I was not to criticise the regular members of the faculty. I responded that I would engage in responsible academic criticism of whomever I wished, and that if he attempted any kind of restriction on my teaching I would broadcast far and wide—especially to the school's accrediting asso-

---

[10] I shall always bless the local banker who agreed to that loan—when we were out of the country and not planning to return to Canada. Needless to say, we paid back that unsecured loan over the next year at Trinity.

ciation—the absence of academic freedom at the Seminary. I heard nothing further from him, but (even after the liberal exodus from Concordia, St Louis, and the restoration of an orthodox faculty) I have never been invited back there, even to deliver a guest lecture.[11]

It will also be noted that during my entire career, though I did a great deal to eliminate the theological liberals from the Missouri Synod during the period of controversy in the 1970s,[12] I have never held a full-time academic position in Synod schools or been featured in denominational activities. This is due to two factors: (1) I supported *Lutheran News* (now *Christian News*), the paper that, more than any other source, revealed to the laity of the Missouri Synod the dangers of theological liberalism and the indifference of the church administration to fighting it (the editor, Herman Otten, is, sad to say, a holocaust revisionist, and just to the right of Genghis Khan politically—but his biblical theology is solid and a statue should be erected to him)[13]; and (2) I was always suspected by the German hierarchy, not having a German name, and actually teaching outside the Missouri Synod—meaning that I did not see the Missouri Synod as coterminous with the Kingdom of God itself. Concordia Publishing House recently refused to print my obituary for Dr

---

[11] One reason may possibly be that, in cross-examination in a Synodical trial defending a sweet, rather naïve charismatic pastor, Leroy Paul, I destroyed on the stand the then president of the Seminary, a Dr John F. Johnson. Johnson had earlier counselled the pastor defendant but then at trial appeared as a witness against him! Showing the court the messy details of this clear conflict of interest was a strong factor in obtaining the pastor's acquittal. Not so incidentally, in the intervening years, the Lutheran Church-Missouri Synod, under the aegis of a church president little interested in doctrinal purity or the protection of the rights of his pastors has managed to eliminate the former adjudication system, which guaranteed due process, and has substituted for it an allegedly "win-win," but in fact weak and dangerous, "reconciliation," i.e., mediation, approach to resolving conflicts in the church body. See my article, "An Invitation to Injustice," *Christian News,* 27 August 2007 (and frequently reprinted).

[12] Cf. my 2-vol. *Crisis in Lutheran Theology.*

[13] See our exchange in *Christian News,* 7 September and 12 October 2009.

Robert Preus, a hero of the struggle against theological liberals in the Synod, because I dared to point out that on the two points just indicated, his position was virtually identical to mine.[14]

Interestingly, James Burkee includes a section titled "Dalliance with Montgomery" in his recent exposé of the Missouri Synod's inerrancy controversy of the 1970's.[15] I am treated rather fairly—considering the author's theme (the controversy was at root political far more than theological and the elimination of the non-inerrantists and the return of the denomination to biblical orthodoxy did incalculable harm to it as a church body). But the research for the book is based almost entirely on interviews and web sources, with a neglect of critical published material. For example, my two-volume *Crisis in Lutheran Theology,* which had a powerful impact on the controversy, is nowhere mentioned. And just before the publication of the Burkee book I received an e-mail request from the publisher to sign off on my interviews with Burkee—when in fact no interviews whatever had been requested or had ever taken place!

During the Trinity years (1964-1974), however, I simultaneously taught at the Concordia Theological Seminary, Springfield, Ohio (now relocated at Ft Wayne, Indiana), by invitation of Jack Preus, who served as its president before becoming president of the entire church body. He was a fine Latinist, but had no time to teach his wife Greek, so I did. He made short work of any liberals or potential liberals at the Springfield seminary. He told me about one Old Testament professor who said: "The Holy Spirit told me that the Bible is a human product and therefore subject to error." Preus replied, "And the Holy Spirit has told me not to renew your contract." One of my students at Springfield was Rod Rosenbladt, who later took his Master's degree under my instruction at Trinity and, on my advice, went on to receive a theological doctorate at Strasbourg; his work in behalf of solid theology and a much-needed emphasis on apologetics

---

[14] It is included in my book, *Christ As Centre and Circumference.*

[15] James C. Burkee, *Power, Politics, and the Missouri Synod: A Conflict That Changed American Christianity* (Minneapolis: Fortress Press, 2011), pp. 80 ff. The Foreword is written by Martin E. Marty, hardly an objective source (Marty, long-time contributing editor of *Christian Century* magazine—left the Missouri Synod over the inerrancy issue and throughout his career has consistently opposed its scriptural position).

Chapter 5

in the Missouri Synod has been simply invaluable. I count him as one of my dearest friends and thank God for giving me the opportunity to impact his thinking and apologetic orientation.

To manage the Springfield teaching along with the regular Trinity appointment was not easy. I flew to Springfield from the O'Hare Airport in Chicago one day a week during term. The aircraft were DC-10 prop planes—virtually indestructible but equally uncomfortable. The weather was often dreadful. More than once, I was so tired on returning to O'Hare that I could not remember where, in the vast airport parking lot, I had left my car—and had to be driven around by the snowplough until it could be located.

I also did a bit of guest teaching in religion at DePaul University, owing to the presence of Robert Campbell, O.P., a conservative Roman Catholic who could not stand the creeping liberalism of his colleagues; he edited *Spectrum of Protestant Beliefs*,[16] to which I contributed, along with fundamentalist Bob Jones, Jr., evangelical Carl F. H. Henry, liberal Bishop James Pike, and death-of-Goder William Hamilton. I characterised my position as "confessional"—solid theologically, stressing the classic creeds of the historic church (the Apostles, the Nicene, and the Athanasian creeds), versus theological liberalisms and radicalisms on the left, and versus sociological conservatisms and pietisms on the right.

In June of 1966, I was one of the participants at the (closed) Wenham conference on the authority of the Bible, organised by Harold John Ockenga, Frank E. Gaebelein, and Russell Hitt.[17] These evangelical leaders were troubled by the movement away from biblical inerrancy principally by certain professors at the Fuller Theological Seminary, and very much wanted a common viewpoint to prevail among evangelical theologians. The conference did not succeed in its objectives: the Fuller people, such as David Allan Hubbard (later

---

[16] Milwaukee: Bruce, 1968.

[17] The surviving records are to be found in the Billy Graham Center Archives at Wheaton College (http://www.wheaton.edu/bgc/archives/GUIDES/032.htm). My contribution to the conference was later expanded into a book, *Ecumenicity, Evangelicals and Rome*—the key essay also forming the Appendix to *God's Inerrant Word*. The John Warwick Montgomery archives at the Southeastern Baptist Theological Seminary also contain valuable documentation concerning the Wenham conference.

to become Fuller's president) and Daniel Fuller (son of founder and radio evangelist Charles Fuller) were convinced that the Bible contained historical and scientific error.

Indeed, early one morning I happened on a discussion between John H. Gerstner and Daniel Fuller in which Gerstner was painfully trying to show Daniel the grounds of biblical inerrancy; to which Daniel replied, "But the mustard seed is *not* the smallest of all seeds"—referring to Mt 13:32 and Mk 4:31. Gerstner pointed out the obvious, that it was more natural to suppose that our Lord was speaking of the seeds present in the ordinary horticulture of 1st century Palestine, not all possible biological seeds on the planet. Late in the afternoon, I found the two men still in discussion. After a particularly strong point made by Gerstner in favour of the entire truth of Scripture, Daniel replied, "But the mustard seed is *not* the smallest of all seeds."

In conversation with Daniel, who had recently returned from Basel, Switzerland, having studied for his doctorate under Karl Barth and having swallowed Barth's neo-orthodox position that one could hold to the gospel whilst also going along with the higher criticism of the biblical texts, I said, wanting to be polite and diplomatic: "It must have been wonderful to study in the shadow of the Swiss alps." Replied Daniel: "My academic experience was frightening. I hope I never see another mountain." Though this will be understood as practicing psychology without a licence, I regretfully concluded that Daniel had been out of his depth in his graduate theological studies. He typified not a few evangelicals with an experience- rather than a doctrinal-centred faith who were blown out of the water by taking doctorates under theologians who deviated from both sound scholarship and historic bibliology—but whose prestige and personal *presence* (at the French language has it) completely overwhelmed them. I wondered if Charles Fuller's emotionally-orientated radio evangelism hadn't unwittingly contributed to his son's movement away from father's Bible-believing fundamentalism.

During the years at Trinity, we worshipped at St Matthew's Lutheran Church in Lake Zurich—just a few miles from Deerfield. The pastor, Harold Krueger, was in every way ideal: doctrinally sound, liturgically literate, pastoral in heart. I served as an assistant pastor, preaching regularly: in the Lutheran Church-Missouri

Synod, unless one is a regular faculty member at one of the Synodical institutions, one can only maintain one's ordination through a pastoral call. Until his death, Harold's father, also a distinguished pastor, was on the staff. If those men could have been cloned, the Missouri Synod would have had immensely less problems! One Sunday, Elmer Towns, then a member of the Department of Practical Theology at Trinity, and later one of the founders of Liberty University, accompanied me to the annual public Confirmation Service at St Matthew's, where the confirmands had to answer doctrinal questions put to them. He remarked afterwards that those teen-aged confirmands knew more systematic theology than most of the students at the Trinity Evangelical Divinity School.

I did a great deal of writing whilst at Trinity, and most of the resulting books were published by Bethany Fellowship in Minneapolis. Bethany was a mildly charismatic Christian community of Lutheran origins, though it eventually took on a non-denominational style with a credo much like that of the Inter-Varsity Christian Fellowship. The president and book editor were entirely on my wavelength in terms of wanting books of serious theology having apologetic impact. Sadly, a generation later, the house shifted to insipid devotional materials and evangelical fiction—and was later absorbed by one of the larger Grand Rapids, Michigan, evangelical publishers.

In my research activity at Trinity, I benefited from fine teaching assistants—in particular Kenneth Harper (later to become a distinguished Presbyterian pastor[18]) and James Moore. Moore was to go through a nasty divorce and spend his career in England with the Open University; he is known today for his publications on the life and thought of Charles Darwin—not quite what I had hoped for him. Other Trinity students to whom I taught apologetics were Ravi Zacharias, William Lane Craig, Mark Noll, John Ankerberg, Erwin Lutzer, John Woodbridge, and Jim Wallis.[19]

During the heady days of Flower Power and "Make-Love-Not-War," Wallis and Moore took a mildly liberal social stance, and one of my professorial colleagues actually said in a faculty meeting that

---

[18] Research essays by him appear in the *Global Journal of Classical Theology* (http://www.newreformationpress.com OR www.1517legacy.com).

[19] Not all of whom, unfortunately, have remained close. In particular, William Lane

he was convinced that they were demon-possessed. (My view was hardly that; but I maintained that Wallis in particular did not—and does not, for that matter—understand sufficiently that the key to social action, as with every sanctification issue, is the personal *justification* of the sinner by the blood of the Cross: only Christ's genuine transformation of the person can result in one's becoming, in Luther's phrase, "a little Christ to one's neighbour." No amount of huffing and puffing per se in the realm of social activism can achieve this.)

The faculty brought together by Kenneth Kantzer was simply stellar: Gleason Archer and Wilbur Smith from Fuller Theological Seminary (which had by now given up its inerrancy platform), Robert Culver, Norman Geisler, Paul and John Feinberg, Walter Kaiser, *et al.* The idea was to create an intellectually untouchable evangelical graduate school of theology maintaining the central creedal verities and unashamedly holding to the inerrancy of the Bible.

The only real tension came from the sociological fundamentalism of the sponsoring church body, the Evangelical Free Church—which had come out of dead Scandinavian Lutheranism. The denomination's Trinity College was on the same campus as the Divinity School, but its president, Harry Evans, was fully on Kantzer's wave-length. The two of them protected me on more than one occasion. In my initial application for faculty appointment, I was advised to be very careful in speaking of my infant baptism: this might trigger a charge of "sacramentarianism" by the Seminary Board. And then there were my elective courses in Christian and modern literature, in which one of the required readings was John Updike's *Rabbit Run*. Updike was a Christian believer,[20] but *Rabbit Run* includes a fair amount of explicit sex. Because of criticism from EFC pastors who came into the Divinity School bookstore and were horrified seeing the book on the shelves, we had to sell it to the students under the counter!

Harry Evans was wonderful. In mid-winter, with snow and ice everywhere, I slipped and fell and a rare 17th-century book I was carrying ended up in a snow bank. I was furious and went to Harry complaining that the campus walks had not been properly cleared. The

---

Craig and Ravi Zacharias have distanced themselves from their former professor.
[20] Updike's superb poem "Seven Stanzas at Easter" is included in my book, *The Suicide of Christian Theology*.

Seminary paid for the book's restoration (at a restorer in Chicago—and this was not cheap). But Harry said to me: "You expect too much of the buildings-and-grounds people. If they were on the intelligence level you are talking about, they wouldn't be doing buildings-and-grounds." He was perfectly right.

Sadly, after his first wife died, and he married a divorcee, he lost his position as president: *he* had not been divorced, but merely marrying a divorced woman was seen as unspiritual. Eventually, he left the EFC and became an Episcopalian. One wonders how many talented believers have been driven away from Bible-believing churches by the sheer legalism and sociological ingrowness that characterises a significant segment of American evangelicalism.

Chapter 6

SEMINARS, DEBATES AND TOURS

During the Trinity years, I began doing apologetics seminars in churches and on college campuses. These were generally organised either through a week (Monday through Friday evenings—but not on Wednesdays, when many churches would have mid-week prayer meetings—and all day on Saturday), or just on a weekend (Friday night, all day Saturday, and Sunday afternoon—with my giving an apologetic-style sermon on Sunday morning). These seminars led to the production of two sets of audiotapes: "Sensible Christianity" and "Defending the Gospel through the Centuries." Eventually, students of mine prepared study manuals to go with the tapes.[1]

Over the years, I probably gave at least thirty such seminars, plus several companion seminars on "Practical Christian Living in Light of the Bible." Some of the locations included: Princeton University's C. S. Lewis Society; Coral Ridge Presbyterian Church, Fort Lauderdale, Florida (Pastor James Kennedy)[2]; Fourth Presbyterian Church, Washington, D. C. (Pastor Richard Halverson); Gloria Dei Lutheran Church, Davie, Florida (Pastors George Poulos and Tony Masinelli); The King's College, Briarcliff Manor, New York; Moody Bible Institute and Moody Memorial Church, Chicago (Pastor Erwin Lutzer); Park Street Congregational Church, Boston (Pastor Harold John Ockenga)[3]; Truro Episcopal Church, Fairfax, Virginia (Pastor

---

[1] These tape sets and accompanying manuals are available from New Reformation Press: www.newreformationpress.com OR www.1517legacy.com. They were initially distributed (and remastered) by the Canadian Institute for Law, Theology and Public Policy, through the good offices and immense labours of blessed Will and Jan Moore.

[2] Kennedy, for all his positive labours for the gospel, was a Calvinist legalist *par excellence*. Without a word or giving me an opportunity to explain my (I contend, scripturally justified) divorce, Kennedy simply dropped me—or, rather, tossed me into outer darkness with gnashing of teeth.

[3] Ockenga was a bit of a New England snob; he never referred to his church as "Park St Church," but always as "*historic* Park St Church."

John Howe); Westmont College, Santa Barbara, California.[4] The most recent of these apologetics seminar presentations took place in October, 2014, at Calvary Church, Albuquerque, New Mexico (Pastor Skip Heitzig and Executive Director Bryan Nixon); it was noteworthy for its impact, with more than three thousand people attending, but also because the bibliophilistic pastor and executive director did the very most to make the speaker's time with them enjoyable--to the point of accompanying him to antiquarian bookstores and picking up the tab for the books he found!

My fame in evangelical circles came about largely because of the debates in which I engaged whilst at Trinity. These led to my regular contributions to the "Current Religious Thought" page of *Christianity Today* under the editorships of Carl Henry, Kenneth Kantzer, and Harold Lindsell.[5] The debating began with my radio encounter with Madalyn Murray O'Hair. Mrs O'Hair had been on Chicago radio with the youth evangelist Jack Wyrtzen, with poor results on the Christian side: she had mentioned the Jewish historian Josephus and apparently Wyrtzen did not know whom she was talking about.[6] Then my home phone began ringing off the hook: the gist of the calls from students and others was "You've got to show everyone that Mrs O'Hair doesn't have the last word!" I vainly pointed out that the Kingdom of God was not likely to fail owing to Wyrtzen's poor showing. A radio encounter was arranged for me to debate Mrs O'Hair.

---

[4] Typical flyers for these seminars can be found in the Appendix, *infra*.

[5] *Après eux, le déluge*. Now the magazine has a far greater popular readership, but it is no longer the scholarly, cutting-edge publication it was under those editors. Cf. my blasts, "The Strange Decline of American Evangelicalism," *New Oxford Review*, September, 1992; "The Descent of Evangelicalism," *Modern Reformation*, September-October, 1997 (and "Response to David Neff," *Modern Reformation*, May-June, 1998). My *Christianity Today* articles are comprehensively listed in Will Moore's bibliography of my writings, included in the Festschrift edited by William Dembski and Thomas Schirrmacher.

[6] Wyrtzen's positive contributions should not be minimised: he had a great impact on Youth for Christ in its early days, and was one of the founders of Word of Life International. By the time of the radio encounter with Mrs O'Hair, he was not exactly in the first blush of youth. In recent years I have been in contact with his son, a fine Christian believer as was his father.

She was quite something. In the first segment, she made sure that she started talking just before the station break, and kept it up to dominate everything right up to the commercials. But I am a fairly quick study and I then used the same tactic for the rest of the programme. It was a great success. Her son William Murray was in the studio with her. He looked a bit like Lurch in the *Addams Family*: stiff as a board and never changing expression. But in 1980, he was baptised and became a preacher. Hopefully, the Montgomery-O'Hair debate made some contribution to this. In point of fact, Mrs O'Hair, who was ultimately murdered by her American Atheists organisation's office manager, was so personally obnoxious that she constituted a significant counter-argument for Christianity: the natural reaction to meeting her was: "If that's what atheism represents, I want the gospel!"

Then came the death-of-God debate with Thomas J. J. Altizer at the University of Chicago on 24 February 1967. The death-of-God movement had captured national and international attention; *Time* magazine devoted lead space to it. My detailed essay on death-of-Godism appeared in a composite volume on the subject published by Random House.[7] Altizer was the movement's most flamboyant representative. He even made fellow religious liberals nervous, and was later eased out of his professorship of Bible and religion at Emory University, to finish his career teaching literature at the State University of New York at Stony Brook.

Altizer was young and very good looking. A public relations lady at the University of Chicago remarked that he was "a living doll." (A decade later he returned to the Chicago area to speak at the liberal Episcopal Seabury-Western Theological Seminary; I was relieved to see that he had developed a paunch and seemed to have suffered the permanent effects of heavy drinking.) The debate took place on a bitter cold February evening. Rockefeller Memorial Chapel was filled to bursting: busloads of people arrived. There were more people in attendance than were present for Karl Barth's appearance there—

---

[7] *The Meaning of the Death of God: Protestant, Jewish and Catholic Scholars Explore Atheistic Theology,* ed. Bernard Murchland (New York: Random House, 1967). My French book, *La Mort de Dieu,* has recently been re-issued by the Verlag fuer Kultur und Wissenschaft.

when evangelical apologist Edward John Carnell was a member of the panel. The debate went very well and some say that it marked, not the death of God, but the death of the death-of-God movement.

One particular reason for the success of the God side of the debate was the fact that I researched Altizer's position in every possible way—whereas he came essentially unprepared. (This has been my experience in all my debates with unbelievers. They are so convinced that believers are simple-minded fundamentalists that they don't believe preparation is necessary. Pride goeth before a fall, yes?) In the course of my research, I learned that Altizer had taken his doctorate at Chicago under the celebrated religious phenomenologist Mircea Eliade and that the subject of his dissertation was analytical psychologist Carl Gustav Jung. So I made an appointment with Eliade and asked him about Altizer. Said Eliade, "he's crazy." At the debate, Eliade sat in the front row, grinning, as I dismembered the death-of-God position.

Even though I hit Altizer's religious philosophy as hard as I could, there was no loss of respect for me on his part. When asked by the religious editor of Lippincott for the name of someone to edit a series of evangelical books on current issues, Altizer recommended me.[8] At Wheaton College, however, the reaction was very different. The student paper piously criticised me for having "crucified" Altizer.[9]

Whilst I am on the subject of Wheaton, I was invited at one point during my time at Trinity to participate in a philosophy seminar on the Wheaton campus. After I had set forth my evidential approach to the defense of the faith, largely in factual, inductive terms, Whea-

---

[8] This was the "Evangelical Perspectives" series of seven volumes. I chose the subjects and the authors (among them, Edwin Yamauchi, Vernon Grounds, and Richard Pierard). I was myself intending to contribute a volume to the series (on a Christian approach to space travel—remember my high school interest in rocketry?), but when I saw that Lippincott was not actively promoting the already published books, I decided against it. A few years ago, I wrote a scholarly article in the general area; it won the 2003-2004 essay prize of the Victoria Institute (the Philosophical Society of Great Britain). The essay is titled, "Did Christ Die for E.T. as well as for *Homo Sapiens*?" It was published in the Victoria Institute's *Faith and Thought Bulletin,* No. 36 (October, 2004), and it is included in my book, *Christ As Centre and Circumference.*

[9] This was especially interesting since, as noted in chapter 3 *supra*, one summer during my undergraduate days I attended a Wheaton summer school—where the spiritual atmosphere was such that I had no problem returning to "pagan" Cornell.

ton's iconic philosopher Arthur F. Holmes remarked, dismissively, "There are, after all, other forms of inference than induction." I replied: "Indeed: for example, deduction, Peirce's abduction or retroduction—and *seduction.*" Half of the audience roared with laughter; the other half were scandalised.

A couple of years after the Altizer debate, the same people who had organised that event set up another debate at the University of Chicago—one between Bishop James Pike and Francis Schaeffer. They told me afterwards that they wished very much that Schaeffer had taken the kind of strong line I had taken with Altizer. They said that Schaeffer's efforts to "love Pike into the Kingdom" (apparently the Wheaton students' approach) had not only failed totally, but that people departing after the debate had said, "Well, the two views are really not that much apart."

In contrast, my approach in public debate has always been to sharpen the issues, not blur them. It is fair to assume that one's protagonist, if he is willing to debate publicly, has pretty much made up his mind and is very unlikely to change as a result of the debate. Therefore, my aim has always been to convince those in the audience whose minds are *not* already made up, rather than focusing on the potential conversion of my opponent.

Halfway into my ten-year tenure at Trinity, I was invited to the University of California at San Diego as a Revelle Scholar. This was a one-term appointment, and I could teach whatever I wanted. I gave courses in Christian philosophy of history and (as I recall) modern theology. The big event during that visiting lectureship was the debate with the father of "situation ethics," Joseph Fletcher, which took place at San Diego State College. As with the Altizer debate, I shall not go into details here, since this debate (like the death-of-God debate) was recorded and can be obtained as an audiotape.[10]

---

[10] From New Reformation Press: http://www.newreformationpress.com OR www.1517legacy.com. Published transcripts of both debates are available as well: the Fletcher-Montgomery debate in book form, and the Altizer debate as a chapter in my book, *Suicide of Christian Theology* (originally appearing as *The Altizer-Montgomery Dialogue: A Chapter in the God Is Dead Controversy* [Chicago: Inter-Varsity Press, 1967]).

Fletcher's tactic was to present himself to the audience as the kindly Episcopal priest, so my aim was to reveal him as he actually was: a utilitarian philosopher with a superficial moral theory directly contradicting the biblical ethic. I finally pushed Fletcher to the point of saying, "Jesus was a simple Jewish peasant. He had no more philosophical sophistication than a guinea pig, and I don't turn to Jesus for philosophical sophistication." This was a suicidal admission. I said nothing at all for half a minute, during which time one could hear the intake of breath on the audience's part. Even non-believers do not want to hear this kind of thing said of Jesus. Fletcher's cover was blown, and starting from that zero point, his path descended rapidly during the remainder of the debate.

During my Trinity years, I commenced leading Christian tours—first to Europe and later to other locations such as the Near East. Eventually we went as far as the antipodes (Australia, New Zealand, Fiji), and even China—where our group was on the last plane out of the Beijing airport before it was closed down owing to the Tiananmen Square massacre.[11]

The tour most repeated was to the Luther sites of East Germany.[12] Every year for a decade I took Christian groups to Berlin, crossing the Iron Curtain into the Marxist German Democratic Republic (a true misnomer)—to visit Eisleben, where Luther was born and died; Eisenach, where he lived as a schoolchild and where the Bach house could also be visited; the monastery at Erfurt where Luther discovered the gospel; Wittenberg, the centre of his reforming activities; the Wartburg castle, where he translated the New Testament; and Leipzig, where his debate with John Eck took place. These trips also included a sobering visit to the death camp at Buchenwald near Weimar, the centre of the so-called German "Enlightenment" of the 18th century.[13] The East Germany tours always left the U.S. on the day

---

[11] See my book, written following that experience: *Giant in Chains: China Today and Tomorrow*.

[12] Typical brochures of these and other tours I conducted are included in the Appendix, *infra*. Some of my Reformation lectures are obtainable on audiocassette from http://www.newreformationpress.com OR www.1517legacy.com; the Montgomery archives at Southeastern Baptist Theological Seminary contain a complete set.

[13] Cf. my *Christianity Today* article, "From Enlightenment to Extermination," reprinted in *Christians in the Public Square* (and elsewhere).

after Christmas and were organised so that we worshipped at the St Thomas Church in Leipzig—Bach's church, where he is buried—on St Sylvester/New Year's Eve. On one occasion, there were almost one hundred tour participants, requiring three busses and my repeating every one of my lectures three times!

Getting those tours in motion was not easy. Initially, I flew to East Berlin and met with Herr Tischer, head of the official East German Tourist Bureau *(Reisebüro der DDR)*. He sat at one end of a long table, I at the other, and on each side were three assistants and three secretaries. I said that I could guarantee a certain number of tourists, but that my conditions were: *I* do the lecturing (theology and church history), and there be no propaganda or visits to tractor factories! Tischer said: "I do not like you or your reasons for coming here, but we need the money; so I agree to your conditions." The only difficulty one year came from a very earnest female representative of the regime (they were always assigned to our busses), who tried to present the glories of Marxism over the microphone. I shut her up in no uncertain terms, and heard later that she had some kind of breakdown—for which I was sorry, but my first responsibility, after all, was to my group.

On one of the East German tours, a young lady discovered—when we were right at the East German border, ready to cross over—that she had left her passport in west Berlin. I found another girl who looked rather like her, positioned that girl in the front of the bus and the girl without the passport toward the back of the bus; after the border guard has inspected the first girl's passport, it was surreptitiously passed from person to person to the other girl, and when the border guard reached the back of the bus, he—without knowing it—inspected the same passport a second time. This worked like a charm as well on the tour's departure from East Germany.

During two of these tour years, I had to stay in West Berlin, sending my groups into East Germany with a trusted colleague. This was because I had been involved in escape attempts (smuggling East German Christians out of that repressive State) and I learned that the secret police—the infamous *Stasi*—had created a file on me. But their bureaucracy left something to be desired and I eventually entered the country again with no special difficulty.¹⁴

A very special tour took place one year to Turkey (Ephesus, where John the Evangelist spent his final years; Pergamon; Istanbul—the ancient Constantinople, with the glorious Church of Santa Sophia; and the region of Mt Ararat, near the Russian border and the then Armenian Soviet Socialist Republic). This tour was the fruit of my own explorations on Mt Ararat in search of the remains of Noah's Ark—a not entirely fruitless quest, as readers of my book on the subject will agree.¹⁵ Those who accompanied me on that tour gave me a handmade, miniature replica Ark, with all their names inscribed on it; this was very touching and I have carefully retained it—along with the piece of hand-tooled, bitumen (pitch) impregnated, 5,000+ year-old piece of wood excavated from the Lake Kop region of the mountain.

Deerfield, Illinois, did not compare with the charms of France (surprise, surprise). I therefore organised, with the blessing of Kantzer and Evans, a quarter abroad for Trinity students at Strasbourg's Faculty of Protestant Theology. This made possible my return to Strasbourg at the beginning of every spring quarter—to direct the programme—with the opportunity to stay on during the summer break. This also provided opportunity for a ministry in Europe, owing especially to invitations from Dr Harold O. J. Brown, then theological secretary of the IFES—the International Fellowship of Evangelical

---

¹⁴ With the unification of Germany and the end of the DDR, the East German *Stasi* files have been opened to the public. My file runs to 305 photocopied pages! With typical German efficiency, there is not only a detailed record of an unsuccessful escape attempt, but even German translations of biographical articles on me appearing in the *Who's Whos*—and a copy of my "95 Theses Then and Now" (later included in my book, *In Defense of Martin Luther*). We trust that the file had evangelistic impact among East German informants and spies! (This *Stasi* file—entirely in German—may be consulted in the Montgomery archives at the Southeastern Baptist Theological Seminary.)

¹⁵ See *The Quest for Noah's Ark*. The paperbound (second) edition contains satellite evidence not available at the time the hardbound edition was published. Theories that the Ark landed somewhere other than on Mt Ararat—or in the foothills—are utterly wrong, though there have been several useless explorations along those lines in the years since my book was published. Oddly enough, they have usually originated from Texas.

Students (the international umbrella organisation embracing the Inter-Varsity Christian Fellowship).[16] I served as one of the speakers at Schloss Mittersill, a castle and IFES conference centre in Austria. One evening, when Joe Brown and I went down to a local bistro, the natives were discussing Hitler: "Don't see why he has such a bad reputation. Why, when Austria voted itself into and was part of the Reich, the trains ran on schedule and the mail was always delivered on time." Those Austrians made redneck Americans look like political liberals.

When my Trinity programme was first inaugurated at Strasbourg, I was invited to lunch by the teaching staff of the Protestant Theological Faculty. This took place at a rather poor-quality restaurant near the train station. (I have learned that academics, in general, have questionable gastronomical standards; that is their one common ground with fundamentalists.) During the lunch, I was seated across from Professor René Voeltzel, whose *forte* was religious education. I remarked that I had recently gone to the cinema in Bischwiller (a suburb of Strasbourg) and that many of the people in the audience seemed to look alike; I wondered if there hadn't been excessive intermarriage in Bischwiller. Looking me right in the eye, Voeltzel said: "I was born in Bischwiller!"[17] One cannot be too careful in one's desultory comments … . But Voeltzel had a fine sense of humour; indeed, one of his many fine books dealt with humour in our Lord's teaching: *Le rire du Seigneur*.[18]

---

[16] Cf. A. Donald MacLeod, *C. Stacey Woods and the Evangelical Rediscovery of the University* (Downers Grove, IL: IVP Academic, 2007), pp. 189–90, 217–18. Joe Brown also solicited articles of mine for the IFES theological students magazine, *Themelios*. In later years, Joe was to lecture regularly for me in my programmes in Strasbourg. In spite of Joe's having been a Harvard man, I counted him as one of my dearest friends, and I miss him very much (he died of cancer in 2007).

[17] My GP in Strasbourg, Dr Baudouin Pfersdorff, is also a writer. In his latest novel, *En attendant Obama* (2009), one of his characters suggests that Bischwiller makes one think of Alfred Hitchcock (!) and the classic anecdote is recounted of the inhabitant of Bischwiller who finally extricates himself from his birthplace and, in some foreign location gets into trouble. He cries (in the Alsatian dialect, to be sure): *"Hilfe! Hilfe! Gibt's jemand uf'm Bischwiller da?"* [Help! Help! Isn't there anybody from Bischwiller around here?].

[18] Strasbourg, 1953.

Chapter 6

As suggested by my touring and the programme in Strasbourg, I was getting a case of Wanderlust. This was compounded by a new interest: legal studies. A new chapter in my life was opening.

Chapter 7

THE JEALOUS MISTRESS OF THE LAW: WASHINGTON, D.C.; LIFE AMONG THE CHARISMATICS: SOUTHERN CALIFORNIA (1974–1980)

In my rare book collection is an early 18th-century Latin thesis, defended at Wittenberg (Germany—where Luther spent his teaching career) on the theme as to *whether one can move from theology to law with a good conscience*. Mercifully, the author concluded that he can.[1]

Whilst at Trinity, I began legal studies with the (no longer existent) LaSalle Extension University. Why legal study? It became evident to me that neither theologians nor philosophers were the best experts on evidence; evidence was the special province of lawyers. And evidence was the key to a powerful apologetic. So it seemed only right to obtain the kind of serious legal training that would give me an apologetics edge not shared in theological circles but of great potential value in defending classic Christian faith. This approach to the defence of the faith has been fully vindicated: a recent work by a Canadian scholar has concluded that my efforts have produced, not just an identifiable style but a distinctive and exceedingly valuable school of apologetics for our time.[2]

A word about LaSalle. It was founded in Chicago in 1908 and had three quarters of a century of success in training students for the bar, for politics, and for business careers. LaSalle's 10th anniversary banquet speaker was William Howard Taft, the only person to

---

[1] *Utrum Studiosus Theologiae Salva Conscientia Theologiae Studium deserere & Jurisprudentiae aut Medicinae se consecrare possit* (Wittenberg, 1711). The president of the jury: the celebrated bibliographer Prof. Dr Johann Friedrich Mayer (1650-1712); the candidate: one Benjamin Potzern from Pomerania. (I should perhaps stress that in taking up the law, I did not, in any event, "desert" theological study!)

[2] William P. Broughton, *The Historical Development of Legal Apologetics* (Longwood, FL: Xulon Press, 2009). The author begins his work with a section titled, "Montgomery: The Leading Apologist of Our Time." Clearly, this is a book which should be in everyone's library! See also Ross Clifford's Australian doctoral dissertation, published under the title, *John Warwick Montgomery's Legal Apologetic: An Apologetic for All Seasons* (Bonn, Germany: Verlag für Kultur und Wissenschaft, 2004).

have been both President of the United States and Chief Justice of the U. S. Supreme Court; Taft had the highest praise for the institution. LaSalle's legal instruction, unlike that of the resident American law schools, was not based on the "case method" as developed and canonised by Christopher Columbus Langdell at Harvard, but on a 14-volume library of "black-letter" treatises: *American Law and Procedure*—very much the classic British approach to legal learning.[3] Instead of attempting to instill a knowledge of legal principles by the inductive study of decided cases, the LaSalle approach was to present the principles themselves in a rigourous, systematic way, illustrating them by decided cases. (What would happen if chemistry teachers taught by expecting the students to discover scientific laws solely by their doing experiments in the laboratory? At best, empirical confusion; at worst, everyone blown up!) The authors of *American Law and Procedure* could not have been more distinguished; among them were Walter Wheeler Cook of Northwestern University, Joseph Walter Bingham of Stanford, James Parker Hall of the University of Chicago, and Roscoe Pound of Harvard. The programme was three years in length, with a fourth year dealing with California law—since, by the time I enrolled, only California would allow a correspondence law graduate to sit for the bar examination without fulfilling other requirements.

Eventually, the American Bar Association killed all American correspondence law instruction by persuading State Bars to allow only graduates of ABA accredited law schools to sit for their examinations.[4] This was very sad, for ABA schools are not necessarily of high academic level and are almost always secular in orientation. In contrast, the jurisprudence (philosophy of law) course in the LaSalle

---

[3] This set, with my (often theological) annotations throughout—together with all my student submissions and rare historical information on the LaSalle law programme—comprises a sacred section in my personal libary.

[4] This contrasts starkly with the British approach. Owing to the absence of so many (civil servants and others) from the British Isles during the days of the Empire, the University of London early made it possible to obtain degrees by taking non-resident examinations, generally administered in British consulates worldwide. Correspondence study was the approved method of preparing for those examinations. In the 20th century, England's Open University has provided a wide range of accredited correspondence degree courses, including degrees in the field of law. I myself have obtained their Certificate in Mathematics and Computing.

curriculum was written by a convinced Christian believer. When I helped the Regent University School of Law to obtain approval from the ABA for a summer programme in Strasbourg, France, the ABA examiners who arrived in Strasbourg were an uncultured lot, whose knowledge of jurisprudence was a real embarrassment. The essence of ABA accreditation is financial: proving that one has such institutional resources that high tuition can and will be charged, thereby ensuring that the law graduate will need (and want) to make money during his legal career. Higher motives of public service and justice are given lip service, but the bottom line is invariably "filthy lucre." Unhappily, this simply reinforces the layman's suspicion of lawyers and their placement close to used car dealers on a scale of ethics and public trust.

Whilst I was working through the LaSalle LL.B. course in what free time I could muster at Trinity, I received an offer from John W. Brabner-Smith, a distinguished Christian lawyer and statesman, to join the faculty at the International School of Law in Washington, D.C.—a new school which he had just founded on a solid Christian basis.[5] Though I was not yet a lawyer, I would hold the chair of jurisprudence, teaching Christian philosophy of law as a required course to all the students. Though this meant giving up my tenured professorship and department headship at Trinity, I could not resist. (I later discovered that owing to bad investments, all the faculty retirement programmes—including mine—at Trinity had gone down the drain, so in leaving I took not a penny of retirement with me after ten years of service. Lesson: never think that sanctification equals intelligence or business acumen.)

Washington, D.C., was a mixed experience. For the bicentennial year (1976), I wrote my book, *The Shaping of America,* dedicating it to a local Lutheran clergyman friend, Art Juergensen, pastor of

---

[5] Brabner-Smith's accomplishments included the drafting of the Philippine Constitution, as well as the charter for the Tokyo War Crimes trials following the end of World War II. The biographical treatment of him on the George Mason University School of Law website (the International School of Law was soon sold to George Mason, a secular institution) is highly inaccurate, turning Brabner-Smith into a kind of "natural law" thinker comfortable with all religious views and beginning his law school with Jewish and Muslim professors! I am nowhere mentioned as one of the original faculty.

Redeemer Lutheran Church in Hyattsville, Maryland, who suddenly passed away from a hereditary heart condition. Another wonderful pastoral contact was the Revd Menzing of Immanuel Lutheran Church, Alexandria, Virginia, where I served as an assistant pastor.[6] When Menzing was dying in a local hospital, he witnessed to every member of the medical staff and the patients with whom he came into contact. But on the negative side, I was appalled by the superficiality of evangelicalism in the nation's capitol (the "prayer breakfasts," etc.), and came down hard on this in a widely-read article.[7]

I stayed with the International School of Law for only two years (1974–1976). The school was not successful in recruiting a sufficiently large student body, so the Board decided to throw the net more widely. They advertised for law students in the New York papers—and, surprise, surprise, a significant number of Jewish students entered. Those students were not happy with a specifically Christian approach to the law, and faced with the conflict of principle and income, the Board chose income.[8] John Brabner-Smith was deeply embarrassed by this turn of events, especially because he had persuaded me to leave Trinity and provide the theological orientation for his new law school. He therefore continued my salary, with no teaching responsibilities for a year, and during that time I wrote my book, *Law and Gospel*, the first edition of which was published by the Christian Legal Society. The book is unique in that it analyses some twenty legal fields, showing their theological connections and significance; it contains extensive bibliography and study questions, thereby serving as a discussion manual on the relationships between theology and law.

It was clear that I needed to find a new position. Two possibilities offered themselves. Jack Preus's brother Robert had become president of the Concordia Theological Seminary, now moved from Springfield, Illinois to Ft Wayne, Indiana. Bob offered me a joint

---

[6] Alexandria was not far from Falls Church, where we lived. On this very attractive community, see Melvin Lee Steadman, Jr., *Falls Church by Fence and Fireside* (Falls Church, VA: Falls Church Public Library, 1964).

[7] "Washington Christianity," *Christianity Today*, 8 August 1975, and reprinted in my book, *The Shaping of America*.

[8] This sad situation is described briefly in my book, *The Shaping of America*—together with the blacklist of those responsible (just so that history doesn't forget them).

professorship in systematic theology and church history. Then Walter R. Martin, with whom I had become acquainted through a very complimentary letter he had sent to me after the Altizer debate, offered me a professorship at the Melodyland School of Theology in Anaheim, California—a school which Walter believed could become the first theologically sound charismatic-evangelical seminary in the country.

I was invited to visit Concordia for a day. The evening was spent at a faculty gathering, during which the conversations never went beyond the internal machinations within the Lutheran Church-Missouri Synod: church politics, seminary infighting, etc. I did my very best to shift discussion to wider issues—the needs of a secular society for the gospel and for a sound, historic theology, apologetics, world affairs; all to no effect whatsoever. Some years later, one of the most ingrown of the faculty members, David Scaer, visited Strasbourg, and had the effrontery to wear a lumber jacket and boots (as I remember) to a fine restaurant to which he had been invited by Bob Preus and myself. It was painfully clear that I would go mad in the Ft Wayne context, as attractive as was the professorial offer.

Then there was California. Though I am entirely convinced that the Holy Spirit did not retire after the first century of the Christian era and that miraculous gifts and healings do indeed continue in the church, I could never classify myself as a charismatic.[9] Thus I had real reservations about going to Melodyland. The name was bad enough, and it was right across the street from Disneyland! But I thought the world of Walter Martin and the idea of serving on a faculty with him was a great draw.[10] Also, California was the only state in which I could, after completing my correspondence law studies, take the bar examination and become a lawyer. So the die was cast: "Go west, young man."

---

[9] Cf. my paper, "Prophecy, Eschatology, and Apologetics"—the concluding essay in David W. Baker (ed.), *Looking Into the Future: Evangelical Studies in Eschatology* (Grand Rapids, MI: Baker Academic, 2001).

[10] To be sure, not all my experiences with Walter were unqualifiedly positive. He once invited me to accompany him on a CRI fund-raising effort at an Austrian castle. The owner, though evangelical, was crazy as a March hare: he thought that he had invented a perpetual motion device. Worse still, he gave Walter no money at all.

Melodyland was indeed an experience. Late one evening, after teaching a class, I was returning to my car in the parking lot, when I was gripped by strong hands, scaring me out of my wits. A student had been "led" to "lay hands upon me." I told the student in no uncertain terms that he had better "test the spirits" by Scripture, as Luther had continually insisted. The key biblical passage in this instance was: "Lay hands suddenly on no man" (1 Timothy 5:22)!

The one truly striking event which occurred during my relatively brief time at Melodyland was an invitational trip to Egypt, Israel, and Jordan. President Anwar el-Sadat of Egypt was deeply concerned that American evangelicals consistently supported Israel no matter what Israel was doing; even war-mongering was acceptable if practiced by "God's chosen people."[11] Sadat wanted peace in the Near East and he invited six evangelical leaders to meet with him to convince them of his sincerity. I was the theologian in the group, whose most well-known member was Jerry Falwell. Geneva, Switzerland, was a stopover on the way, where I dined at the wonderful Restaurant des Eaux-vives. Unfortunately, the first course, unbeknownst to me, contained buckwheat flower, to which I am deathly allergic; the night was spent at the cantonal hospital; in the morning, after morphine injections, I proceded, white and shaking, to my flight to Cairo.

A state dinner was held for us in Cairo. I noticed, on entering the lavish dining hall, racks of Châteauneuf du Pape wine—1964 vintage. My table location was across from the head of French television for Egypt, and we discovered that we had some common acquaintances in France. The conversation was going swimmingly and I was getting in a good witness, when I realised that no wine was being served at our table. I enquired of the waiter, who said, "The head of your delegation said that wine was not to be served to your group." I asked (knowing the answer that would come): "And *who* is this 'head of our delegation'?" It was, of course, Falwell. Said I: "Firstly, there

---

[11] In my personal view, it is one of the gravest hermeneutical errors to confound current Israeli political decisions with the activities of God's chosen people in the Old Testament. The Israel of the Old Testament was a unique phenomenon—maintained for the purposes of the coming of Messiah. To give Israel some kind of divine *imprimatur* in the realm of today's politics leads either to a naïve Christian Zionism or to Calvinist "Reconstructionisms."

is no 'head' of our delegation: we are individual invitees. Secondly, *bring on the Châteauneuf du Pape!"* Later in the trip, Jerry said to me, "If you hadn't done that, I could have financed future Ararat expeditions for you." I replied, "I can live with that. After all, our Lord turned water into wine at Cana, not the reverse." In fairness to Jerry, however, his father was an alcoholic, and like many American fundamentalists, Jerry was incapable of distinguishing drunkenness (rightly condemned in Scripture) from the moderate use of alcohol as a food (not condemned anywhere in the Bible).[12]

We met President Sadat at his home in Ashwan. I was deeply impressed by him.[13] He said that whilst he had been in prison he had read Thomas Costain's novel, *The Robe,* and that the portrait of Jesus there had stuck with him. Sadat wanted to built a common place of worship on Mount Sinai—for Jews, Muslims, and Christians. In personal conversation with him, I tried to get across the uniqueness of Christ, who said, "I am the way, the truth and the life: no one comes to the Father but by me." A year or so later, Sadat was murdered by right-wing Moslem religious fanatics.

When Prime Minister Begin of Israel and Crown Prince Hassan of Jordan heard about our invitation to visit President Sadat, they immediately got into the act. Our return journey was by way of Israel and Jordan. Begin was anything but impressive; I could well understand that he had been a violent revolutionary against the British mandate. Prince Hassan, an Oxford man, had the effrontery to lecture to us—using a blackboard—as if we were ignorant students needing to be brought up-to-date on Near Eastern affairs.[14]

Walter Martin's efforts to ground the theology at Melodyland in the inerrant Scriptures rather than charismatic experience came to naught. A professor of systematic theology, who later would go to Pat Robertson's Liberty University, had been converted when serving on a liberal theological faculty; he saw no reason why his conversion should mean a rejection of the higher criticism of the Bible. After all,

---

[12] On Falwell, see Susan Friend Harding, *The Book of Jerry Falwell: Fundamentalist Language and Politics* (Princeton: Princeton University Press, 2000).

[13] Cf. President Sadat's book, *Those I Have Known* (London: Jonathan Cape, 1984).

[14] I wrote up this trip in several places: in the short-lived *Inspiration* magazine (1978) and in *Christianity Today* (2 and 23 March 1979).

wasn't his experience of Christ-in-the-heart the important thing, not issues of the historical reliability of the biblical texts? Walter tried to get the pastor of the Melodyland Christian Centre, Ralph Wilkerson, to shore things up theologically at the seminary, but to no avail. Walter told me that the situation was becoming hopeless, and that he was going to negotiate a year's salary for me in conjunction with my resignation, and that he would himself leave Melodyland not long after that. He did not want his Christian Research Institute to suffer guilt by association.[15]

---

[15] Later, the entire Melodyland complex was sold. The buildings were razed and the location is now, I understand, a parking lot. Owing to its disappearance and to the ease with which my connection with the operation could be misunderstood, I have not included any reference to my time at Melodyland in my biographical entries in the Who's Whos (*Who's Who in the World, Dictionary of International Biography, Who's Who in America, Who's Who in American Law, Who's Who in France, Debrett's People of Today, Contemporary Authors,* etc.). As for the history of Walter's Christian Research Institute after his death in 1989, see Jay Howard, *Hard Questions for the Bible Answer Man* (Logan, OH: Religious Research Project, 2009).

Chapter 8

LEGAL EAGLING AND THE SIMON GREENLEAF SCHOOL OF LAW (1980–1987)

Having passed the California bar examination (a perfect terror, the hardest bar examination in the world, with a 40% pass rate even with Harvard law graduates taking it),[1] I moved into new territory. First, I began to deliver guest lectures, often under Inter-Varsity or Campus Crusade sponsorship, at secular universities, using legal evidence in the defence of the faith. In Canada, my lectures impacted such law students as Dallas Miller, later to become a Canadian Queen's Counsel and Judge of the Court of Queen's Bench in Alberta.[2] Secondly, I entered into partnership with John Moen, an ordained Lutheran pastor and lawyer, and Jack Golden, a lay Christian believer, to form the law firm of Moen, Montgomery, and Golden. Among our successes was the (at the time) largest personal injury verdict rendered in Orange County. Thirdly, I determined to fulfil John Brabner-Smith's failed vision and create a genuinely Christian law school. With Walter Martin on its first Board, the Simon Greenleaf School of Law came into existence in 1980.

To promote the school, I commenced a local talk radio programme that lasted for a decade: "Christianity on Trial." For two hours on Sunday nights, I took any and all religious questions, especially those with some legal connections. Halfway through each programme, there was the "Legal Loon Award"—given for the nuttyish

---

[1] I had also taken and passed the Virginia bar examination, but that was possible, not on the basis of my LaSalle studies but owing to an "apprenticeship" in a law office. As a result of the continual pressure exercised on State bars by the American Bar Association, there are only five or so States that still allow one to take the bar examination on the basis of apprenticeship in a law office. Abraham Lincoln could not today become a lawyer in Illinois through self-study or apprenticeship.

[2] The Millers and the Montgomerys have become very close friends, in spite of an ocean separating us.

religious notion of the week. Generally, this went to religious liberals, but not necessarily (TV evangelists of the "get rich by faith" variety were frequent recipients).[3]

Radio led to television. My friend Charles Manske, the founder and first president of Christ College (now, Concordia University), Irvine, California, became moderator of a "Christianity on Trial" show sponsored by Trinity Broadcasting Network—the Jan and Paul Crouch operation. These programmes consisted of panel discussions, with me always as a panel member, on current theological and social issues. Later, I was to do 26 programmes in Israel on the historicity of the life of Christ,[4] as well as 13 programmes on the Protestant Reformation filmed in Germany. These were shown all over the world on the TBN network. At a Sherlock Holmes Society of London event years later, a Greek lady recognised me immediately from seeing some of those programmes on Greek television.

Of course, Jan Crouch was crazy and Paul was a sitting duck for charismatic faith ministries. One of the few times Walter Martin and I disagreed was as to whether I should be appearing on the Trinity network. Walter was dead against it. My argument was that he himself was always appearing on secular TV—being interviewed by non-Christians—so how could he object to solid theology à la Manske-Montgomery on the Trinity network? He retorted that we were aiding and abetting heresy. In any case, after a decade, Jan Crouch finally got around to watching our programmes. Since she didn't understand a word of what was going on, the programmes were canceled. But the impact had been tremendous, and Chuck Manske somehow got the rights to all the programming vested in him, so that these shows can now be purchased and used in churches as a means of very sophisticated evangelism.[5]

---

[3] A representative recording of a "Christianity on Trial" programme is available on cassette from http://www.newreformationpress.com OR www.1517legacy.com and other historic programmes can be found in the Montgomery archives at Southeastern Baptist Theological Seminary.

[4] Contacts with Israel have been strong over the years. For example, I participated in Carl F. H. Henry's Jerusalem Conference on Biblical Prophecy in 1971. In the Appendix are two photos of interest: one with Halvor Ronning, my favourite Christian tour guide and Hebrew language specialist in Israel—and the other with a camel.

[5] Dr Manske can be contacted by e-mail; his electronic address is: USCLuther@aol.

Legal Eagling and the Simon Greenleaf School Of Law (1980–1987)

Simon Greenleaf began with a dozen courageous students.[6] During our first year of operation Pastor Chuck Smith gave us free classroom space at his Calvary Chapel in Costa Mesa; we subsequently moved to the campus of Trinity Lutheran Church in Anaheim Hills, where Simon Greenleaf board member Pomeroy Moore, the pastor, was a faithful supporter.[7]

My inaugural oration at the opening of Simon Greenleaf cited the incident in London during the Second World War when de Gaulle, in exile, said to his companion-in-arms René Cassin (later to draft the Universal Declaration of Human Rights), *"Cassin, nous sommes la France"* [Cassin, we *are* France]. Though few in number, they represented what France really stood for. I argued that the law required a theological foundation, and we were going to provide it.

The School had three foci: legal instruction leading to the practice of law (J.D. degree); apologetics employing legal reasoning (M.A.); and human rights (summer programme in Strasbourg, France, at the seat of the European Court of Human Rights—in conjunction with the International Institute of Human Rights, of which I was Director of Studies under its then Secretary-General, A. H. Robertson, an English barrister).

Speaking of the English bar, I myself commenced English legal studies so as to qualify. In England, as in some Commonwealth countries, there are two legal professions, not just one: the *barrister* is a legal specialist, particularly in high court advocacy (barristers wear wigs in all criminal proceedings and in some civil actions), whereas the *solicitor* is a general practitioner, much like the American lawyer; it is the solicitor who consults and hires the barrister when confronted with the more difficult cases and those involving complex litigation. Until recently, no residency was required for becoming a

---

com.

[6] I appropriately named the school for the 19th-century Harvard law professor and Christian author of the *Testimony of the Evangelists,* a work showing that the New Testament witness to Jesus Christ would hold up in any common-law court; this monograph is reprinted in my book, *The Law Above the Law.* Greenleaf's classic treatise on common-law evidence remained the standard, in England and America, for a century.

[7] Cf. Pastor Moore's autobiography, *How I Became a Lutheran Pastor in the LCMS: A Journey with Christ* (rev. ed.; Raleigh, NC: Lulu, 2011), pp. 39-40, 66-67.

barrister, but one needed to pass an "academic stage" examination (English constitutional law, Contract, Tort, and Crime), followed by the regular bar examination. Over a three-year period, I succeeded fulfilling these requirements, and was called to Bar of England and Wales in 1984. I also won the Inns of Court School of Law Kapila prize for the best essay submitted that year. My topic was "The Rights of Unborn Children"—a powerful defence of the right to life—and the essay was published in Vol. V of the *Simon Greenleaf Law Review*.[8]

One of the reasons for immersing myself in the English legal scene was to give an English tone to instruction at Simon Greenleaf. In England, barristers have a powerful Christian tradition behind them. Barristers must be members of at least one of four "Inns of Court"—medieval foundations that grew out of the crusading orders. One must eat a certain number of dinners at one's Inn before call, thereby having intimate contact with practicing barristers and high court judges. I was called at Middle Temple, in the great hall of that Inn, a 16th-century edifice with a glorious hammer-beam ceiling, where Shakespeare himself was in the company performing his play, *Twelfth Night*. Later I also joined Lincoln's Inn, of whose chapel John Donne had been preacher in the 17th century, and where, at the death of a "bencher" (board member of the Inn), a bell tolls. This is the source of the reference in Donne's well-known and profound line (of whose profundity Hemingway was not especially aware!): "Each man's death diminishes me, for I am involved in mankind. Therefore, send not to know for whom the bell tolls, it tolls for thee."

Dinners at the Inns are preceded and following by Trinitarian graces, and one must be present for both for the dinner to be counted. So much the worse for unbelievers: England has a state church, so there is no "separation of church and state" to contend with in maintaining a thoroughly Christian legal tradition in this way. The consequence for legal practice is less stress on money, more stress on values.[9] I instituted such dinners at Simon Greenleaf.

---

[8] This essay has also been reprinted in my book, *Christ As Centre and Circumference*.
[9] This is not to say, however, the money plays no role in the barrister's profession. On one occasion, I was invited by Lord Mackay of Clashfern, the then Lord Chancellor, to lunch with him at the House of Lords (he succeeded Lord Denning as president of the Lawyers' Christian Fellowship, and for many years I was one of that society's vice-presidents). In passing I mentioned that it would be grand to become a "QC" (Queen's

Legal Eagling and the Simon Greenleaf School Of Law (1980–1987)

Reading for the bar in England gave me personal contact with the great contemporary Christian leaders of the law: Lord Diplock, member of the Judicial Committee of the House of Lords and regular worshipper at the Temple Church, owned jointly by Inner and Middle Temple (the Judicial Committee was the closest thing in England to the U. S. Supreme Court, and in 2009 was replaced by the Supreme Court of the United Kingdom); Lord Hailsham, the Lord Chancellor (whose Christian testimony and apologetic for the faith we reprinted with permission in the *Simon Greenleaf Law Review*), and Lord Denning, the most influential English judge in the second half of the 20th century and president until his death at age 100 of the Lawyers' Christian Fellowship of Great Britain.[10] I was myself later to become one of the vice-presidents of that society and to do apologetics seminars with the late Val Grieve[11] and on one occasion served as co-conferee with Sir Norman Anderson, in his time the foremost Christian specialist on Islamic law.[12]

Counsel). He countered: "How much do you make as a barrister?" Never expecting such a question, I mumbled something about being an academic and taking primarily *pro bono* religious human rights cases. He said, "No sense in your applying. One must prove worth by clear evidence of success in the profession." To be sure, Mackay was a Scot, so perhaps his philosophy in this regard can be attributed to genetics ... (That the questionable association of money with legal ideals is by no means limited to the U.K. scene is evidenced in my Appendix article, *infra,* on becoming a member of the Paris bar.) It is only fair to add that more recently new rules for becoming a QC have been introduced, in part to deemphasise the financial factor; however (1) the new rules require more evidence of cases argued before English judges in English courts than I could produce, and (2) as a result of the self-funding nature of the new system, the candidate must himself or herself pay 6,000 Pounds sterling (approximately $10,000) just to engage in the process! Lord Mackay, by the way, had such high respect for me personally that he later nominated me (unsuccessfully) to become an "honorary" QC. (By that time, he was no longer Lord Chancellor, the political climate had changed, and his recommendation had no effect.)

[10] My obituary for him ("Lord Denning (1899–1999): An Appreciation") appeared in *Faith and Thought* [Victoria Institute], no. 26, October, 1999.

[11] Manchester solicitor and author of the popular books, *The Trial of Jesus* (Bromley, Kent, UK: OM Publishing, 1990) and *Your Verdict on the Empty Tomb* (rev. ed.; Bromley, Kent, UK: OM Publishing, 1996). When we were introduced as speakers, and my several degrees were mentioned, Val would always say: "My one Oxford degree is worth all of those!"

[12] Sir Norman (who also wrote as J. N. D. Anderson) was director of the prestigious Institute of Advanced Legal Studies of the University of London and the author of several popular books relating law to theology. His evangelical theology has recently

I also had the opportunity to preach in the Temple Church, where William Sherlock, the father of Thomas Sherlock, the great 18th century apologist, had been Master (i. e., chief pastor).[13] As a result, I became a close friend of the then Master, Joseph Robinson,[14] and well acquainted with his successor, Robin Griffith-Jones.[15] Later, I would also preach in the Lincoln's Inn Chapel and become a friend of the fine evangelical Preacher to the Inn, Bill Norman.[16]

At Lincoln's Inn, if a barrister reserves for Sunday lunch, immediately following Morning Prayer in the Lincoln's Inn Chapel, he sits at high table with the benchers of the Inn, the judges, and their guests. During term time, when the students are present, fulfilling their dining requirement, the lunch is held in the Great Hall, and everyone must wear legal dress (the black barrister's robe). As those at the high table enter the hall, the students rise and bow to them individually, and the occupants of the high table return the bow to the assembled students. This is, of course, in the Oxbridge tradition, and the Inns of Court are regarded as England's "third university":

---

been studied in detail: David H. Mcilroy, "The Theology of Law of Norman Anderson," *Law & Justice: The Christian Law Review,* No. 163 (Trinity/Michaelmas, 2009), pp. 110–26. On his contributions to the Institute of Advanced Legal Studies, see the chapters by William A. Steiner and Aubrey L. Diamond in *Law at the Centre: The Institute of Advanced Legal Studies at Fifty,* ed. Barry A. K. Rider (The Hague, Netherlands: Kluwer Law International, 1999), especially pp. 7–8 and 22–23. Of Sir Norman, Steiner writes: "He was an eminent theologian and lay preacher and a leading member of the evangelical wing of the Church of England. ... He conducted a fortnightly Bible study group at the IALS. He devoted a great deal of time to any necessary pastoral care of members of the IALS."

[13] Thomas Sherlock's *Tryal of the Witessses of the Resurrection of Jesus* is reprinted in my *Jurisprudence Reader.*

[14] A moving and excellent obituary for him was published in *The Times* [London] on 9 July 1999; in it one reads, *inter alia,* "Robinson was really rather a private man, and sometimes a very blunt one. 'Only two major heresies this morning,' he told a colleague who had just been preaching."

[15] When "Da Vinci Code" tours arrived at the Temple Church, Robin Griffith-Jones gave them pointed lectures showing the historical nonsense of the book—in contrast with the solidly historical portrait of Jesus in the canonical Gospels; from those talks came Griffith-Jones's little book, *The Da Vinci Code and the Secrets of the Temple* (Norwich, UK: Canterbury Press, 2006)—a fine witness to naïve occultists and their ilk.

[16] Bill graciously contributed one of his sermons to my Festschrift.

the University of the Law. Barrister's rank is considered a degree: "the degree of the Outer Bar." After my call to the English bar, I frequently enjoyed this experience and the contacts that came with it.

Thus, on several occasions at Lincoln's, I met and conversed with Tony Blair, the Prime Minister, and Cherie Blair, his wife. Both are barrister members of Lincoln's, though Tony never practiced. Cherie is well known for her human rights cases, so we had something in common. She is a strong Roman Catholic, and Tony converted from Anglican to Roman Catholic after leaving office. Though on a number of occasions Tony has publicly affirmed his stance as a Christian in politics, his time as head of a Labour government was a period of increasing secularisation in England, and the reforms he introduced (such as the elimination of most hereditary peers from the House of Lords) hurt the country badly.

After being called to the English bar, I was one of a small number of barrister members of Middle Temple invited to dine with the late Princess Diana.[17] The Princess of Wales was charming in every way. I gave her a copy of my book, *History and Christianity*, and—since rumours of Charles' extramarital activity with his future second wife were in the wind—a copy for the Prince of my *Situation Ethics* debate with Joseph Fletcher. I received a nice note afterwards from the Princess's equerry (personal secretary), thanking me for my gift to her. It goes without saying that I did not receive a comparable note from Charles.

There were also the lighter moments. Ordinary dinners at the Inns of Court are arranged in "messes of four": four at a table. It is common for a member to try to sit at a mess with three Muslims: he then has the bottle of table wine all to himself! Once in while, my mess companions were Oxford or Cambridge men, who would say to me, "Ah, an American. Over here to learn the language, wot?" To which I would always reply, "No, as a matter of fact. Over here to teach you the more evolved form of the language."

During the seven years of my deanship at Simon Greenleaf (in effect, presidency, since the CEO of an independent law school is traditionally so named), we grew to over one hundred students and an impressive pass rate on the California bar examinations. Our

---

[17] For a photo of the event, see the Appendix *infra*.

M.A. students included Craig Parton, who has written and lectured extensively in legal apologetics, has become a dear friend, and is now American director of my International Academy of Apologetics, Evangelism and Human Rights; and Frank Beckwith, who, whilst going on to a Ph.D. at Fordham and doing important work in defending the right to life, returned recently to the Roman Catholicism of his childhood.[18]

The particular strength of Simon Greenleaf lay in our faculty and guest lecturers. Besides Walter Martin and I, there was Harold Lindsell, who had recently retired from his editorship at *Christianity*

---

[18] In his published apology for his conversion (*Return to Rome: Confessions of an Evangelical Catholic*), Beckwith has nice things to say about his Simon Greenleaf experience. However, his passing criticism of my epistemology shows no acquaintance with my *Tractatus Logico-Theologicus,* and his theological self-justifications painfully display a total lack of formal theological (seminary) training. It is disturbing that Beckwith never once discussed with me the issues involved in returning to Rome; he took that route without any in-depth examination of the Reformation alternative. I should also perhaps respond here to his epistemological swipe (p. 59 of *Return to Rome*): "Montgomery, unfortunately, seemed smitten by a particular way of doing Christian apologetics that bought into a view of rationality that the Reformed thinkers rightfully, I believe, saw as not only philosophically flawed but deleterious to Christian faith. Montgomery is a self-styled 'evidentialist.'" *What is really* "philosophically flawed" and "deleterious to Christian faith" is the insistence by those "Reformed thinkers" that one must always begin with the metaphysical issue of God's existence in order to make meaningful the evidential case for Jesus Christ. They forget that "classical," Thomistic-style arguments for God's existence (1) have never saved any one, since "the devils also believe [in God's existence] and tremble"—without being saved (James 2:19), (2) are so abstruse that convincing the unbeliever of them can take until just after the Last Judgment—when, presumably, they will not be important, and (3) are hardly the evidential approach Jesus took: Philip to Jesus: "Show us the Father." Jesus: "Have I been so long with you and yet you have not known me? He who has seen me has seen the Father" (John 14:8-9).

Whilst on the subject of Rome, I should observe that, *pace* the late vitriolic anti-Catholic John Robbins, it is absolutely untrue that "Montgomery [displays a] compromise with Rome" owing to alleged reliance on Thomas Aquinas! (Foreword to J. H. Thornwell, *Sacramental Sorcery: The Invalidity of Roman Catholic Baptism* [Unicoi, TN: Trinity Foundation, 2006], pp. 8–9). First, I am not, and have never been, a Thomist. Secondly, when Robbins condemns R. C. Sproul and Norman Geisler on the same basis, he makes a severe category mistake: to agree with Aquinas' *apologetic approach* (which I don't, but they do) does not at all mean that they agree with Aquinas' *theology*. True, Geisler has swallowed more Aquinas than I believe to be healthy, but the kind of poor scholarship and bad logic Robbins represents does Protestantism no favours.

Today. Lindsell had fought hard and long against the deterioration of evangelical bibliology, particularly at the Fuller Theological Seminary, where he had been a professor in the halcyon days of Edward John Carnell and Wilbur Smith. Through my contacts over the years, I brought in as guest lecturers such luminaries as Gleason Archer, Jr, powerful advocate of the historicity and inerrancy of the Old Testament (Gleason Sr had been a law school dean, and Gleason Jr studied law and became a member of the Massachusetts bar, but never practiced law; said he on one occasion: "I defend only one client: Jesus Christ"); Stanley Jaki, Gifford lecturer, physicist and apologist for God's existence; Arthur Henry Robertson, English barrister and author of *Human Rights in Europe*[19]; Armand Nicholi, Harvard psychiatrist; and Graham Leonard, bishop of London (who would, in utter disgust with the increasing liberalism of the Anglican Church, later become a Roman Catholic priest). Honorary doctorates granted by Simon Greenleaf were accepted by, *inter alia*, Erwin Lutzer, pastor of the Moody Memorial Church in Chicago, and Lord Chancellor Hailsham of St Marylebone—mentioned above—the highest ranking legal luminary of the United Kingdom.[20]

For seven years, I edited the *Simon Greenleaf Law Review*. This publication contained seminal articles in support of right-to-life and apologetic defenses of Christian faith. Volume III was entirely devoted to my Master of Philosophy in Law thesis, accepted at the University of Essex, England, on "The Marxist Approach to Human Rights: Analysis and Critique." Harold Lindsell supplied the Introduction. The final (7th) volume of the *Simon Greenleaf Law Review*—just before I resigned my deanship—contains the story of my successful defense-of-evangelism case in Greece; this material, together with the pleadings in later evangelism cases won at the European Court of Human Rights, is the subject of my book, *The Repression of Evangelism in Greece: European Litigation vis-à-vis a Closed Religious Establishment*.

---

[19] After Bill Robertson's sudden death, I was successful in securing all his personal papers for the library of the Simon Greenleaf School of Law. This was an important coup, since Robertson had had much influence in the founding of the European and the American regional systems of human rights protection. The papers instantly gave Simon Greenleaf status as a research institution.

[20] Flyers representing typical activities at Simon Greenleaf in its halcyon days are to be found in the Appendix, *infra*.

Chapter 9

ANNUS HORRIBILIS AND NEW BEGINNINGS (1988–1991)

By 1988, my marriage had deteriorated to the zero point. Arguments were daily fare. Joyce no longer prepared meals; I had to eat out in restaurants. She refused categorically to accompany me to Europe during the annual Simon Greenleaf summer human rights programmes in Strasbourg, and when, after summers of loneliness abroad, I returned in the fall, I would find that we were in precarious condition because of her spending whilst I was away. She also refused to join my tour to Australia, New Zealand, and Fiji, which was the last opportunity my sister Mary and I had to give our father an experience he had always longed for.[1] For some seven years, I had spent a great deal of what little money we had on marriage counselling with Dr Ron Rook, a Christian psychologist.[2] (Before that, Dr Paul Fairweather, a distinguished psychologist friend of Professor Rod Rosenbladt, after a single session with Joyce and with me, had said that she would never accommodate to the marital role, but I had refused to give up hope.) I was certainly not the easiest person to live with, but I did believe in working through the problems.

Ultimately, things became so bad that I moved out of the house and into a one-bedroom apartment. I became convinced that Joyce, by refusing to engage in a meaningful marriage, had entered into a

---

[1] Because my kid sister Mary married young, after her first year in college, and spent her entire married life in New York City with her husband, banker Robert Schumacher, we had had relatively little contact. Mary passed away from cancer in 2008. She was a stalwart at one of the most influential Episcopal churches in New York City, and Bob continues to guide the Calvary-St George's parish in these difficult financial times. A member of the church's clergy staff, the Revd Jacob A. Smith, was one of twenty registrants in our International Academy of Apologetics, Evangelism and Human Rights programme in Strasbourg in July, 2009. Lany and I were in the States at the time of my sister's death and I was able to speak briefly at the memorial service for her.

[2] My article, "Getting Hold of Our Feelings," on Rook's approach (rational emotive therapy), appeared in *Christianity Today*, 2 October 1981.

state of "constructive desertion" (1 Corinthians 7:15).[3] I sent a letter, apologising for my own contributions to the problem and offering to finance the completion of her bachelor's degree at the University of California at Irvine, and then to do the same for a master's degree (she had complained that this had not been possible)—all to no avail.[4] So I filed for divorce.

When I informed members of the Simon Greenleaf board of this, all hell broke loose. Two of the members, one of whom was the chairman of the board, had been strong supporters of my ministry, though never financially. The chairman, David Berglund, was a very successful plaintiff's personal injury attorney with no theological training,[5] and the other board member, one John Wanvig, was a prissy, bachelor lawyer who ironically had graduated from Simon Greenleaf. These self-styled inquisitors told me that a divorce would not do: "a bishop must be blameless, the husband of one wife … one that ruleth well his own house" (1 Timothy 3:2–4). I got nowhere pointing out that what the passage was actually prohibiting was bigamy—and that it was impossible for me to "rule," much less to live in, my house under the existing circumstances. (I did not go into the question as to whether or not I was a bishop.)

My church body, the Lutheran Church-Missouri Synod, is one of the very strictest in the area of clergy divorce. A divorce not on scriptural grounds (adultery or malicious desertion) leads to the defrocking of the clergyman. My district president (equivalent of a bishop) investigated my marital situation in depth, even interviewing my wife. He was satisfied that my divorce was biblically justified and my

---

[3] See my article, "Church Remarriage After Divorce," in *Christ Our Advocate*, giving, *inter alia*, Luther's position. The Reformers argued, on the basis of Matthew 19:9 and 1 Corinthians 7:15, that there were only two scripturally allowable ways a marriage between living persons could be ended. A classic treatise on the subject was Theodore Beza's *Tractatus de repudiis et divortiis* (Leiden: F. Moyard, 1651); cf. Robert M. Kingdon, *Adultery and Divorce in Calvin's Geneva* (Cambridge, MA: Harvard University Press, 1995).

[4] The original of that letter exists in Montgomery archives at Southeastern Baptist Theological Seminary.

[5] Among Berglund's other activities was his tooth-and-nail fight to prevent a legislative cap on personal injury awards in California—a position not exactly devoid of self-interest.

ordination was therefore not imperilled. Walter Martin was also a great support, having done all in his power to aid in the preservation of my marriage, but ultimately recognising that this was impossible.[6]

The two arbiters of morals on the Simon Greenleaf board would not rest until I was removed from the law school I had founded—and where, to make ends meet—I had taken less than my appointed salary almost every year to ensure that the books would balance. In a real sense, I have to take a certain responsibility for what happened, since I myself had agreed to the choice of those board members: I was desperate for supporters who would contribute financially to an academic ministry that could not obtain the broad-based support of an orphans' home or foreign missionary work[7]; but the hurt in being cast into outer darkness was no less because of that.

When the majority on the Simon Greenleaf board decided to judge me as a recalcitrant sinner—over the objections of my pastor, who pointed out the obvious, that a law school is not a church—I turned the matter over to the Christian Conciliation Service (CCS) of the Christian Legal Society. A professor of criminal law at Simon Greenleaf, Laurence Donoghue, whose daytime job was that of an assistant district attorney in Los Angeles, prepared a lengthy brief in my behalf, and the M.A. faculty petitioned the board not to remove

---

[6] Walter himself had been divorced. I once met the first wife (a real harridan, who ran away with her hairdresser—of all people). A few years thereafter, the fundamentalist president of an Oregon bible college tried to prevent Walter from speaking at a major conference of the Council for Biblical Inerrancy simply because he had been divorced; I managed to persuade those in charge to keep Walter on the programme.

[7] We never had the money to hire a professional fundraiser at Simon Greenleaf. Walter suggested that we use the services of Hank Hanegraaff, whom he had begun to use in that capacity at the Christian Research Institute. However, we were strongly warned away from Hanegraaff by Harvey Milkon, a distinguished retired financier and friend of Simon Greenleaf, who had personally witnessed some doubtful financial activities by Hanegraaff. After Walter's death at the relatively young age of sixty (he was diabetic and overweight), Hanegraaff, who had given "memory" seminars and never took a single earned degree, ingratiated himself as Walter's designated successor to head CRI and become the new "Bible Answer Man." The result was the alienation and departure of a number of Walter's key researchers. Even Walter's second wife and widow finally came to see the error in allowing Hanegraaff to take over CRI. Hanegraaff's books are invariably "researched" (i. e., written) by others. One of his co-authors, Dr Paul Maier, has said that he would never do another book with Hanegraaff.

me. That faculty document cited 66 instances of the board's "lack of leadership, inefficient management and negligent inattention"—plus 18 cases of "poor judgment and misdirected focus," together with 24 instances of "unethical and unbecoming behavior" on the board's part.[8] Strong and consistent support came from Dr Robert Meyer, a mathematics professor in the California state university system.[9] The Revd Pomeroy Moore, who—it will be recalled—had graciously made his Trinity Lutheran Church educational facility in Anaheim Hills, California, available to Simon Greenleaf for its classes during its early years,[10] did everything in his power to persuade the board to keep me as head of the School.[11] Further support came from a Christian CPA in Santa Ana, Ramon Raugust, who had served on the Simon Greenleaf board in the early years of the institution. The eminent theological bibliographer Cyril J. Barber, a member of the Simon Greenleaf faculty, wrote to me:

> I volunteered for the opportunity to work with the CCS so as to insure that you were not given the "shaft." ... Well, the CCS never advised me or any of the others of when we could meet with them. ...
>
> Please let me acknowledge, therefore, your immense contribution to the Simon Greenleaf School of Law. It could not have been started without your vision, and it could not have attained any degree of recognition without your indefatigable efforts![12]

---

[8] Letter of 7 November 1988, in the Montgomery Archives at Southeastern Baptist Theological Seminary.

[9] Dr Meyer is now one of the patrons of the International Academy of Apologetics, Evangelism and Human Rights, which I direct in Strasbourg, France; more on it in a later chapter.

[10] See Chapter 8, at note 6.

[11] A revealing letter from Pastor Moore to David Berglund is to be found in the Appendix, *infra*. The John Warwick Montgomery Archives at Southeastern Baptist Theological Seminary contain a full history of the matter by way of original documents.

[12] Letter of 19 December 1988, in the Southeastern Baptist Theological Seminary archives.

Chapter 9

The conciliator informed my adversaries that they had no legal grounds whatever for removing me; but he emphasised, at the same time, that the controversy (which by then had hit the newspapers) would destroy the School if I stayed.

I therefore resigned, leaving the School in possession of my personal law library which I had originally deeded to the School to allow for its founding (assets of $50,000 were essential to obtain a charter for a California law school), but which I never thought that I myself would lose the right to use. I was able to extract the non-law, apologetics part of the collection, together with my 16th-, 17th-, and 18th-century rare books—except for (the board insisted) an edition of Richard Hooker's 16th-century classic *Of the Lawes of Ecclesiastical Politie* which bore the original signatures of Joseph Story and Simon Greenleaf—and which I had personally found and purchased through a European antiquarian book dealer.

The final conciliation agreement contained a confidentiality clause—which Berglund promptly violated by going on local Christian radio. This was picked up by two unprincipled religious radio muckrakers—one John Stewart (whom I as a pastor had married to a lovely, believing wife he subsequently divorced on non-scriptural grounds)[13] and a freelance writer, William Alnor of Philadelphia (who had married a disgruntled former secretary of mine and apparently thought of himself as the Bob Woodward of evangelicalism).[14] My law partner Jack Golden did a herculean job in blocking much, but not all, of the inaccurate and malicious fallout.

---

[13] Interestingly, John Stewart's admission to the California bar was delayed for years owing to his record of dubious financial dealings in real estate. As a licensed California real estate broker, I entered into transactions years before with Stewart and he taught for two years at the Simon Greenleaf School of Law. When I discovered the shady nature of his dealings, I ceased entirely to work with him and terminated his employment at the Christian law school. His subsequent attempt to ruin my reputation was not unrelated to this unfortunate history. (It should be noted, however, that John Stewart's brother Don Stewart was a model of the Christian popular writer; he co-authored several books with Josh McDowell.)

[14] Just one example of Alnor's sleazy journalism: without any evidence whatever, he accused my pastor, the Revd Pomeroy Moore, of unethical financial dealings in conjunction with the work of the Simon Greenleaf School of Law. Pastor Moore was in fact a man of consummate integrity and had nothing at all to do with the School's financial affairs. For a balanced, independent account of Alnor's irresponsible journalism, including a brief description of his attempt to deep-six my ministry, see

In the subsequent years, Simon Greenleaf hit an all-time low, and was ultimately taken over by Trinity International University—the umbrella organisation embracing Trinity Evangelical Divinity School, where I had served from 1964 to 1974! Trinity had been looking for a West Coast base, and purchasing Simon Greenleaf gave them this opportunity. But the ex-Simon Greenleaf School of Law—Trinity dropped the name—was never to be the same again. True, California state accreditation, which I was on the verge of securing for the School when I resigned, was successfully obtained. But the apologetics emphasis was dropped in favour of Trinity's existing philosophy-of-religion M.A., and the human rights programme in Strasbourg degenerated into the mere opportunity for students to attend the summer sessions of the (secular) International Institute of Human Rights—which they could have done in any case, even without being enrolled at the law school.[15] Our glorious annual Commencement ceremony, always held in a fine, Lutheran liturgical setting, with the first hymn "Praise to the Lord, the Almighty, the King of Creation," and ending with the Vaughan Williams version of "Thine Be the Glory," passed into history—as did the traditions of the English bar.

And that wasn't the end of scandal. A few years after I left, one Winston L. Frost, the then dean of the School, was discovered to have engaged in outrageous plagiarism. To create a published article with his own by-line, he cobbled together a lecture by legal scholar Jerome Shestack that he had heard in Strasbourg at the International Institute of Human Rights and a portion of the human rights article from a recent edition of the *Encyclopaedia Britannica*—and then added footnotes, most of them to my book, *Human Rights and Human Dignity!* When I learned this, I telephoned the president of Trinity International University and insisted that the man be fired. (At the same time, I insisted that their website do the honest thing, and state, which it did not, that I had founded the School.) Clearly,

---

http://www.equip.org/articles/breaking-the-silence-alnor-as-news-editor/ Alnor died prematurely on 20 March 2011; one hopes that he is not disappointed by the inutility of muckraking in heaven.

[15] This situation has improved in recent years. Andrew DeLoach, one of the graduate Fellows of my International Academy of Apologetics, Evangelism and Human Rights now directs the Trinity Law School's foreign program at the IIHR.

Trinity had hoped for a more diplomatic, less public solution for the plagiarism incident, but they did finally give their dean his walking papers. In more recent years, the former Simon Greenleaf has overcome this blotting of their copybook and appears to be gaining influence and support again. I wish them well. "Wherever Christ is preached, I therein do rejoice, yea, and will rejoice" (Phil 1:18).

What, however, was I to do? The first thought was start an independent "Institute for Theology & Law" which would continue the apologetics emphasis we had had at Simon Greenleaf. Drs Frank Diegmann and Beverly Loo, a local veterinarian couple (cat specialists, no less), who had thought highly of my work at Simon Greenleaf and had pledged to endow a $400,000 chair for me there after I had stepped down as dean—this, to be sure, never coming about, since the board forced me to cut all connections with Simon Greenleaf—generously offered to support the new Institute. They also paid the costs of the divorce, which were considerable, owing to the fact that Joyce, never thinking that I would go through with a divorce, now decided to clean me out.

On visiting a second-hand bookstore in the area, I was surprised to discover a number of books identical to those in my home library; they turned out in fact to be my own books, which Joyce had sold without my knowledge whilst I was conducting my final summer programme for Simon Greenleaf in Europe. The book dealer, worrying about a lawsuit, allowed me to buy back at cost what I could (I didn't have the money to buy everything back).

The Diegmanns were willing, for the sake of getting the divorce out of the way rapidly, to employ an expensive route: the property settlement to go before a California rent-a-judge (a retired judge acting as an arbitrator, his decision having the same force of law as would be the case in a regular court action). Joyce's attorney was a feminist terror and, in order for me to retain my book collection (what was left after the legal part stayed at Simon Greenleaf), I was compelled to give up our house in Orange, California and the apartment in Strasbourg, France.[16] Joyce also tried to obtain title to the tiny pied-à-terre in London, but our dear friend Raymond Baron,

---

[16] Joyce's attorney, one Lisa Hughes, engaged in such unethical conduct that I later made a formal complaint against her to the California bar—typically without effect.

who lived in the same building and served as an administrator for the building, was willing to fly to California and testify as to the real value of the flat. The judge left me with that flat and my books—and nothing else.

A subsequent irony was that after Joyce obtained title to the house and sold the Strasbourg apartment, she mortgaged the house and spent the money from the mortgage and from the Strasbourg apartment in buying what was intended to be income property in Orange County; but the market collapsed almost immediately thereafter (this was the infamous 1980s' property decline in California) and she lost everything—sadly, needing to live with friends for the rest of her life.

By the terms of the divorce, I was also required to pay alimony.[17] But there was also a clause requiring Joyce to inform the court and me if she subsequently obtained employment. I learned independently a few years later that she had found a professional position as programme director of a retirement community but had never said a word about it. I therefore stopped paying alimony. But being out of the country, I did not go back to court to obtain a technical modification of the original decree of maintenance. Years later, when I returned for a week from England to Orange County to deliver apologetics lectures at Concordia University, Irvine, Joyce had me served during a break in the evening with a writ for non-payment of alimony.[18] This required my making a second transatlantic flight

---

[17] It is vital to realise that allegations appearing in divorce petitions and responses represent *only the claims of the parties*. Over the years, certain persons who have wanted to hurt my reputation have occasionally repeated such allegations as if they were proven facts. Just as one needs to hear both sides in counselling, so one should never simply accept the claims of a disgruntled spouse as they appear in divorce papers. This is a basic principle in law, but is not widely recognised by laymen (especially journalists?).

[18] Her attorney was the same ghastly Lisa Hughes who had represented her in the original property settlement. Hughes took Joyce's alimony case on a contingency fee basis, receiving $25,000 (1/3) of the $75,000 settlement. Providentially, the dollar dropped in value against the pound sterling right at that point (by then I was receiving an English salary), so that managing the payment did not cause the misery that would have been the case otherwise. From Joyce's death certificate, I ultimately learned that she had had her remunerative position as a professional programme director of a local retirement community for at least the final 11 years of her life (and therefore that she should not ethically have been receiving most of the alimony

Chapter 9

to meet a court date—otherwise I would have been in contempt and would have acquired a criminal record in California. A compromise was entered into in which I did not have to pay more than a small portion of back alimony but did have to resume payments—since Joyce claimed that by then she no longer had a remunerative position.[19] Two years later, in 2007, she passed away from cancer, bitter to the end, blaming me for all her difficulties.[20]

To say that I was lonely would be a vast understatement. I briefly dated a professor of biology at Chapman College, but this went nowhere. However, in attending her little Episcopal church one Sunday, I was spotted by a friend of hers, who, for reasons unknown to me, took an interest in me. That friend, Lanalee de Kant, a professional harpist[21], asked the biology teacher for my phone number. The biology prof checked with me, and I was flattered to death. Result: Lanalee and I started dating, and Lo! a storybook, whirlwind romance. The next month, I was scheduled to conduct one of my European tours. Before I left, I proposed and asked Lany to fly to Europe, meet me in Paris, and marry in Strasbourg. Unbelievably, she agreed. The wedding took place at the historic Lutheran Eglise

---

for which she sued).

[19] I was assisted in this very difficult situation by a fine lawyer friend of Dr Rod Rosenbladt: Tom Garrett, Esq.

[20] Scripture promises that in the eschaton "every tear shall be wiped away" (Rev. 21:4). Joyce was a believer and I know that in eternity there will be reconciliation. The same will be true in regard to the children of the marriage, two of whom have sadly gone their separate ways. (Should they read this, they are to be reminded that their father's house—in both senses—remains always open to them.)

[21] Lany had played under the greatest of 20th century orchestra conductors, both before and during her tenure as principal harpist of the New Orleans Symphony Orchestra and the Vancouver Symphony Orchestra (example, Pierre Monteux, who gave her a signed photograph). In 1954, during Ralph Vaughan Williams' final visit to the United States, shortly before his death, she was his chosen harpist for a concert he directed at Cornell University. During his four-month visiting professorship of music on the Cornell campus, Vaughan Williams encountered a music student at the antipodes of Lany's musical philosophy: this "unfortunate young student ... played over to him a movement from a somewhat dissonant quartet on the piano, at the end of which he simply peered down his glasses and observed: 'If a tune *should* occur to you, my boy, don't hesitate to write it down'" (James Day, *Vaughan Williams* ["Master Musicians Series," 3d ed,; London: J. M. Dent, 1975], p. 69). A modernist conductor in Vancouver once forced Lany to play one half-note apart from another harpist; her comments on this experience were unprintable.

de St Pierre le Jeune. Arrangements such as the reception were made by my dear friends Robert and Patricia Francineau, and we honeymooned in Lucerne, Switzerland—an old English watering hole with swans on the lake and a funicular and cable car ascent to Mt Pilatus or Mt Rigi. During my time of extreme loneliness, a clergyman said to me, "For the Christian, crucifixions are always followed by resurrections." How right he was!

The local Episcopal church with which Lany was connected was a real anomaly. Her father (already deceased) and mother were Bible-believers in the great tradition of the Thirty-Nine Articles.[22] But that little church, overlooking the ocean in lovely San Clemente (Nixon territory), had acquired as rector a former car salesman who surely typified the current condition of the American Episcopal denomination—demonstrating why that church body in recent years has suffered conservative defections right, left and centre. The fellow wore a cowboy hat between services and was "the clergyman on the hot, tin roof"—having affairs with women in his parish. When Lany told him that this was utterly inconsistent with Christian profession, he said that if she would marry him, he would cut it out—and not marry another woman in the congregation to whom he had recently proposed!

I saw him only briefly (he understandably did not warm to me when I began dating Lany), but I was even more troubled by the sight of a really ugly nun-like creature on the church staff. This person was eventually revealed to be quite notorious: as the only person to have been dishonourably discharged from the U. S. Marine Corps both as a man and as a woman. "It" joined as a man, was discharged for homosexual activities, had a sex-change operation, joined as a woman, and was discharged again for fraud and deception in not revealing "its" true identity. All this came out when "it" attempted to found a spiritual order of some kind at the church and *Sixty Minutes* got a hold of the story. The local Roman Catholic parish immediately broke off all ecumenical contact with the church; the Anglican

---

[22] Lany herself had suffered divorce. She had been married to Ronald de Kant, also a professional musician (clarinettist). After years of marriage, he ran off with one of his music students. Lany, née Litz, has retained the name *de Kant*, it being her established professional name.

bishop revised the rector's sabbatical plan to go to Oxford by sending him to a mission in Mexico City; and Lany was persuaded to become Lutheran!

But the Institute I had contemplated never got off the ground. The Diegmanns, who had a history of blowing hot and cold in their support of Christian causes, cooled toward us without our ever knowing why. Their financial assistance was critical to any new project. So the Revd Pomeroy Moore, who had graduated from the independent Lutheran Faith Theological Seminary in Tacoma, Washington, suggested that I take up a position there. He predicted that this would not be permanent, owing to the fact that Reuben Redal, the president of that Seminary, who was also pope (whoops, pastor) of the Central Lutheran Church in Tacoma, had a long history of autocratic rule and many professorial heads had been severed on his personal guillotine. But at the moment he was looking for a name to further the accreditation of his school. Moreover, some years before, I had acted as counsel for his church in its controversial departure from the liberal American Lutheran Church (the ALC),[23] and was therefore a hero of sorts to Redal.

Lany and I therefore made the trek, with all our possessions, to Tacoma, where we bought a lovely Victorian mansion within fifteen minutes driving distance from the Seminary. Lany's mother, Letetia Litz, accompanied us, living with us there and later in England until she passed away. She was a wonderful person, solid in theology

---

[23] The transcript was privately published as a 299-page book: Reuben H. Redal and Paul G. Vigness (eds.), *The Rape of a Confessional Church* [Tacoma, WA, 1981]. This ecclesiastical trial was a real hoot. Among my expert witnesses was the late Dr Eugene Klug, a fine Lutheran scholar on the faculty of the Concordia Theological Seminary, Ft Wayne, Indiana (had even a majority of the faculty there been like him—or like Dr Robert Preus—I would never have gone to Melodyland!). In my cross-examinations of ALC bureaucrats, I revealed the local ALC bishop as inconsistent, hypocritical, and a liar: he had suspended Central Lutheran Church for calling as an assistant pastor a conservative who had not graduated from a seminary approved by the ALC, but he had no problems accepting even liberal non-Lutheran clergy to serve in pastoral roles in his congregations whenever the spirit of ecumenicity moved him. He only admitted to this after learning that, whilst I had had him sequestered, those liberal clergy had themselves testified as hostile witnesses that the bishop had welcomed them into the pulpits of ALC churches in his district. I have included in the Appendix, *infra,* the key portion of my cross-examination for the delectation of the reader.

and possessing a gift of healing. She would sometimes spend hours on the phone helping an acquaintance who had spiritual difficulties, and be utterly exhausted from the strain of her counselling and prayers for others.[24]

On the negative side, there was the cultural spectre of John Candy playing "Tom Tuttle from Tacoma."[25] And Tacoma suffers from the endemic odour of local beer manufacture, reminding me of the same industrial phenomenon in Waterloo, Ontario. (What have I done to deserve two entirely independent sojourns in beer country?) Also, there was the Norwegian cultural commitment—if one can use the word "culture" in this context. Redal's Lutherans were Norwegian to the hilt, and for the first time I could appreciate the ironies in Garrison Keillor's *Lake Wobegon* narratives. (At a social evening at our house, I played a Keillor "Prairie Home Companion" episode dealing with Lutherans; Redal was not amused.) Particularly appalling was the annual congregational *lutefisk* dinner; that fish dish, made using caustic lye soda, is truly "the piece of cod that passeth all understanding."

The one outstanding faculty member at Faith Seminary was the historian Dr Paul Vigness, who had taken up a post there after retiring from a distinguished academic career at several universities, where he had received numerous awards for his teaching.[26] He got along with Pastor Redal by simply allowing Redal to run the show. Paul died whilst we were in Tacoma, and it was a great loss.

Among my students was one Edward Hogg, who at that time had a hippie-like appearance, but who was later to become the (non-ponytailed) president of the Trinity College and Theological Seminary in Newburgh, Indiana. As will be seen, I would later serve as a faculty member of that distance-learning institution. Ed was (and is) a polymath: licensed pilot, law student (he passed the University of London's first-year law examinations entirely by correspondence), holder of a business doctorate.

---

[24] Lany's father, Stanton Litz, who had died before I met Lany, was also a fine Christian believer, as is her one brother, Stan Litz, now retired from a challenging teaching career in the Los Angeles inner city high schools.

[25] In the comedy film, *Volunteers* (1985).

[26] Vigness was author of *The Neutrality of Norway in the World War* (Stanford University Press, 1932).

Chapter 9

During my first year in Tacoma, I studied for and passed the Washington State bar examination, which differs from most other state bar exams in being entirely of an essay character: virtually all other American jurisdictions employ the one-day Multistate multiple-choice test (the MBE) as one-half of their total requirement. Also, the Washington State bar includes environmental law as a part of its syllabus, which is not common elsewhere. After passing the examination, I carried on a wills practice whilst teaching at the Seminary.

I also taught a human rights course for one quarter at the Puget Sound University School of Law in Tacoma. This was very discouraging—though I learned a good deal about the insignificance of American Bar Association accreditation of law schools. Puget Sound was fully accredited, yet the students cared for nothing but grades. One student actually wanted to know how she could be *assured* of receiving an A grade in my course! The dean was a strange one, a libertarian who told me, when we were having lunch at the prestigious Tacoma Club, that he did not believe in state licensing of doctors. His view was that in a free market the good ones would succeed and the poor ones fail. I immediately thought of brain surgery: he was of course correct that after the surgeon botched a few operations and a few patients died, people would hesitate to go to that doctor!

Though I had been called as a barrister in England, I was not yet able to practice there, since the English practice certificate could only be obtained after a "pupillage"—normally one year of increasing responsibilities under the watchful eye of a senior barrister. This is serious bottleneck for the hopeful barrister, for the number of available pupillages is far less than the number seeking them—at least in London, the centre of English legal activity. In my case, because of my academic qualifications and my experience in legal practice in the States, I was exempted from half of the normal pupillage time. So, in contracting with Faith Seminary—i.e., with Redal—the Seminary agreed to give me a paid leave of six months to satisfy this requirement. Off I went to London, whilst Lany held the fort in Tacoma.

My pupilmaster was embarrassed to death by my presence, and saw no reason why I should be doing a pupillage at all. He knew about my human rights teaching responsibilities in Strasbourg in July of each year, so he said, "We'll go through the routine for the coming three months; then you will go to Strasbourg for three months; and afterwards I'll sign anything you want to validate the pupillage." So that is exactly what I did.

But back in Tacoma, things were not peaceful. Redal had not liked the fact that during the academic quarters when I had been teaching I had not spent a certain number of hours in my office on campus—in effect, punching a time clock. He believed, as a tightwad Norwegian, that he was not getting his money's worth. And then—horror of horrors—the Seminary was paying me whilst I was in England! Providentially, Lany was led one day, when she had intended just to go to the bank, to circle back to the Seminary, and she overheard Redal in his office with the door open talking to his minions: "We've got to get rid of Montgomery. He's costing us too much." That evening, Lany phoned Redal at his home and arranged a meeting the following day. At that meeting, she told him in no uncertain terms that he would not get away with violating the terms of my contract. He said simply that he was not going to renew it. Lany then contacted Harry Trembath in California, one of the chief donors to the Seminary—who with his family had gone on one of my European tours and who was forever thankful to me for witnessing to one of his daughters who had become a Baha'i.[27] Trembath was incensed and insisted that Redal pay me a fat severance bonus. Subsequently, the Trembaths ceased to support Faith Seminary.

So: Lany and her mother in Tacoma, I in London, and suddenly no teaching position or source of income for the next academic year.

---

[27] Sadly, that daughter stayed with the Baha'i, and their son Kern swallowed the "higher criticism" of the Bible (cf. his book, *Evangelical Theories of Biblical Inspiration*). Harry was one of the strong financial supporters of the Concordia Seminary, St Louis, and one wonders if, were that Seminary providing any kind of meaningful instruction in apologetics, the children of Missouri-Synod Lutherans would not so easily be shot out of the water by non-Christian ideologies.

Chapter 10

MERRIE OLDE ENGLANDE (1991–1996)

In perusing the London *Times' Educational Supplement,* I noticed an advertisement of the Luton College of Higher Education, seeking a senior or principal lecturer in law. I applied, went through a rigorous process of interviews, and, *mirabile dictu,* won the position. And here a few words of explanation are needed concerning the English university system.

Aside from Oxbridge (Oxford and Cambridge) and the Inns of Court (the "universities of the law"), which operate in lofty quasi-independence, the English higher education scene has traditionally consisted of the regional or urban universities, the polytechnics, and the colleges of higher education. Shortly before I did my pupillage, the polytechnics were absorbed into the university sector—without their having to demonstrate university-level competence. For a college of higher education to become a university, however, it had to undergo rigorous quality tests in two areas: teaching and research. Luton was engaged in this process, and so were looking for new faculty who could reinforce Luton's argument that they deserved to be reclassified as a university. Thus, their interest in me.

I was told later by the College's head of personnel that one of the losing candidates for the position I won was suing the school for discrimination (he was black). Said the head of personnel: "This is going before an Industrial Tribunal. We knew that sometime such a thing would happen. Thank heaven it occurred with you as the successful candidate. With your record, we can't lose." And they didn't.

Ranking of faculty in the English higher educational system is also quite different from what one finds in the United States. The "line" ranks (those relating to a specific salary scale) are, from bottom to top: lecturer, senior lecturer, and principal lecturer. Most faculty members never get beyond these. But there are also "staff" ranks, which involve no increase in salary, but carry great prestige: reader, and professor. I was brought in as a principal lecturer, two years later raised to reader, and a year after that designated professor (recommended by Luton's vice-chancellor—equivalent to the president of an American university—and requiring the approval of a panel of three academics from other institutions who interviewed me in depth). As a result, I became one of only six professors—out of some five hundred teaching faculty at Luton. So rare are professorships in England (even at Oxford, most of the faculty are only ranked as "fellows and tutors") that there is a small national society whose members are limited to those holding professorial rank.

During my time at Luton, the college became a university, and later changed its name to the University of Bedfordshire.[1] This was a good move, since the city of Luton—north of St Albans and therefore due north of London—has not had a reputation for urban attractiveness. In the 19th century, the city was famous for its hat industry, and that brought in many Irish immigrants. Today, its major industry is the Vauxhall automobile factory, employing many workers from the East Indian subcontinent.[2]

When Lany arrived in London—having taken care of the herculean task of packing up and shipping all our worldly goods halfway across the world[3]—we did house hunting, and quickly determined that we did not want to live in the city of Luton. We found a little cottage in the village of Lidlington, between Luton and Bedford (the centre of John Bunyan's activity in the 17th century). Lidling-

---

[1] The standard work on the early history of the county is Joyce Godber, *History of Bedfordshire, 1066-1888* (Luton: Bedfordshire County Council, 1969).

[2] See James Dyer and John G. Dony, *The Story of Luton* (3d rev. ed.; Luton: White Crescent Press, 1975).

[3] Including not only two automobiles (one of them my 1954 Citroën 11-B *Traction avant*) and a vast number of rare books, but also our Teddy Bear collection, headed by Winston. (See the Appendix for photos.) Winston, incidentally, entered the Montgomery household during an ecclesiastical trial in which I defended a mildly charismatic Missouri Synod pastor, Leroy Paul, who was being boiled in oil by inquisitorially minded colleagues. One of my expert witnesses was Dr Rod Rosenbladt. Winston was in the shop of the St Louis, Missouri, hotel where we were staying and it was love at first sight (between Winston and me, note well, not between Rosenbladt and Winston, much less between Rosenbladt and me; these days, one cannot be too careful). On the plane back to California, after winning the case, we put Winston in the seat between us, with an open newspaper in front of him. The air stewardess said, "Oh, how cute! Who does he belong to?" I replied, "Winston is Winston. How would you like someone to ask, 'Whom do *you* belong to?'" We didn't see the stewardess for the rest of the flight.

Chapter 10

ton, incidentally, is mentioned in the 11th-century Doomsday survey of England commanded by William the Conqueror.[4] This meant a 15-minute train ride to the University and 45-minute travel to London (where I was now a member of barristers' chambers)—no great strain.

The University of Bedfordshire has in its student body a significant number of the offspring of ethnic families with non-Christian religious backgrounds. On one occasion, I successfully defended the father of one of my ethnic students in an industrial tribunals case—to the family's unending appreciation. Interestingly, in my courses in English legal system, jurisprudence (=the philosophy of law), and human rights, even though I provided a consistent and explicit Christian approach to the subject matter, I never received a single ideological complaint.

One of my law school colleagues, however, who was an atheist and one of the rare Marxists still around after the disappearance of the Soviet Union, refused to speak to me after I received my professorship (he was a lecturer and so poor in the classroom that his electives attracted on average but five or six students).

The Muslim student society on campus didn't mess with me; they were content to distribute a tract with a photo of the then Bishop of Durham, David Jenkins, in which they pointed out (quite correctly) that even Anglican bishops could deny the unique Sonship of Jesus, and therefore indirectly support the Quranic picture of Jesus. (Jenkins had made himself so objectionable with his deviant theological ideas that when, three days after his consecration as Bishop of York—6 July 1984—lightning struck the historic York Minster, it was widely suggested that this occurred because the Lord was sick and tired of the Bishop's views.)

Which brings me to my personal encounter with the Bishop. My wife and I became staunch members of the Sherlock Holmes Society of London, and at one of the annual banquets Jenkins was the invited speaker (he had remarked, on a "Desert Island Disks" television pro-

---

[4] *Domesday Book: Bedfordshire,* ed. John Morris (Chichester, England: Phillimore, 1977), sec. 11 (XI). Cf. John Bottoms, *et al., Lidlington: A Historical Guide through the Bedfordshire Village of Lidlington (AD 275-1997)* (Lidlington: Lidlington History Society, 1977). In our Appendix, *infra,* we have reproduced from this book a photo of the house where we lived—the historic "Old School House" of the village.

gramme that were he on a desert island, he would read the Holmes stories). What he didn't realise was that the practice of the Society was to assign a member to respond after the invitational talk. Being a theologian, I was asked to provide that response. Jenkins, a great egotist, used his time to talk about himself, with only a passing Sherlockian reference to an Indian he had once known who had much the same inductive powers as the Great Detective. I then spent ten minutes eviscerating him (the Bishop, not the Indian). I titled my remarks, "The Bishop and the Detective," observing that whereas the Bishop was engaged in the destruction of classical Christian theology by swallowing, hook, line, and sinker, speculative German higher criticism of the Bible, Sherlock Holmes had been dead against speculation. He held that it is always "a capital mistake to theorise in advance of the facts."[5] And the historical facts were that Jesus lived a perfect life, performed numerous miracles, died on the Cross for us, and rose again, demonstrating that he was the very divine being he had claimed to be. The Bishop was sitting at high table, next to my wife, and after I finished he grumbled to her, "Well, if I had wanted to, I could have talked about Holmes, too."[6]

At the Inns of Court School of Law in London, under the auspices of the Lawyers' Christian Fellowship, I debated Shabir Ali, an *imam* from Toronto, shipped in for the occasion. His thrust was to use biblical higher criticism, which he had learned from the German theologians (with friends like these, Christians need no enemies), to downgrade the historicity of the portrait of Jesus in the New Testament. I pointed out that even if he were right (which he certainly

---

[5] I later did an entire book of Holmesian essays, containing strong apologetic emphases, as the title suggests: *The Transcendent Holmes*. I also wrote an apologetically relevant Sherlockian piece for Vol. 52, no. 2 of the renowned *Baker Street Journal* (Summer, 2002): "How Many Holmeses? How Many Watsons?"

[6] A sad event occurred whilst we were active in the Sherlock Holmes Society of London: the apparent suicide in March, 2004, of the Conan Doyle scholar Richard Lancelyn Green, who had given my book, *The Transcendent Holmes*, a glowing review. We counted Richard as a personal friend. His father was the noted children's author and Christian writer Roger Lancelyn Green. Richard's death became the subject of a major *New Yorker* magazine article and various scurrilous attempts by journalists to explain the suicide have been rife. In point of fact, Richard, though eccentric, was a Christian believer and we do believe for the world that his death was other than an accident or a product of deep depression.

wasn't, on scholarly grounds alone), this would hardly show that the Quranic picture of Jesus as no more than a prophet was correct! And I had much fun with the following analogy: Suppose someone in our century—over 500 years after the event—claimed that America had not actually been discovered by Christopher Columbus, but by his nephew Alfonso. What historian would accept this? Yet, you—Imam—are saying that the historical picture of Jesus in the New Testament, provided by eyewitnesses and close associates of eyewitnesses, is wrong, whilst Mohammed's portrait of Jesus in the Quran, written well over 500 years after the time of Jesus, and which contradicts what the New Testament says, *is* correct![7]

When I became a practicing barrister, I joined the distinguished Tanfield Chambers, near Gray's Inn, whose head of chambers at that time was Alan Tyrrell, Q.C. On my being promoted to a professorship at the University, Alan remarked, "That's the academic equivalent of becoming a Queen's Counsel!"[8] Among my interesting cases was one against the Church of Scientology. An English couple converted to evangelical Christianity from Scientology and began distributing anti-Scientological literature. They were immediately sued (standard Scientology practice). Our defense strategy was to go to the judge and request all the foundational Scientology records—on the ground that, to defend against the defamation suit and restraining order, we had to be able to show that what the couple said about Scientology was in fact true (defense of justification). The judge agreed and—as we expected—the Church immediately dropped the suit. If you were a Scientology executive, you wouldn't want to reveal what the organisation was actually up to, would you?

A law degree in England, like medical and theological degrees, is a first degree—unlike the American situation, where one first obtains a general degree in arts or in the sciences, and then a graduate law degree. Therefore, my law students at the University of Bedfordshire

---

[7] The debate was recorded and can be obtained on audiotape from http://www.newreformationpress.com OR www.1517legacy.com. I have written up the event in an article originally published in the *New Oxford Review* and reprinted in my book, *Christ As Centre and Circumference*.

[8] We have mentioned "Q.C." earlier: Chapter 8, note 7. I am now a barrister member of 1 Gray's Inn Square Chambers—to which a number of former members of Tanfield Chambers have emigrated.

were all undergraduates. (After obtaining the LL.B., they would then need to attend bar schools to become a barrister, or, more usually, the law society's course to become a solicitor.) Among my students was Ashton Doherty, now with Howard Kennedy, the distinguished firm of solicitors off London's Oxford Street, and Alex Dos Santos, who, as a practicing barrister dealing especially in criminal matters, has been my junior in all my cases before the European Court of Human Rights—and who has become a dear personal friend and friend of the family.

One of those cases warrants an excursus: *Bessarabian Orthodox Church v. Moldova*.[9] I shall not bore the reader with the technical legal details, but merely note here a few personal aspects of the case.[10] Moldova was part of the old Soviet Union, and, until July, 2009, its government was still in the hands of former Marxists who retained the habit of taking all their cues from Moscow.[11] The powers-that-be therefore categorically refused to register an independent Orthodox Church under, not the patriarch of Moscow but the patriarch of the Romanian Orthodox Church, claiming that such a church was a covert operation to return Moldovan territory to Romania. My opponent in the case was the Moldovan Minister of Justice, who wore an ill-fitting, black suit (the uniform of Communist party bureaucrats), and who spoke only Romanian. The official languages of the European Court of Human Rights are French and English, so Moldova had to pay for translators from Romanian to French and English, and back again.

After the Minister argued that two Orthodox Churches in the country would cause it to implode, I countered that (1) I apparently had more confidence in the Moldovan people than its Minister of Justice did, since I was certain that the country could live with

---

[9] A photograph taken following the oral hearing in the case may be found in the Appendix, *infra*, together with my draft oral arguments.

[10] The legal details of the case are recounted in my article, "Life Can Be Difficult If You Are Bessarabian Orthodox," *Law and Justice: The Christian Law Review*, no. 151, Trinity/Michaelmas, 2003 (available in a revised and more complete version in my book, *Christ As Centre and Circumference* [Bonn, Germany: Verlag für Kultur und Wissenschaft]).

[11] The London *Times*, in its 31 July 2009 issue, reported the narrow election victory of pro-European coalition parties over the incumbent Marxist-Leninist government.

two Orthodox Churches, and (2) in any event, the function of the European Court of Human Rights was not to prevent Moldova from imploding, but to implement the European Convention (=Treaty) of Human Rights, which, by virtue of its Article 9, guarantees religious freedom and the right to choose one's religious affiliation. The Court—including the Moldovan judge, who sat *ex officio*—voted unanimously in our favour. I have heard that subsequently the Moldovan government removed that judge from the bench. Following the Court hearing, and wanting to be civil, I said to the Minister of Justice, "I hear you are going from Strasbourg to Paris. How wonderful—the City of Light. Would you like some recommendations of fine restaurants and must-see attractions?" He grumpily replied: "I am going there only because there is an international procurators meeting which I am attending." Who says one's worldview doesn't influence every aspect of one's existence?

Another interesting aspect of the Bessarabian case was that it brought about the end of my relationship with Jay Sekulow of the American Center for Law and Justice. I had joined his operation to assist him in the creation of a corresponding European Centre for Law and Justice in Strasbourg. Years before, I had met Jay at the TBN studios when we were both appearing on an interview programme. Jay had asked my advice as to whether he himself should argue a U. S. Supreme Court case. He said that everyone had advised him to give the case to seasoned counsel. I listened to his account of the case and told him that it was a sure winner and that he himself should argue it; he did so, and his reputation was made.

The dedication ceremony for the new European Centre featured a talk by Pat Robertson, shipped in for the occasion since his money was bankrolling the operation. On the spot, I was asked to translate Robertson's 20-minute speech into French for the largely French audience. Robertson never paused as a courtesy to the translator; he delivered his entire address and then turned to me to translate— which I did, having a fairly good memory. Robertson had ranted and raved against "socialism" and used Thomas Jefferson as a prime example of American Christian values. The mayoress of Strasbourg at that time was not only a solid Lutheran but also a (mild) socialist, as was the city government; and, to be sure, Jefferson had been a deist—anything but a Christian believer. So *(mea culpa)* I dropped all references to Jefferson, and substituted "secularist" for "socialist" in my translation—thus saving Robertson's bacon, though he hardly deserved it.

In any event, the cases accepted by Jay's European Centre were invariably "dogs"—chosen mostly for publicity value when reported on Jay's radio programme back in the United States. In one case, a charismatic church in Germany, with an expatriate American pastor, had not paid taxes for years, and when prosecuted by the German tax authorities screamed "religious discrimination"! And then Jay insisted on being seated as counsel in my Moldova case before the European Court of Human Rights—even though most of the pleadings and documents were in French (which he did not speak) and although he was not a member of the bar of any European jurisdiction. I told him gently that I would never have asked to sit with him as counsel in one of his U. S. Supreme Court cases; but he would not listen. So I resigned from the European Centre for Law and Justice—and won the Moldova case.

That case was one of the most important ever decided by the European Court of Human Rights. In his Sir Thomas More Lecture at Lincoln's Inn (17 October 2002), the then President of the European Court of Human Rights, Sir Nicolas Bratza, listed the five or six most significant cases which had come down since the implementation of the new structure of the Court by way of Protocol 11 (1 November 1998); the single example he gave under Article 9 of the European Convention—the Article guaranteeing religious freedom—was my Bessarabian Church case. And in Vincent Berger's standard work analyzing the leading cases that have come before the Court, only eight cases under Article 9 are listed; the Moldova case is the most recent of them.[12]

As a direct consequence of this victory, I was invited to Romania and given the Patriarch's Medal of the Romanian Orthodox Church. Romanian Orthodox are much more biblical in their theological style than are the Greek or Russian Orthodox, and a dinner with the elderly Patriarch at his palace in Bucharest was a fine experience. I lectured in French to theological students at the University of Bucha-

---

[12] Vincent Berger (ed.), *Jurisprudence de la Cour Européenne des Droits de l'Homme* (11th ed.; Paris: Sirey/Dalloz, 2009), no. 203, pp. 553–55.

rest and attended a fair number of Orthodox church services, where one stands—not sits—for hours at a time.[13] Three of my books are now available in Romanian translation, and a thesis on my apologetic has been successfully defended at the University of Bucharest's Faculty of Baptist Theology.[14]

There were some—but only a few—positive aspects to the time with the European Centre for Law and Justice. First, it was through the organisation that I came into contact with the distinguished European evangelical theologian Prof. Dr Thomas Schirrmacher and his wife Dr Christine Schirrmacher. Thomas is the head both of the Bucer Seminar (a theological seminary in Bonn, Germany, with branches elsewhere in Europe) and of the Verlag für Kultur und Wissenschaft, which now publishes several of my scholarly books in German, French, and English; he is also Ambassador for Human Rights of the World Evangelical Alliance and Executive Director of its International Institute for Religious Freedom—of which I myself am now Honorary Chairman of the Academic Board. Christine is the foremost Christian specialist on Islam in Germany and is frequently consulted by the German government on Muslim problems in the country. The Schirrmachers would later teach at the International Academy of Apologetics, Evangelism and Human Rights in Strasbourg (during its 2010 session).[15]

Secondly, through the ECLJ, I was invited to lecture at the Kwasizabantu Mission in South Africa.[16] The Mission provides a major outreach to the Zulu. Lany and I spent ten days there and the time was very productive. The only downside was that, very much like the contact with YWAM years before (in connection with the trial of

---

[13] There is the Lutheran adage concerning sermons: "No one is saved after the first twenty minutes."

[14] Damian Liviu. *John Warwick Montgomery: și necesitatea istoriei în susținerea adevărului teologic; Tratat de epistemologie teologică evidențialistă* (June, 2007). Professor Liviu provides an English-language treatment of my philosophy of history in Vol. 12, No. 2 (2015) of the *Global Journal of Classical Theology* (www.globaljournalct.com). Of considerable interest also is the excellent doctoral dissertation by Wesley Scott Thompson: *The Influence of a Christian Worldview on John Warwick Montgomery's Educational Practice* (Southeastern Baptist Theological Seminary, 2013).

[15] http://www.apologeticsacademy.eu

[16] http://www.kwasizabantu.com

the "Athens Three"), the leaders of the Mission seemed to be a rather closed spiritual group, and we never felt that we were part of the inner circle. Since our visit there, the Mission has never re-contacted us or endeavoured to maintain any kind of continuing relationship.

Thirdly, I had the privilege of influencing the release of a Turkish evangelical believer jailed in a small town near Izmir (the biblical Smyrna). He had been distributing Christian literature, chiefly material published by Campus Crusade for Christ. The books and tracts were not critical of Islam, nor did they denigrate Muhammed, but he was arrested anyway. I flew to Izmir and met with the judges before the hearing. I pointed out to them that (1) Turkey had been a secular state ever since its modern re-founding by Atatürk in 1923, and (2) Turkey had ratified the European Convention of Human Rights, compelling the country to allow religious freedom, including the right to change one's religion—and that, in turn, entailed the right to distribute religious literature even if that literature represents a minority viewpoint. I said that if they did not release the accused, I would take the case to the European Court of Human Rights—to the acute embarrassment of the Turkish state. They whined that the area was strongly Moslem, etc., but finally gave in.[17]

Not so incidentally, Islam has been an appalling source of human rights violations, especially in the religious sphere. If a country is officially Moslem, there is little or no toleration of other faiths and draconian punishments for religious deviation, sometimes including the death penalty for apostasy. But in non-Muslim, western countries, Islam insists on the freedom to propagate its ideas and relies on its high birth rate to grow in influence. Western nations appear generally oblivious to the dangers this will surely produce for civil liberties in the future.[18]

Whilst at the University of Bedfordshire, I also taught at the BPP School of Law in London. This was one of six schools preparing students for the (old) English bar examination. (The system has now

---

[17] Not so incidentally, the youngest child of my first marriage, Catherine—and the only one to maintain contact with me—after obtaining a French master's degree at the University of Strasbourg, has served for many years as the chief international financial officer for Sekulow's American Centre for Law and Justice.

[18] Cf. the section on Islam in my book, *Human Rights and Human Dignity*.

been changed—for the worse, I believe—in that there is no longer a bar examination as such; students must all take a year's resident course, with continuous assessment. I am strongly in favour of a comprehensive examination to focus one's legal knowledge at the end of formal instruction and before one commences practice.) My area was what is known as Conflicts of Law (or Private International Law)—the fascinating subject treating how courts in one country (or, in the U. S. in one state) handle legal matters where the law of another country or state needs to be taken into account. Many of my students came from Commonwealth or former Commonwealth countries, where the English common law still forms the basis of the legal system. This included countries where a premium is not exactly placed on civil liberties (Singapore, for example). I had a fine opportunity to argue for the western Christian understanding of human rights—and for a Christian perspective. The mother of one of my Taiwanese students insisted on one occasion to invite Lany and me to a lavish—and very expensive—hotel restaurant in London, to show her appreciation for the instruction given to her daughter. Short radio programmes I did for BPP can still be accessed through my personal website.[19]

The University of Bedfordshire was very good to me. On appointing me, they had provided a significant stipend for the shipment of our possessions from Tacoma to England (the farthest shipping point possible from the States, unless one lived in Alaska or Hawaii!). They also did the paper work so that Lany and I could, over a four-year mandatory waiting period, become naturalised British subjects, meaning that we became and now are dual citizens—and servants of Her Majesty! My only complaint relative to the University was that, in accord with general higher educational practice in England (before the recent implementation of European anti-age-discrimination directives), I was put out to pasture at age sixty-five, after six years of service, becoming the first and, at that time the only, emeritus professor of the University of Bedfordshire.[20]

---

[19] http://www.jwm.christendom.co.uk
[20] See the Vice-Chancellor's official letter to me in the Appendix, *infra*.

A few years after leaving the University of Bedfordshire, I was waiting at a tube (underground) station in London, and a young man—whom I did not recognise—jumped off his train, shoved a piece of paper in my hand, and jumped back on his train just in time before it took off for the next station; the paper read: "I was one of your law students at Luton. You were the best teacher I ever had in my life. Thank you for all you did for me."

Chapter 11

LA BELLE FRANCE (1997–)

Emeritus status at the University of Bedfordshire meant that the university would still benefit from my publications in their research exercises, but would not continue to pay me (a nice arrangement for the University). But what, then, would constitute income?

Two sources providentially appeared on the scene. First, a dear Christian friend, Dr W. Howard Hoffman, eminent pathologist in Las Vegas, Nevada, commenced subsidising my ministry abroad. Howard had himself studied for a time in Oxford and had a passion for serious apologetics. He realised that the defense of the faith was not a drawing card in evangelical circles and yet was desperately needed in a secular society. The value of his assistance over the years has been inestimable.[1]

Secondly, Edward Hogg, then in charge of the (Newburgh, Indiana) Trinity College and Seminary's distance-learning operations, asked me to join their faculty.[2] I was to design theology courses around my books and direct resident seminars for Trinity in the United Kingdom. Hogg made my book, *The Suicide of Christian Theology,* required reading for every Trinity student. Since Trinity already had students enrolled from every continent, this meant a tremendous impact. A single example: one of our students, Susan Haden-Taylor, lived on the island of Jersey and was a neighbour of the adventure novelist Jack Higgins, especially famous for the book and film, *The Eagle Has Landed.* Susan was so persistent in witnessing to Higgins and presenting the Christian apologetic to him that she became a character in one of his novels: "The person he's seeing is a friend of mine, a lady called Haden-Taylor.

---

[1] And not just financially. For example, see his Afterword to my Festschrift.
[2] Trinity Newburgh is to be distinguished from the Trinity International University and the Trinity Evangelical Divinity School, whose headquarters are located in Deerfield, Illinois.

She's not only a psychiatrist, but a professor and an ordained priest of the Church of England. She operates out of Harley Street—or St Paul's church, around the corner, if you can't afford to pay."[3]

The summer human rights programme in Strasbourg I had created and directed for the University of Bedfordshire (and which, in turn, was modelled on the programme I had developed at the Simon Greenleaf School of Law) was redone to feature Christian apologetics and thereby to attract Trinity student participation. The programme received a new title: the International Academy of Apologetics, Evangelism and Human Rights. Craig Parton, Esq. became the Academy's American director and my right arm; the programme celebrates its twentieth successful year in 2016.[4] The Board of Reference includes such notables as John Ankerberg, John Bloom, Ross Clifford of Australia, William Dembski, Gary Habermas, Craig Hazen, Michael Horton, Gregory Koukl, Charles Manske, Josh McDowell, Angus Menuge, Dallas Miller, Will Moore, J. P. Moreland, Rod Rosenbladt, Thomas Schirrmacher, Gene Edward Veith, and Oliver Wilder-Smith. The guest lecturers each summer in Strasbourg are selected from the membership of the Board of Reference. Every year twenty-five registrants—maximum—are accepted for this elite "institute of advanced studies" in the defence of the faith. Graduates have included pastors, student workers, foreign missionaries, doctors, lawyers, judges, educators, business leaders, and statesmen—from as far away as Scandinavia, Romania, Africa, Jamaica, and New Zealand.

Soon after Lany and I were married, we happened into a fine clothing store in Strasbourg. The major salesperson, Jean-Marie Mueller, was a distinguished looking and well spoken young man. We got into conversation and discovered that he was a serious Christian believer with a problem: his fiancée needed accommodations in Strasbourg to complete her final university year, in order to be licenced as a biological technician. Since we were then not using, except in summers, the apartment we had managed to purchase (after the loss of the other one

---

[3] Jack Higgins, *Bad Company* (London: HarperCollins, 2003), p. 105. Susan inscribed a copy of the book to me, with the words: "Thank you for all the help you have given me and other students from all over the world—to understand Jesus Christ."

[4] http://www.apologeticsacademy.eu. For a typical brochure of the annual sessions in Strasbourg, see the Appendix, *infra*.

to Joyce in the property settlement), we agreed to rent the apartment to Jean-Marie's fiancée, Laurence. This was the beginning of a wonderful relationship with the two of them.

Eventually, we succeeded in adopting Jean-Marie: French law, unlike the law of most countries, allows for the adoption of an adult. This is termed *adoption simple*, but it is anything but "simple." The notion goes back before the French Revolution, and was a way by which a nobleman could preserve his line even though he did not have natural children. The adoptee does not lose his natural family or the legal advantages that relationship carries; he acquires, in addition, all the advantages related to the adopting parent. In a real sense, he obtains a second family. This requires the consent, not just of the adoptee, but that of his natural family. Normally, the family name becomes a hyphenated one—in this case, Mueller-Montgomery or Montgomery-Mueller. But it is possible to substitute the name of the adopting parent as the entire surname. This Jean-Marie did, with the blessing of his natural parents, thereby assuring the continuation of our Montgomery family name.[5] And, indeed, Lany and I are now grandparents: there is wonderful little Sarah (whose English can stand some work; she insists on saying, "How do you do—you do—you do") and grandson William who appeared on the planet 2 February, 2010—to continue the Montgomery line.[6]

Jean-Marie is a remarkable personal witness for Christ: he has clearly received a divine gift in this regard. He is now the major salesman at the most prestigious men's clothing store in Baden-Baden, Germany, just across the Rhine from the Alsace. (Both Jean-Marie and Laurence are perfectly fluent in German.) In conversation with his customers, Jean-Marie always looks for open doors to present Christ. Baden-Baden was a watering hole (literally: *Bad* in German means "spa") for the European aristocracy between the First and Second World Wars, and today boasts more millionaires than any other city in Germany. In 2009, together with Strasbourg, it hosted the NATO

---

[5] The dropping of the name Mueller was in accord with a comment in E. Wetterlé's delightful book, *Le Professeur Kurt Oscar Muller* (Paris: Edition Française Illustrée, n.d.), p. 8: "Les Muller forment une innombrable tribu et leur nom est de vaine pâture."

[6] On adoption in general, see Russell D. Moore, *Adopted for Life: The Priority of Adoption for Christian Families and Churches* (Wheaton, IL: Crossway, 2009).

summit of heads of state and government at which Obama, Sarkozy, and other world leaders were present. Jean-Marie's clientele includes movie stars (Hugh Grant), Saudi princes, and the political greats (Helmut Kohl). A Saudi prince was so impressed that he invited Jean-Marie to a personal dinner with him. When the owner of the store, Herr Wagoner, desperately wanted to talk with Helmut Kohl, Kohl shooed him away: the discussion of the gospel with Jean-Marie was too interesting to be cut short.[7]

So strong has the relationship become with our adoptive son and daughter-in-law, and with their natural parents and relations,[8] that Lany and I finally decided to sell the Lidlington house and move close to Jean-Marie and Laurence. With their help, we found a house in Soufflenheim,[9] a pottery village 15-minutes from their home in the nearby village of Niederroedern and only a half-hour from Strasbourg. The Soufflenheim home is almost entirely settled after more than a decade (we settle in slowly), the important element being the busts of Luther and Bach in the forecourt!

Our official residence (legal *domicil*) remains that of the United Kingdom, but we have taken on a French *persona*. The reader may well wonder how such a thing is possible. Have not the English and the French hated each other ever since the Hundred Years War (and maybe before that)? Do not the English call the French "frogs" and the French call the English "*les rosbifs*," demonstrating the culinary gulf separating the two peoples? In fact, the European Union, with all its unfortunate bureaucracy, has softened the tensions somewhat. And, in any case, we find the French tons of fun, very easy to get along with, and stimulating in conversation and social relations.[10]

---

[7] Jean-Marie is also no mean poet. One of his Christmas poems was featured in the family's 2008 Christmas card. His ode to me on Father's Day, 2009, can be found *infra,* in the Appendix.

[8] The family includes Jean-Marie's natural parents, Marlène and Alphonse Mueller (strong evangelical Catholic believers, Alphonse, sadly, now deceased); Jean-Marie's brothers, among them Guy, a fine singer; and Laurence's parents, Marthe and Willy Fullhard (Willy, a retired technician, will give you a full history of any machine or machine part, starting with its use on Noah's ark).

[9] Lucien Sittler, Marc Elchinger, Fritz Geissert, *Soufflenheim, Une cité à la recherché de son histoire* (Strasbourg: Société d'Histoire et d'Archéologie du Ried Nord, 1987).

[10] Illustration: On one occasion in Paris, Lany and I dined at La Fontaine Gaillon, one of the restaurants owned by the movie star Gérard Départdieu. He was on the

Much of this has to do with a very strong public educational system, in which successful graduation from high school entails the country-wide *bac* examinations, a genuine rite of passage. Prominent in those examinations is a four-hour philosophy paper. When my dear friend, Dr Willy Humbert, now retired from France's National Centre of Scientific Research, took his, the subject given to him (providentially for a Christian) was "Evaluate the concept of love as set out by St Paul in 1 Corinthians 13." No English (or American) high school student goes through anything like this. The only—and minor—parallel in my personal experience was the Regents examinations, which, in my day, were required of high schoolers in New York State.

To be sure, the French can be difficult if one doesn't speak the language. It has been said that the French are the only people who consider a grammatical fault to be a moral fault. And there is the celebrated line, "The French don't care what they say, as long as they say it correctly." But we find that refreshing—particularly in the face of split infinitives, dangling participles, and the (mis)use of the direct object after the verb "to be"—all characterising the average English speaker today.[11]

But hardly had we begun to immerse ourselves in francophilia when everything suddenly changed at Trinity Newburgh. Dr Hogg had worked like a Trojan to achieve Mid-West regional accreditation for the school, but the Trinity board, including its chairman Thomas Rodgers and one Howard Hunter, a Baptist evangelist, neither put up enough money themselves nor secured from contributors the needed funds to accomplish this. (And Rodgers was not—and is not now—exactly poverty-stricken. He owns homes in Newburgh and in Florida—and a yacht.) When the accreditation did not go through, the board blamed not themselves but Hogg, and summarily dismissed him, actually locking him out of his office.

---

premises and we had a delightful conversation over wine. He told us that his vinological skills had been gained in part when he was filming in Italy with Burt Lancaster. Dépardieu was much impressed with Lany's professional career as an orchestra harpist.

[11] For a fine series of recent discussions on "l'esprit français," see *Philosophie Magazine*, No. 30, June 2009.

Rodgers himself took over (he had been president before Hogg and remained *éminence grise* during the Hogg years). Trusting implicitly in one Revd Thomas Patton, a extreme rightist Northern Irishman—supporter of Ian Paisley—and a fellow who could sell refrigerators (whether they worked or not) to Eskimos, Rodgers accepted the idea of simultaneously registering for Trinity degrees foreign students in the U.K. who were already enrolled in storefront, essentially immigrant "business colleges." He thought that this would be a windfall and would solve Trinity's financial problems. There were overwhelming reasons not to do this, however, to which Rodgers and Patton paid no attention whatsoever. First, these institutions were not part of the British university system, even though they called themselves "colleges"; they often had no academic status whatever. Connecting with them, therefore, was an invitation for devaluing if not killing Trinity's hard-won academic reputation in the U.K. Secondly, these business colleges were not infrequently channels of illegal immigration, opening Trinity to serious potential problems with British governmental authorities. Thirdly, the students at these institutions were rarely Christian, so, to rope them in, a different kind of Trinity programme had to be created for them: Rodgers, with a bachelor of business administration undergraduate degree, attempted to solve the problem by slapping together a Trinity business degree. The result of all this was inevitable. Trinity, which had lost its British accreditation a few years before with the University of Liverpool, largely on the basis of Patton's questionable recruiting practices, now lost its accreditation through Canterbury Christ Church University—which Hogg and I had achieved at tremendous effort.

Then Hunter took over as president of Trinity, with Rodgers' blessing. All at once, I received word (by e-mail) that I was being summarily terminated. It required legal action on my part to recover monies owed to me by Trinity and to obtain a severance package honouring my contract. A number of years before, I had been given a retirement commitment, signed by the Trinity board and the administration, and I had fulfilled all the conditions of it (10+ years of service, etc.). I then discovered that the plan had never been funded and that I would receive nothing. I was, however, able to extract the copies of my publications stored in Newburgh; get Trinity to pay a whopping bill, owed for over two years, to the Canadian Institute for Law, Theology and

Public Policy; and to remove from its website the online journal (the *Global Journal of Classical Theology*) which I had created and edited for Trinity for a decade—making it possible for me personally to retain the rights to the *Journal* and all of its archived issues.

I later learned that Trinity had tried, after their U.K. accreditation debacle, to work out a degree-approval arrangement with the University of Wales. This operated for about a year, until Wales learned of the mess Trinity had created with the business colleges and that Trinity had failed in obtaining U.S. regional accreditation. Wales thereupon dropped Trinity like the proverbial hot potato. This was a great relief to me, since I am an alumnus of Cardiff University (holding the Cardiff LL.M. and LL.D. degrees), and until very recently when it became entirely independent, Cardiff was under the aegis of the University of Wales.

Again, therefore I needed to seek other educational connections. I had happened to watch a BBC television programme on Patrick Henry College in Virginia, close to the nation's capitol, Washington, D.C. I expected the BBC to do a number on this evangelical institution, but the treatment of it was very objective: the College was shown as conservative theologically, with great success in intercollegiate debating (they beat Oxford University both at home and at Oxford!), and committed to putting believers into positions of influence in government. A book entirely devoted to the College and written by a non-Christian journalist had recently been published; its title, significantly, was *God's Harvard*. In checking the College website, I learned that Gene Edward Veith, a Lutheran literary scholar and cultural apologist, had just taken up the post of provost. I therefore contacted the College and offered to work out a research professorship involving teaching on their campus one semester per year—with the summer apologetics programme in Strasbourg receiving academic credit through the College and the *Global Journal of Classical Theology* being moved to the College's website.[12]

---

[12] The *Global Journal* is now sponsored by New Reformation Press and can be consulted at http://www.globaljournalct.com The Associate Editor for many years was Dr Edward Martin; it is now my esteemed colleague at Concordia University Wisconsin, Dr Kevin Voss.

I was invited to deliver a lecture on the PHC campus in conjunction with the national conference of the Evangelical Theological Society the following November, where I was scheduled to present a paper. The lecture went very well. A "distinguished research professorship of philosophy and Christian thought" was offered, and I accepted it. Later I discovered that the president of PHC, Graham Walker, had years before been influenced by my book, *History and Christianity*, and was therefore very pleased with my coming to Patrick Henry. During the academic years 2008 through 2012, I taught an apologetics course, required of all students, and an elective course in philosophy of law and human rights on PHC's Virginia campus.

The location was ideal—close to the nation's capitol and not far from the historic triangle of Williamsburg, Jamestown, and Yorktown. Though hardly a Revolutionary (how could I be, as a servant of Her Majesty?), I am deeply impressed by the colonial traditions of the Commonwealth of Virginia and her respect for sound historical and legal values.[13] An interesting sidelight of the Patrick Henry College experience was our housing there: on two occasions the College rented a house for us that had belonged to Catherine Marshall, the inspirational author and widow of Senate chaplain Peter Marshall; her biography of her late husband, titled *A Man Called Peter*, was made into a popular Hollywood film in 1955 starring Richard Todd. The history of the house offset the unwelcome presence of its other inhabitants

---

[13] The College of William and Mary in Williamsburg boasts the oldest law school still in operation in the United States. It was founded through Thomas Jefferson's appointment of George Wythe to a chair in law in 1779. The founding was a good idea, but Jefferson's motivation for doing so was as questionable as his deistic religious views: he hated the fact that most American lawyers had been receiving their training either at the Inns of Court in London (horrid royalists!), or by staying at home and reading Sir William Blackstone's *Commentaries on the Laws of England* (Blackstone being not only a conservative politically, but also a convinced Christian believer). When I took and passed the Virginia Bar Examination, it was a truly civilised experience. The examination was held in the John Marshall Hotel in Richmond; I stayed at the hotel and had my lunch, between the morning and afternoon sessions, delivered to my room by a uniformed waiter. At that time, one was required to dress for the examination "as in a court of record," meaning with jacket and tie. This was in stark contrast with the (far more difficult) California bar examination, where the candidates entered the examination room in shorts and tee-shirts, looking like death-warmed-over.

(mice) and the fact that the house seemed to be a kind of slave quarters on an unpaved road behind the "mansion"—owned now by Catherine Marshall's stepson. We were never invited to the main house.

To be sure, every institution in a fallen world has its downside. My experience with the Patrick Henry students was a mixed blessing. Most of them are homeschooled—giving them a basic education well above the level of the American public school system.[14] But homeschool families tend to be counter-cultural and anti-authority (not just versus the federal government but against authority in general). Thus the students expect high grades and have little respect for professorial authority. Couple that with immaturity and the result is that teaching them did not constitute an unqualified blessing. And the school made the great mistake of acquiring, from Biola University, an "executive vice-president" thoroughly disliked by faculty there—who referred to him as "Darth Vader"; his chief activity at PHC was to cut expenses (for example, adding keys to copy machines so as to identify the sources of the copying). He clearly resented having to find and pay for our housing during the annual teaching semester on campus. The Patrick Henry administration in general allows the inmates—here, the students—to run the asylum, in that the students are regarded as "customers" having a "contract" with the school and its professors to give them "their money's worth." It is not hard to imagine former homeschoolers' attitudes toward assignments and grades in light of such a notion—which is (mercifully) entirely absent from European university philosophy.

For the fun of it, during one of my last semesters at PHC, I did an anonymous survey of the students in my class. There were 60 students in the apologetics course, most of them seniors and juniors, and they therefore represented 20% of the entire 300-member student body. The results of the survey were most revealing. 81% favoured the election of a Mormon president in the just-held national election—demonstrating, it would certainly seem, that their theological convictions were of less importance to them than their right-wing political com-

---

[14] Out of the goodness of my heart (even though I favour the Lutheran parochial school over any form of homeschooling), I edited and contributed to *Homeschooling in America and in Europe: A Litmus Test of Democracy* (Bonn: Verlag fuer Kultur und Wissenschaft, 2012).

mitments. 32% believed that "the United States is constitutionally a 'Christian nation'"—in spite of no mention whatever of Jesus Christ or of his gospel in the founding documents of the nation. 10% said that "electing conservatives to public office" was a "more important corrective for the secular condition of our country" than personal evangelism. Not surprisingly, therefore, a third of those surveyed admitted that they had not even once "presented the gospel to a non-Christian in the last year"; less than half had done so more than once in the previous twelve months. Clearly, a significant number of those former homeschoolers remained in the ghetto in which they had grown up, with little appreciation of the desperate need to enter into and witness to a lost world. More than two-thirds of those surveyed (68%) said that they would not have enrolled in an apologetics course had it not been required for graduation.

PHC stands not just "for Christ" but also "for liberty" (its motto being *"Pro Christo et Libertate"* –"liberty" being understood as the equivalent of American nationalism and conservative politics). My International Academy of Apologetics, Evangelism and Human Rights, meeting in Strasbourg, France, understandably did not attract many attendees from the College. PHC's founder, Michael Farris, a fine lawyer with a string of cases before state and federal courts, including the U.S. Supreme Court, is nevertheless just to the right of Genghis Khan: he opposes the influence of foreign law on the American legal system, most international organisations such as the UN, and the ratification by the U.S. of international treaties. Incredibly, he worked very hard to kill ratification even of the UN Convention on the Rights of Persons with Disabilities! It goes without saying that he is dead against the international Covenant on the Rights of the Child, critiquing it as reducing parental and family rights. Last we heard, however, our Lord declared that "of such"—little children, not their parents—"is the kingdom of heaven."

But no institution is perfect, and I had a fine relationship with several (but certainly not all) PHC faculty, for example, scientists Neal Doran and Mike Kucks and musician Steve McCollum and his wife, educator Laura McCollum, and with several outstanding students (James Barta, who went on to graduate study at the Georgetown University School of Law, particularly comes to mind).

Chapter 11

The crisis for us at Patrick Henry came in the spring of 2013. Like most evangelical institutions, PHC does not have tenured professorships. My contract, as a full professor, was a three-year one. After one renewal, I was suddenly and without warning or discussion offered a less than half-salary contract involving two weeks of intensive apologetic lecturing on campus. I was no longer to be instructor-of-record in my own apologetics course; it was to be turned over to a distance-learning instructor in Colorado![15] (Colorado, among a very few states, had not implemented new federal standards for correspondence instruction, so PHC could get away with this without legal sanctions.)

The logic was apparently this: we radically limit Montgomery's contact with the students (thus no more grousing from students about his heavy reading assignments, required class presentations of controversial apologetics issues, and tough examinations); we save more than half the salary we have been paying him; we also eliminate having to pay housing for him and his wife one semester a year—and we *still* get the benefits of his name and reputation for our fundraising, accreditation requirements, and recruiting![16] Lany had wanted to instruct in harp in the music department, but the head of the liberal arts faculty quashed that—it would have interfered with their limiting my lecturing to only two weeks per annum on campus.

---

[15] The result could have been worse, however—at least for one academic year. My replacement was Steven Hein, a Lutheran much influenced by my evidential apologetic. He subsequently taught at one of the Strasbourg International Academy of Apologetics sessions, and used two of my books as required texts in the PHC apologetics course. But Hein lasted only one year; he was replaced by "team-teaching," consisting of a local pastor plus a Campus Crusade staff member. In practice, the level of my course was reduced to that of high-school, Sunday School instruction in apologetics. The students in the course are no longer required to engage in any live presentations or defense of Christian faith—a far more comfortable situation for most of them, who, as average homeschooled students, have never witnessed to a non-Christian and instead spend their time with fellow believers at conservative churches and campaign to bring about the Kingdom of God by electing Republicans to public office.

[16] This, as a matter of fact, turned out to be a classic example of "penny wise, pound foolish." On receiving the half-salary contract, we immediately revised our wills. These had designated PHC as the favoured recipient of my 25,000+ rare book library (including some 500 books earlier than the 19th century) and evaluated by theological bibliographer Cyril J. Barber, author of *The Minister's Library* as worth a million dollars twenty years ago—when the collection was half its present size. Our wills now expressly prohibit the library from going to PHC by gift or purchase.

Provost Veith[17] and President Walker did nothing to keep this from occurring; indeed, Walker appeared to be behind it.[18] An Arminian of the legalistic, fundamentalist variety, with a charismatic-styled Episcopal church connection (services there were almost too much for an orthodox Lutheran to bear), it was he who recruited "Darth Vader" from Biola without ever checking that faculty's opinion of him, and made sure that when Lany and I were invited to attend the 10th Anniversary celebration for the College we had to pay personally for the wine we consumed at our motel restaurant!

A confirmation that I have not been evaluating Patrick Henry through creeping paranoia came from the experience of another PHC professor—no longer at the College now, having found greener pastures. He wrote to me shortly after I had received the half-salary contract:

> The day before the Faculty Appreciation Reception, I received an "accidental" email. My student said she was trying to delete it and hit the wrong button. It was supposedly a letter circulating among students that contained a list of complaints against me. ... It said that I was one of three professors on a "hit list" among students. ... No, I am not a perfect teacher. I admit it. But I do have students who thank me and I simply do not believe I deserve this kind of vitriol. ... A literal "hit list" speaks of both violence and hatred. This metaphor is unnerving. At the least this speaks nothing of the love and grace I expected at a Christian institution.

So a word of warning: where fundamentalist legalism has roots at an academic institution, always watch your back. They may dine you (never wine you, of course); but if they can save money by reducing

---

[17] Note well: I have nothing but good to say about Dr Veith's scholarship and theological orientation; indeed, we are co-authoring a book for the 500th anniversary (2017) of Luther's Reformation. He may not have had the power to prevent what was done in my case. But if a College provost has that little power, what does this say about the way the academic institution operates?

[18] I found apropos a recent interview with the celebrated and now retired French movie star Jean-Paul Belmondo. Interviewer: "In your view, what is the most attractive quality in a person?" Belmondo: "Honesty. I can pardon mistakes. Betrayal, never." (*Le Figaro,* 12-13 October 2013.)

your influence, they will surely do so. And since the students provide the income, and you don't, the administration will do everything it can so as not to offend their "customers." Spirituality (much talked about, but far less practiced) is but an exceedingly thin layer on the surface. Thus, no one in the College administration cared about radically cutting the Montgomery salary—at a time of economic downturn far more severe for us living in Europe than for those in the U.S. where there were at least some signs of recovery. And how about that biblical requirement of hospitality? Only two faculty members ever invited us to their homes during our six-year teaching experience at PHC. We sent Christmas cards to most of our colleagues, but never received more than one or two from members of the Patrick Henry community ...

In 2014, therefore, having reached the end of our patience, we severed our connection with the College.

Romans 8: 28, however, still holds true. Dr Angus Menuge, our dear friend, faithful alumnus of the International Academy of Apologetics in Strasbourg (Fellow and Diplomate, thereof), solid Lutheran, and distinguished President of the Evangelical Philosophical Society, made the contacts necessary for a new position to be offered at Concordia University Wisconsin—the largest of the universities of my church body, the Lutheran Church-Missouri Synod.

The position: Distinguished Research Professor of Philosophy. Concordia has highly valued our Strasbourg Academy programme, with no fewer than three of its professors besides Dr Menuge (Drs Don and Mary Korte and Dr Kevin Voss) having become Fellows of the Academy and the Kortes' contributing a science scholarship every year. The University has now committed itself to take over the academic sponsorship of the International Academy from Patrick Henry College. At Concordia, moreover, we benefit from the solidity of Lutheran theology—and we can actually order wine when carrying out University functions and not have to pay for it!

The University is located in Mequon, a small city just north of Milwaukee. So we packed up our belongings stored on the PHC campus (including Lany's concert harp, never used by her for teaching at Patrick Henry) and made the trek to the Midwest to begin autumn semester instruction commencing in August, 2014. Survival among the Lutherans is more likely (and far more palatable) than survival among the evangelical homeschoolers.[19]

The Concordia University Wisconsin teaching position, however, did not turn out to be an unmixed blessing. Mary Korte had warned me that the University's president, in obtaining his position of administrative control years ago, had stressed that he was "not an elitist." Translation: he was for numbers, not for excellence and certainly not for creating a Christian Harvard or Yale to impact our secular society for Christ at the highest leadership levels. This meant that he had little appreciation for my scholarship and never regarded me as more than a mere "visiting professor"; I lasted at Concordia only three years. Here's an article of mine published shortly after my departure:

A Not-So-Pleasant Teaching Experience at Concordia University Wisconsin

After six years at Patrick Henry College, under the deanship of Gene Edward Veith, I decided to take a 50% salary cut to teach at a university of my own church body, The Lutheran Church-Missouri Synod.

At CUW, I received a two-year renewable contract, which was renewed once for a single year. This year, renewal was not offered.

The reason? *Finances*, according to the Vice-President for Academics, Dr William Cario.

Then, *mirabile dictu*, a LC-MS layman offered to pay my full salary and housing expenses for a five-year extension of my contract. (He considered it demeaning that I had had to go to the administration with my hat in my hand seeking contract renewal. He was particularly impressed that at the University of Bedfordshire, England, UK, where the faculty numbered some 500 and there were only 6 full professors, I was one of them.) This donation would have totaled a quarter of a million dollars for the five-year period.

---

[19] Cf. my book for the 500th anniversary of the Reformation in 2017: *Where Christ Is Present: A Theology for All Seasons* (New Reformation Press).

The CUW president, Dr Patrick Ferry, did not even speak to the potential donor, but shunted him off to Dr Cario, who promised to consult on the gift and get back to him. Dr Cario never called the potential donor back, so the donor had to phone him (a second time, at the donor's expense). Cario's response: we are not going to accept your offer.

Now, as I observed in a subsequent meeting with Dr Ferry, there are but two rational explanations possible for this refusal: (1) Montgomery was not doing his job, or (2) arbitrary stupidity (since the University had nothing to lose and everything to gain by accepting the donation).

Could it be that Montgomery was not doing his job? During the three years at CUW, my "Rate Your Professor" score was the highest in the philosophy department; I published three books, all carrying the CUW byline; I received a prestigious award at an international cybernetics conference in Germany this very year; all three years at CUW I gave papers to enthusiastic audiences at the Evangelical Theological Society's annual conferences; my relations with fellow CUW faculty and students could not have been more positive.

So what really motivated the decision? Age? But in three years of instruction, I never missed a single class because of illness. The Kloha debate?[20] Makes one wonder. Did anyone holding Synodical office or someone at a Synodical institution suggest to Ferry that I was a dangerous person, uncontrollable by bureaucracy? There is no way of knowing, since Ferry would not say. But if the reason was ideological, that would be an egregious violation of academic freedom and could jeopardize the University's status with its regional accrediting association--a powerful reason for refusing to give any explanation for non-renewal of contract.

---

[20] In October, 2016, I debated former Concordia Theological Seminary (St. Louis, Missouri) professor Jeffrey Kloha in Chicago on his "plastic" view of the New Testament text. In my view, his philosophy of lower criticism (thoroughgoing/reasoned eclecticism) introduces such a level of subjectivity into the textual critic's activity that it eviscerates any meaningful doctrine of biblical inerrancy. The (new) third volume of my *Crisis in Lutheran Theology (1517 Legacy/New Reformation Press) provides in full my analysis and critique of Kloha's position. Of the debate, one periodical report was titled:* "The Great Historic 21st Century Debate on the Bible: Montgomery Won but Kloha is Winning the Battle for the Bible in the LCMS."

Sadly, I was simply lied to. The non-renewal of the contract was NOT because of finances--or the donation would have been joyfully accepted.

Now a word about how CUW is run. My department head badly needed my continuing services. I offered two unique courses, one of them important also in the Bioethics area of the curriculum. The philosophy department is very small (only four faculty members beside myself) and no one had the background to teach my two areas. But central administration (Ferry, Cario) didn't care and paid no attention whatever to my department head's recommendation. CUW is run as a sinecure by its central administration, with departmental and faculty concerns regularly ignored--including, *inter alia*, complaints of nepotistic administrative hiring.

All of the above characterises the CUW atmosphere (and, I have been told, many of the same problems can be found at other schools in the Concordia system). Tenure no longer exists, so all faculty are at the mercy of the higher administration. No one dares to oppose even arbitrary, stupid policies for fear of being sacked.

Donations are ignored, leaving the university at the mercy of a "tuition-driven" philosophy. Efforts are concentrated on building up the student population (and thus the financial intake). This year at CUW there was a shortfall of incoming students, producing severe cutbacks. Science departments could not renovate essential laboratories.

A tuition-driven institution cannot maintain a consistent policy of rational growth, for any dip in enrollment invariably causes panic. This means, in a secular society, recruitment will occur without a Lutheran or even a Christian focus. The result will be a steady increase in the proportion of non-Christian students on campus. Many faculty members in such a context are far more interested in the subject matter of their discipline than in how to integrate faith and learning. Do we wonder that denominational colleges and universities move inexorably in a secular direction, becoming indistinguishable from their non-Christian counterparts?

Years ago I was the founding dean of a Christian law school, and, having held faculty positions in both secular and Christian institutions in four countries on two continents, I know how a university ought to be run--and how to sustain its Christian (and Lutheran) character. The current administration at CUW, sadly, does not seem to have a clue.

P.S. It took me only a single phone call to obtain a higher paying, better housed professorship elsewhere--where there is still comprehension of Luther's philosophy of Christian education. Contact 1517: The Legacy Project.

*****

What, you ask, is 1517: The Legacy Project? It is an independent Lutheran operation, headquartered in Southern California, with the particular aim of helping Christians of evangelical persuasion to consider the theological and worship advantages of Lutheran faith. Its publication arm, New Reformation Press, has taken over the dissemination of virtually all my books, audiotapes, and videotapes. It utilizes a considerable number of podcasts, including a revival of my radio series "Christianity on Trial."

My activities as Professor-at-Large and Senior Fellow at 1517 Legacy have not required displacement to California. We remain in France and my podcasts are recorded there. My leadership of the annual and independent International Academy of Apologetics, Evangelism and Human Rights, held in Strasbourg and now (2020) in its 24th year of teaching sessions, continues with the superlative assistance of American director Craig Parton, Esq. and his wife Ellen.

Key players at 1517 Legacy are Rod Rosenbladt (Senior Fellow and my former student); Kurt and Debbie Winrich; Scott Keith; "Oz" Osborne (the techie guru); and Steve Byrnes (the masterful head of publications).

1517 Legacy has been the subject of some nasty and unfounded criticism from the Lutheran far-right. It has been claimed, unjustly, that the organization is against the so-called "Third Use of the Law," i.e., empirical sanctification; that it wishes to reduce all theology just to the central Lutheran teaching of justification by God's free grace; that it is weak on biblical inerrancy, etc. Were any of this true, I would never have touched the organization with the proverbial ten-foot pole. In fact, 1517 Legacy, whilst not a church body, is unqualifiedly committed to historic Christian faith, the Ecumenical Creeds, and the Lutheran Confessions. Like the radio show on which I have appeared for years, Issues, Etc., it endeavours to spread Reformation theology as widely as possible in an age of secularism, religious indifferentism, and ecclesiastical superficiality and weakness.

So the Montgomerys continue to hold forth in Europe—especially France. Indeed, after two years of documentation and interviews, I have become a French citizen. Not an easy row to hoe, by the way. Listen to the personal itinerary.

As a dual American and British citizen, living happily in France by way of the European Union, I had no reason to tackle French citizenship. But then came the referendum in the UK to leave the EU. BREXIT (=British Exit) was confirmed by Parliament and was followed by three years of chaos, owing to the controlling Tory Party's inability to decide on the conditions for leaving the EU. One commentator said that she had named her cat "Brexit," since the cat scratched and scratched to get outside, and then, when the door was opened, just sat there and couldn't make up her mind. I anticipated this situation, since I had long observed an unfortunate aspect of the English mentality—lack of appreciation for European values combined with an overblown commitment to British national sovereignty. So I immediately started the French naturalization process.

I submitted tons of required documents, including, *inter alia*, my deceased parents' *birth certificates* (just try getting these from the Clerk's office in Wyoming County, New York State); proof that I had no criminal record in the United Kingdom; evidence that I owed nothing to the city of Paris (where we have a *pied-à-terre*). In achieving the latter, after my phone calls were never answered, I took the TGV to Paris, went to the local government office, found the proper cubbyhole, and was told that they *never answer the phone*! I extracted the needed attestation from a zombie-like creature whose mumbling was almost incomprehensible, had a great lunch at Lasserre's,[21] and returned home.

My fat dossier of documents (arranged in five folders, with an index on the cover of each) was returned to me six months later with a covering letter to the effect that I needed to have paid income tax in France for five years before such an application could be submitted.

---

[21] See my latest book: *A Gastronomic Vade-Mecum (Irvine, CA: 1517 Publishing, 2018)*.

Chapter 11

However, I knew that the *Code Civil* contained an exception directly applicable to me: if one holds a French university degree, the required period is reduced to two years. My dossier had in fact included proof of my French doctorate, and the examining *fonctionnaire* had missed it entirely. So, this time, I somehow reached the powers-that-be by phone and got the matter cleared up. I then resubmitted everything—by registered mail with return card—by way of a second expensive mailing.

Another six months passed and I finally received a date for my oral interview/examination. This required bringing my original doctoral and bar certificates to the examination; since mine had been framed, I had to remove them from the wall at home and lug them to the Préfecture. During the interview, one must show a good general knowledge of French history, geography, politics, and culture—and be able to converse fluently in French, since the interview is conducted entirely in the national language—declared to be such in the French Constitution. (It is said that the French are the only people on earth who regard a *grammatical* fault as a *moral* fault.) Since I was already a member of the Paris bar and hold a French doctorate, the interview was no problem for me; and as a convinced pedant, I insist on linguistic precision anyway. The examiner, a very pleasant woman, could not have been more gracious. On the way out, I asked: "With the length of the entire citizenship process, how many candidates die of old age before being naturalized?" She had no answer, but her staff and she got a real kick out of my question.

From the local Préfecture, the dossier and the examiner's report go to a national government office (now in Nantes, a bureaucratic horror, where just changing my British driver's license for a French one took almost two years).

Some four months later, I received a mysterious phone call from a lady at the civil register who asked two questions: (1) Was "John Warwick" a single first name, requiring a hyphen? (2) Should my place of birth (Warsaw, New York) be listed as *Varsovie* (the French translation of "Warsaw," as in Poland)? I replied (1) I possess *two* Christian names, not a single compound first name like my son Jean-Marie--so no hyphen should be used. She then wanted to use a comma, but I scotched that. (I later learned, from examining my daughter-in-law's French passport, that commas are used administratively between two independent Christian names. *However*, in my case, down with *vir-*

132

gules.) (2) I explained that Warsaw, New York had nothing to do with Warsaw, Poland; indeed, there have apparently never been any Poles living in my birth town. "Warsaw" had to be kept "Warsaw." The lady was very courteous and encouraged me to phone her if I had any other problems. But, in fact, *those* problems hadn't originated with *me*.

Two months after the "hyphen" phone call, and almost a half-year after the naturalization materials had reached Nantes, I received the magic letter: my French citizenship had been granted and recorded in the *Journal Officiel*. A ceremony at the Strasbourg's mayor's office was still to take place—some six months after citizenship had been finalized. Thank heaven, my official welcoming letter from the President of the Republic is signed by Emmanuel Macron and not by his ghastly socialist predecessor, François Hollande.

But why France? you ask. At the beginning of this autobiography, the Norman French roots of the Montgomerys were described in some detail. BREXIT was certainly the precipitating factor for going French, but, quite frankly, the seeds had long been planted. There is a Dutch saying to describe a happy life: "living like God in France." And here is W. Somerset Maugham's telling description of finding one's true home--from his novel, *The Moon and Sixpence,* chapter 50:

> I have an idea that some men are born out of their due place. Accident has cast them amid certain surroundings, but they have always a nostalgia for a home they know not. They are strangers in their birthplace, and the leafy lanes they have known from childhood or the populous streets in which they have played, remain but a place of passage. They may spend their whole lives aliens among their kindred and remain aloof among the only scenes they have ever known. Perhaps it is this sense of strangeness that sends men far and wide in the search for something permanent, to which they may attach themselves. Perhaps some deep-rooted atavism urges the wanderer back to lands which his ancestors left in the dim beginnings of history. Sometimes a man hits upon a place to which he mysteriously feels that he belongs. Here is the home he sought, and he will settle amid scenes that he has never seen before, among men he has never known, as though they were familiar to him from his birth. Here at last he finds rest.

Chapter 12

PRESENT AND FUTURE

Since my "retirement" from full-time teaching, I have been carrying on a number of personal projects along with the professional activities just described. Here is a sampling, more or less in chronological order.

Over a two-year period, I studied for an LL.M. in canon (i. e., Anglican and Roman Catholic ecclesiastical) law at Cardiff University in Wales. This is the only academic programme in canon law since Henry VIII abolished instruction in the subject in the 16th century. The course involved weekend residential seminars, regular submission of academic essays, and a thesis. Most of the essays became chapters in my book, *Christ Our Advocate*. The thesis was published as *The Repression of Evangelism in Greece* and was based on my successful cases against Greece in Athens and at the European Court of Human Rights in Strasbourg.

Having received the Cardiff LL.M., I was able to submit my most important publications to the University for consideration for the higher doctorate, the LL.D. In England, the Ph.D. is a lower doctorate, the higher doctorates being based on an extensive and important record of scholarly publication, which is evaluated by examiners external to the university where one is seeking the degree. The English LL.D., then, is an earned degree, unlike the American LL.D., which is honorary—like the American D.D. and the Litt.D. (One thinks of Pastor Fiddle, who received the honorary doctorate in divinity and became "Fiddle, D.D.") The LL.D. was granted to me in 2003.[1]

---

[1] As a matter of interest, I am also the recipient of an honorary doctorate—from the Institute for Religion and Law, Moscow. This was granted because of my activities in defense of religious liberties and the freedom to evangelise.

In the post-Bedfordshire years, I also qualified for the Advanced Certificate of the (English) Heraldry Society by completing a treatise on *Heraldic Aspects of the German Reformation*.[2] And I obtained a Certificate in Mathematics and Computing from the Open University in England—making good on a promise to myself to study calculus and differential equations (I had not gone beyond advanced algebra, trigonometry, and solid geometry in high school), and also to extend my knowledge of computer programming. As to the latter, I reached the point, using the Pascal language, to create a couple of simple apologetics programmes, which can be found on my website.[3]

My most important writing project after becoming Emeritus at Bedfordshire was the completion of my *Tractatus Logico-Theologicus,* begun thirty years before when I was teaching apologetics and philosophy of religion at the Trinity Evangelical Divinity School. The early propositions circulated in typescript, and I had long promised myself to finish the book. This was a herculean task, finally entailing more than two thousand propositional entries, and serving as a comprehensive apologetic for Christian faith and the truth and relevance of the Holy Scriptures. The style is a bit off-putting, since it is based upon the construction of Ludwig Wittgenstein's *Tractatus Logico-Philosophicus,* but the merit of it lies in the cleanliness of the argument. So often theological writing employs emotive rhetoric and sermonising in a manner that obscures the logic (or the illogic!) of the arguments being presented. The structure of my *Tractatus* makes ambiguity virtually impossible and thus offers a far greater apologetic precision than one finds in most of the literature in this field. Believers as well as non-believers should find this, at minimum, refreshing—and hopefully persuasive.

In 2008, I studied for and passed the required examinations to become an international Certified Fraud Examiner (CFA).[4] This coordinates well with my legal training, and was suggested by one of my lawyer-students in Strasbourg (John Tollefsen), who pointed out

---

[2] Published by the Verlag für Kultur und Wissenschaft, Bonn, Germany.

[3] http://www.jwm.christendom.co.uk. It should not go without saying that, though I have PCs and can operate with Windows' operating systems, I am fundamentally a Mac person. The Mac is to the PC what a Rolls Royce is to a Ford.

[4] http://www.acfe.com

its potential apologetic value. I have since introduced a "fraud" unit into my apologetics courses, showing why one cannot successfully argue that the testimonies to Jesus Christ in the New Testament are the product of fraud or deception. My interest in fraud goes back several years. In 1995, I gave an invitational keynote lecture on "The Alleged Myth of the Mafia" at the Seventh International Anticorruption Conference, held in Beijing, China. My argument in that paper was that, *pace* the views of some criminologists, there is plenty of good evidence for the existence of the Mafia—though that evidence is inferior to the historic case for Jesus Christ! It was a great pleasure to present that theme in Beijing, and my Chinese translator said that my paper was one of the clearest and most appreciated by the audience.[5]

I have not given up debating—but I am limiting myself to events of real importance. In 2008, I headed the team, joined by Dr Angus Menuge, that won a significant "God debate" at University College Dublin, Ireland. The opposition—arguing that it is irrational to believe in God—featured a California Institute of Technology theoretical cosmologist and the executive secretary of the American Humanist Association. The University's Literary & Historical Society, which hosted the debate, had been founded by John Henry Newman in the 19th century, and has a *cachet* similar to that of the Oxford Union and Cambridge Union debating societies in England. My detailed write-up of the Dublin debate has been published both in the U.K. and in the U.S.[6]

In 2009, after two years of intense study of French law, I received permission to take the oath to become a French lawyer—an *avocat à la Cour de Paris*. This had entailed passing a four-hour written examination in French criminal law, plus three oral examinations (commercial law, administrative law, and legal practice and ethics). The orals were a gruelling experience before juries consisting of a

---

[5] The paper was published, in English and in Chinese, in the conference proceedings. The English text appears in the Trinity/Michaelmas, 1996, issue of *Law & Justice: The Christian Law Review,* and has been reprinted in my book, *Christ Our Advocate.*

[6] *The Christian Lawyer* [U.K.], Spring, 2009; *Modern Reformation* [U.S.], January-February 2009. This article is reprinted in my recent book, *Christ As Centre and Circumference.*

retired member of the Paris bar council, a law professor, and a practicing lawyer. I had hoped to avoid the examinations on the basis of my prior legal activities, but the French legal profession is very protectionist and especially suspicious of those coming from an Anglo-American rather than from a European civil law background. But the examinations were indeed a character-building experience![7] And induction at the glorious First Chamber of the Court of Appeals in the Paris Palais de Justice—where the trial of collaborationist Pétain of the Vichy régime took place—was worth all the effort.[8] Since, unlike the English barrister and the American lawyer, the French *avocat* must be in active practice to employ the title, I am now connected with a fine practice in Paris with two Christian lawyers, Eric Noual and Nicolas Duval, and with the *cabinet* of Thierry Edmond in Strasbourg. I had worked with the distinguished solo practitioner Jean-François Legendre until he retired and became an *avocat honoraire,*

An important ministry has consisted of regular appearances on the Issues, Etc. American radio broadcast. This programme was previously the mainstay of the Lutheran Church-Missouri Synod's radio station KFUO in St Louis, Missouri: the station made famous throughout the United States by the broadcasts of the great Walter A. Maier. Then the current Synod bureaucracy suddenly cancelled Issues, Etc.—apparently because of the programme's openness to non-Lutheran evangelicals and its courage in criticising the happy-clappy tendencies of certain Synodical folk. The Issues, Etc. host, the Revd Todd Wilken and its producer, Jeff Schwarz, then went independent—to the Missouri Synod's loss. These gentlemen spend an arm-and-a-leg roughly once a month interviewing me long-distance in France or England on theological topics and current issues. Many of the taped programmes have been archived and can be obtained

---

[7] The following judgment (still true today) appears in Lincoln's Inn barrister Robert Jones' Preface to his *A History of the French Bar, Ancient and Modern* (Philadelphia: T. & J. W. Johnson, 1856): "There [in France], no distinction, rank, or privilege is to be obtained by the legal aspirant, but by long and arduous study; and whatever position the Student holds, or may afterwards hold, whatever may be the ultimate title affixed to his name, he ... may fearlessly assert that he has fully earned it."

[8] My article on becoming a French *avocat* is reproduced in the Appendix. It was originally published in *Amicus Curiae: Journal of the Society for Advanced Legal Studies* [U.K.], Issue 80 (Winter 2010), pp. 14-16. I am a Fellow of that Society.

from Issues, Etc.[9] Todd Wilken has taught for us at the International Academy of Apologetics, Evangelism and Human Rights. He tells us that Strasbourg, France is far more exciting than St Louis, Missouri.

Professional and lecturing activities have continued apace. I co-chaired with my dear German lawyer friend Dr Friedrich Toepel a section on freewill and punishment, and delivered my own papers on these subjects, at recent international conferences of the IVR—the World Congress of Philosophy of Law and Social Philosophy—held in a different country every two years. In 2007, the sessions to which I contributed were in Kracow, Poland; in 2009, in Beijing China.[10] I have recently been named honorary chairman of the Academic Board of the World Evangelical Alliance's International Institute for Religious Freedom, headed by Prof. Dr Thomas Schirrmacher, whom we mentioned in the previous chapter. In 2010, I was appointed Consultant Editor for Religion and Law of *Amicus Curiae: Journal of the Society for Advanced Legal Studies,* University of London.

During September of 2010, the Christian university in Tonga held the first ever Pan-Pacific Apologetics Conference. I was the keynote speaker. The island kingdom (known also as the "Friendly Islands" owing to the fact that the natives did not kill and eat Captain Cook!) was missionised by Methodists—in the days when the Methodists still believed in the biblical gospel and the authority of the Scriptures as Wesley did. Some fifteen hundred attended from Australia, New Zealand, Fiji, Hawaii, and many other locations in the South Pacific. I was invited as honoured guest owing to the fact that the president of the university, when studying as a foreign student years ago at the University of Melbourne, Australia, was overwhelmed by the death-of-God movement—until he got a hold of my debate with Altizer and other theological writings. During our time on the island, Lany and I were feted lavishly, received many gifts (such as a Tongan war club to aid my apologetic endeavours!), and had an audience with one of the Tongan royal princesses, a solid Christian believer.

---

[9] http://www.issuesetc.org. One can listen to current programming via webstreaming by clicking "Listen Now."

[10] These two papers have been published by the IVR and also appear in my book, *Christ As Centre and Circumference.*

Christmas, 2010, was a particularly gratifying time. I was invited to deliver the French-language sermon at the major Protestant-Catholic International Carol Service at the Cathedral in Marseilles, in the presence of the Archbishop and city officials.[11] At this afternoon service, there were some 800 in attendance. This is a major evangelistic outreach to the Marseilles community. My theme was along the following lines: "Plus ça change, plus ça reste la même chose?" Is it true that "the more things change, the more they stay the same"? That was the classical Greek, pagan philosophy of history (also Nietzsche's "myth of the eternal return"). Often Christmas seems like this. So we need to get focused—to go from the "background of the photo" of Christmas to its centre: the unique incarnation of Christ—his miraculous birth, death for our sins on the Cross, resurrection. Why is this so essential? Because our lives are not "cyclical" (Heb. 9:27) any more than is history in general, we need a salvation that is settled and sure. I quoted two of Luther's Christmas sermons, in which he stresses that in the Isaiah chap. 9 prophecy of the coming of the Saviour and in His birth narratives, the important words are "for you": if this good news is not made personal by an act of faith, it might as well not have happened at all.

In March of 2013, I served as keynote speaker at the International Consultation for Religious Freedom Research sponsored by the International Institute for Religious Freedom of the World Evangelical Alliance. The sessions were held in Istanbul—a particularly appropriate location in light of the politically-motivated arrest—at 4 a.m.!—on 18 January of that year of fifteen Turkish lawyers in Istanbul, Izmir, and Ankara. Modern Turkey was created as a secular state by Kemal Atatürk after the defeat of the Ottomans in World War I, but the country has remained deeply Muslim: an Islamic-leaning but pragmatic political party (the AKP) came to power with a landslide victory in 2002 and has steadily increased its share of the popular vote in succeeding years—to the great and legitimate concern of western nations.

I must admit that whilst in Istanbul I did not focus solely upon civil liberties issues. I could not resist dinners at two of the most celebrated restaurants of the city (as recommended, to be sure, by

---

[11] For photos of the occasion, see *infra,* the Appendices (No. 24).

French gourmets): Rami, featuring Anatolian cuisine in a candlelit atmosphere with a stunning view of the Blue Mosque; and Leb-i-Derya, on the glass-fronted top floor of the Richmond Hotel, providing a panoramic view of the Bosphorus and the Golden Horn and famed for its 40-spiced beef filet.

The year 2014 saw the publication of a collection of apologetics essays under the editorship of Korey D. Maas and Adam S. Francisco.[12] As Gene Edward Veith notes in his Foreward, the contributors represent, in almost every case, first- and second-generation disciples of my Reformation-based, evidentialist apologetic. It is immensely gratifying to see the fruits of one's labour where, prior to my work, virtually no apologetics scholarship was being produced in Lutheran circles, and where evangelicals were so often led away from a solid apologetic by the siren songs of presuppositionalism.

My extracurricular activities in recent years have not been limited to the academic. For example, I spent two years building, from a subscription kit, a very detailed model of the historic vessel, *The Bounty*. This involved a psychologically debilitating creation of detailed rigging and the painting of all the minuscule figures of the crew.

I have also become a bit of an expert on vintage Apple computers, having obtained and learned to operate an Apple IIe and IIgs, a Macintosh 512Ke, a Performa 5320, a Macintosh 7600, etc. I do not limit myself to Apple Macs (I also have the Texas Instruments 99/4A system), but I am convinced that the PC—and all its works and all its ways—will be officially prohibited during the Millennium.

I have been inducted into one of the historic London livery companies, the Worshipful Company of Scriveners, which holds banquets of no mean consequence every year. My sponsor was Archbishop George Carey, a liberal evangelical whose views on the reliability of the Old Testament could stand much improvement, but who was a vastly better head of world Anglicanism than his successor, Rowan Williams.[13] I also became a Freeman of the City of London in an impressive ceremony at London's Guildhall.

---

[12] *Making the Case for Christianity: Responding to Modern Objections* (Saint Louis, MO: Concordia, 2014).

[13] A parish near our home in Lidlington wrote to Williams at the time of his appointment to enquire how, in view of the Anglican Church's explicit rejection of the

My London clubs are the Athenaeum and the Players'. The Players' Theatre Club revives the London music halls of the Victorian and Edwardian eras. The Athenaeum is the most "intellectual" of the London clubs, with special emphasis on theology, law, science, and medicine. Bishops of the Church of England are automatically granted membership. Others must apply and undergo a considerable waiting period. The club boasts an impressive number of Nobel Prize winners. Founded in the mid-19th century, its membership has included such notables as Sir Humphry Davy, Michael Faraday, Charles Dickens and William Makepeace Thackeray; indeed, in 1863, Dickens and Thackeray famously resolved a longstanding feud at the foot of the Athenaeum's grand stairway. After becoming a member, I was invited to give one of the Athenaeum's formal "talk dinners," this one chaired by the late evangelical hymn-writer Canon Michael Saward.[14] My subject was "Why Human Rights Need Religion"—offering a neat opportunity to witness in that distinguished context.

I am also a member of the Académie européenne des Sciences, des Arts et des Lettres (the European Academy of Sciences, Arts and Literature), and, owing to them, I have become a published poet! On the 30th anniversary of the founding of the Academy, an international poetry anthology was published: *Enchantons la vie. Glorifying Life* (Antibes, France: AESAL, 2010; ISBN 978-2-9537468-0-8). I am one of the fifty-seven represented in the volume, and my poem appears to be the only specifically Christian contribution. I wrote the poem in French and then provided an English translation.[15]

Whilst on the subject of memberships, I should mention that I am one of the fifty living members of the Académie Internationale des Gourmets et des Traditions Gastronomiques, Paris. My inaugural lec-

---

ordination of practicing homosexuals, he could in good conscience take the Archbishop's oath when he held the opposite view. He wrote back saying that these were indeed two incompatible viewpoints, but that he would of course uphold the Church's existing position. I immediately thought of the medieval Averroist belief that something could be true in theology and false in philosophy, or vice versa, at the same time, yet both could be acceptable. Should this perhaps be called intellectual schizophrenia?

[14] His most well-known hymn is the magnificent "Christ Triumphant, Ever Reigning." Canon Saward graciously contributed an original hymn to my Festschrift, edited by William Dembski and Thomas Schirrmacher.

[15] The poem, with English translation, appears in the Appendices (no. 26), *infra*.

ture was on the subject of Bertrand Guégan, the French translator of Apicius, for whom my chair was named, and in the lecture I stressed the need for all gastronomes (and non-gastronomes, for that matter) to accept the garments of Christ's righteousness in order to participate in that Great Banquet at the end of time when our Lord returns.

Along the same line, I am a *maître* (master) of the Confrérie St Etienne, the Alsatian wine society, where ranking is based on blind taste tests.[16] And since I am now on the subject of wine, I must mention an apologetic work by a distinguished 18th century German classical scholar and bibliographer, arguing that the special features of *water* demonstrate the existence of Divine Providence.[17] In my view, a far better case can be made for *wine*; after all, our Lord turned water into wine at Cana—not the reverse. And I have frequently predicted an eventual ecumenical union of theological liberals and fundamentalist pietists, where there will be an acceptance of the higher critical supposition (based, as are all such, on zero manuscript evidence) that in the original, unredacted text of John 2, Jesus actually turned wine into water!

I must also mention my classic cars: all but two a Citroën—my 1924 C-3, the 1925 B-14, my 11-B Traction avant (the French gangster car of the 1930's), and the glorious DS-21 with hydraulic suspension and front lights that turn with the steering wheel.[18] What I paid over the years for all of these would not today total the cost of a single sports car. The two non-Citroëns in my stable are a Lincoln Mark V (after riding in my archivist Jim Lutzweiler's, I could not resist find-

---

[16] My wife Lany, as a celebrated international harpist, was inducted into the society as an honorary member, and did not have to take any tests at all. I was not so lucky, and by reflective drinking eventually rose through the ranks from Apprentice and Journeyman to that of Master—as in the medieval gilds.

[17] The book is best known in a contemporary French translation with additional documentation: Johann Albert Fabricius, *Théologie de l'eau* (2d ed.; Paris, 1743).

[18] In journalist Stephen Clarke's hilarious book, *Talk to the Snail: Ten Commandments for Understanding the French* (London: Transworld/Black Swan, 2007), the author makes the outrageous comment that the Citroën DS is "shaped like a flattened frog" and is "the only road vehicle in the world guaranteed to give all passengers instant carsickness." Nothing could be further from the truth! The hydraulic suspension provides the most comfortable ride of any car—and in February, 2009, the DS was voted by a 20-member panel of leading automobile designers the "most beautiful car ever" (*Classic & Sports Car* magazine).

ing one in near-mint condition near Strasbourg) and a DeLorean—that amazing vehicle of *Back to the Future* fame with gull-wing doors. The car was designed by John DeLorean who lost everything when the British government reneged on their commitments to support his Belfast manufacturing plant, and who, after beating a U.S. federal prosecution for allegedly seeking drug money to save his project, was converted and became an evangelical believer.[19]

What of the future? (Not DeLorean's; that's now settled. I am referring to my own!) I intend to keep my nose to the proverbial grindstone: teaching apologetics, philosophy of law, and human rights, and directing the International Academy of Apologetics, Evangelism, and Human Rights summer sessions in Strasbourg. Nothing is more gratifying—or of more long-term value—than to impact the lives of students. I am well aware of the impact my teachers have had on me.

In that connection, I want to provide a different kind of model from that common in the evangelical community. The average evangelical values the heart over the head, is suspicious of too much education, has little appreciation for the theology of the Reformation or the worship experiences of the historic church, thinks that "being conservative" (in politics and economics as well as in theology) is a divine requirement, is often a chauvinistic American who believes his country can do no wrong and that things foreign and international are per se suspect. He is also often so narrow-minded in his interests that "he can see through a keyhole with both eyes simultaneously." If I can offer something better—and far more biblically justifiable—than this, I am convinced that I will be doing evangelicalism an important service.

Of course, statistically speaking, the duration of my earthly future cannot be more than a quarter of a century at very most, even for a typically long-lived Montgomery.[20] So: what of the next world?

---

[19] Cf. John Z. DeLorean, *DeLorean* (Grand Rapids, MI: Zondervan, 1985).

[20] And there is the disquieting (but not really!) recent news report: "More than 65 million years ago, a huge asteroid plummeted to Earth, destroying nearly all life on the planet. Astronomers now know that large asteroids collide with the Earth every 500 years or so. They've even identified one that's likely to come close to Earth on April 13, 2029, and may return to hit us 7 years later."

Chapter 12

C. S. Lewis says somewhere that "no good thing is ever lost"—and that affirmation appears fully justified by Holy Scripture. Moreover, the theme of bodily resurrection runs through the entire Bible. Therefore, I see no problem in hoping for all sorts of wondrous contacts—and reunions—in the next world, or, if the Reformers are right, after a time of rest "in Abraham's bosom," on the return of Christ and his transformation of this sorry globe into a "new earth." It goes without saying that I want some good chats with St Paul, Augustine, Luther, Pascal, Dr Samuel Johnson, *et al.* I also hope that I shall be greeted at the registration desk by Walter Martin as chairman of the welcoming committee, consisting of—at very minimum—my grandmother Flora Watrous, my great grandfather John Warwick Montgomery, Herman John Eckelmann, and Harold O. J. Brown. (Walter, by the way, always addressed me, when he telephoned, as "Great One." How I long to hear his voice uttering those words again!)

Other images include entering into that very lovely garden pictured in the children's book I mentioned in Chapter Two—maybe even being knighted as a "good and faithful servant" along the lines of the illustration in my long-lost scout manual. I would certainly like to meet my dear Putty again (and what's the matter with a pet receiving immortality on the basis of our love for the animal—just as we receive immortality by God's love for us in Christ?). I look forward to barbecues with the family, paralleling those in our back garden in Soufflenheim—and, even more so, to that Great Banquet at the Marriage Supper of the Lamb at the end of time. I also very much want to find that in the next world those who have been unhappy with, or hurt by, my activities during my lifetime on earth have found it in their hearts to forgive me.

As for the value of this autobiography, aside from what I hope will be the fun of reading it and the incentive on the reader's part to formulate important goals for himself or herself, I trust that it will drive home at least two important theological lessons.

The first relates to the operations of providence in the believer's life. My apologetic works have stressed the objective evidences for the truth of the gospel story and for the Bible as the unique and veracious revelation of God. In defending the faith, I have stayed away from the Christian's personal experience, owing to its largely subjective character and the ease with which unbelievers dismiss it. But in my own life, as outlined in this book, I have been simply amazed by the clear evidences of guidance. People I would never have met in the ordinary course of affairs (for example, my wife Lanalee, my adoptive son Jean-Marie, my maecenas Dr W. Howard Hoffman) entered into my life at the crucial time. Ideal new opportunities for Christian service appeared as if by magic just when they were needed (the professorships at Trinity Deerfield, at the University of Bedfordshire, and at Concordia University Wisconsin). Will Moore of the Canadian Institute felt a burden to keep my books in print and to distribute widely my taped lectures; Ted Rosenbladt (son of Prof. Dr Rod Rosenbladt) and New Reformation Press took over that task in 2012 and expanded it through mp3 offerings of my lectures and debates.[21] Broadman & Holman, the distinguished Southern Baptist publishing house, published the Festschrift for me edited by Thomas Schirrmacher, world-renowned theologian and religious liberties spokesman for the World Evangelical Alliance, and William Dembski, the most sophisticated living advocate of Intelligent Design—even though I was not a member of their ecclestiastical communion.

It should therefore go without saying that Romans 8:28 has proven its truth to me over and over again. Unbelievers dismiss this sort of thing simply because they have not experienced it. The promise of that Romans passage applies solely to believers. For the non-Christian, life is indeed, as Shakespeare classically described it, "a tale told by an idiot, full of sound and fury, signifying nothing."[22] To find a meaningful existence in the hands of a loving Father, one must first admit that one cannot save oneself and then accept the sole remedy: the gospel of our Lord and Saviour Jesus Christ.

In the second place, I would hope that this book reinforces for the reader the truth of the Lutheran doctrine of *simul justus et peccator* (=the Christian believer is a sinner and justified at the same time). One of the greatest theological weaknesses of evangelicalism is its Wesleyan notion of perfectionism—that once saved we can be free of sin. Since sinlessness is in fact impossible in this life (1 John 1:8-10),

---

[21] That move would not have been possible without vital assistance of Kurt and Debra Winrich—whose blessed aid to the International Academy of Apologetics and to the Montgomerys personally can never be adequately repaid.

[22] *Macbeth*, Act 5, Scene 5.

the evangelical so often engages in a process of self-deception and hypocrisy—in fact sinning but rationalising it away. As mentioned in the Preface, Harold Lindsell refused to write his autobiography for fear that it would reveal guilty secrets about evangelicals that would better be left alone. Some of the incidents recounted in my autobiography are hardly to the credit of those involved, but they are consistent with the nature of a fallen race and should be expected even among believers. This is no criticism of the gospel or of our Lord's saving work on our behalf; it is, rather, a realistic evaluation of existence in a fallen world.

Am I saying that the life of the saved person differs in no way from that of an unbeliever's? Hardly. But the difference does not lie in quantifying the believer's level of empirical sanctification. The difference, rather, is one of life-orientation: the non-Christian centres his life on false gods, generally that archetypal false god, himself; whereas the believer, by definition, makes Christ the centre and circumference of his existence. All in all, believers are more honest, more trustworthy, and more loving than the pagans; but not always. Background, environment, and the individual personality all enter into the equation.

So I leave you, gentle reader, with that oft misquoted and misunderstood aphorism of Martin Luther: *"Pecca fortiter"*—"Sin bravely"—but which he followed immediately with the words (invariably left out) *"sed fortius fide et gaude in Christo, qui victor est peccati, mortis et mundi"*—"but believe and rejoice in Christ more boldly still, for he is victor over sin, death and the world."[23] Luther's point is that none of us should deceive ourselves as to our sinful character; what we need to understand is that our only hope rests with what Christ has done for us by taking away the penalty of our sins through his perfect sacrifice, thereby giving us the immeasurable gift of eternity with him. So, in evaluating the events of my life and the people described in this book, I trust that you will take them all "more bravely still" to Calvary's cross and to Easter morning's empty tomb.

---

[23] Luther, in a letter to Philip Melanchthon, 1 August 1521.

Il faut qu'en Dieu l'on se confie:
La paix du coeur se trouve en lui.
On ne peut prolonger sa vie
Par ses tourments, par ses soucis.
Mais en réponse à notre foi,
A toutes choses Dieu pourvoit.

Au coeur humain la joie et bonne
Et le Seigneur le sait aussi.
Pleine et parfaite, il nous la donne
Dans le moment qu'il a chosi.
Il est celui qui sait le mieux
Ce qu'il nous faut pour être heureux.

Puisqu'il me garde sur ma route,
Craindrai-je encor de défaillir?
Je prie, je chante et ne redoute
Ni le présent, ni l'avenir.
Il est fidèle et tous les jours,
Je peux compter sur son amour.[24]

---

[24] L. Levis-Baudin (1976): *Alléluia* (Lyon: Editions Olivétan, 2005), 47:12.

APPENDICES

1. LIKES AND DISLIKES

Item	Likes	Dislikes
Theology	Classic Lutheran, Evangelical	Any theology demeaning the historicity and/or full authority of the Bible
Worship style	High liturgy, especially Anglican	Happy-clappy, particularly if employing overhead projectors and marimbas
Political leadership	Lincoln, Teddy Roosevelt, Churchill, Reagan, Thatcher, Sarkozy[1]	FDR, Clinton, and all heads of state with Messianic complexes and loose personal morals
Architecture	Baroque[2], gothic, romanesque, 18th C. colonial[4]	Rococo, Bauhaus, 1960s utilitarian-functional[3]
Music: classical	Bach, Händel, Mendelssohn, John Stainer	Rostopovich, Gustav Mahler

---

[1] In spite of his choice of mate, who simply cannot sing—and whose romantic history leaves a great deal to be desired.

[2] As in Christopher Wren's glorious London churches.

[3] As in London's Barbican and southbank Royal Festival Hall. (Here—*and only here*—we agree with the views of Prince Charles. We are disgusted when he says that, as sovereign, he could be "defender of faith," but has problems being "defender of *the* faith.")

[4] As in Williamsburg, Virginia.

1. Likes and Dislikes

Music: popular	Bing Crosby, Perry Como, Nat Cole, Tony Bennett[5], Charles Aznavour[6], Mireille Mathieu[7], Richard Anthony, *The Seekers*[8]	Rock, hard or otherwise
Music: lowbrow	Victorian music hall (Players' Theatre, London),[9] Minstrel shows	Karaoke
Reading: classical	Milton, *Paradise Lost*	Proust
Reading: midbrow	Thornton Wilder, *The Eighth Day*	Hemingway
Reading: lowbrow	Alexander McCall Smith's "Ladies Detective" series, Greg's Achille Talon BDs	Evangelical romantic fiction, as currently published by Bethany
Theatre: highbrow	Puccini's *Turandot*	Wagner, in any form[10]

---

[5] Attend his concerts whenever possible.
[6] Ditto.
[7] Attend her concerts whenever possible (they are now very rare).
[8] Attended their wonderful farewell concert at London's Albert Hall in 1994, and wrote an article about it ("Back to the Sixties?," *New Oxford Review*, July/August, 1994). The article is reprinted in my book, *Christ As Centre and Circumference*.
[9] Under the chairmanship of my late, good friend Dominic LeFoe.
[10] One of the worst theatre evenings in my life was spent at the Teatro alla Scala in Milan, subjected to four hours of the Ring: *Götterdämmerung*. The title was well chosen.

Appendices

Theatre: midbrow	*Les Misérables*, Lloyd Webber's *Phantom of the Opera*, Sigmund Romberg's *The Student Prince*.[11]	Ibsen and Strindberg, in any form
Cinema	*The Wizard of Oz, Snow White and the Seven Dwarfs* (Disney), any film with Mickey Rooney[12], *The Verdict* (with Paul Newman).	*The Texas Chainsaw Massacre*, any film starring Tom Cruise
Television	*Songs of Praise* [U.K.], Law and Order, Alf	All quiz and reality shows
Restaurants	Pont de l'Ill (Strasbourg/La Wantzenau), Lasserre (Paris)[13], Rules (London), Fangshan (Beihai Park, Beijing)	All Döner Kebab takeaways, and all vegan operations

---

[11] And operetta in general.
[12] Attended his pantomime performance (at age 86!) at the Sunderland Empire Theatre in December, 2007.
[13] My son and I are members of their Club des casseroles.

1. Likes and Dislikes

Foods	Tournedos Rossini, escargots, cuisses de grenouilles à la persillade, crêpes Suzette, virtually anything with caviar or black truffles.	Egg rolls[14], anything containing buckwheat flour or pistachio nuts[15], falafel, merguez (or any other North African dish)
Wines: red	The great French Bordeaux reds, as listed in the 1855 classification	Anything with a Baron de Rothschild label
Wines: white	Pouilly fumé, (dry) Alsatian whites	(Sweet) German/Mosel whites
Wines: sparkling	French crémants, Especially crémant d'Alsace	All vins mousseux, all pretentious champagnes
Transport: autos	Citroëns, the DeLorean	Anything constructed in Japan or Germany[16]
Transport: air	Ryan Air[17]	China Air[18]
Transport: public	The TGV, Eurostar, the Paris Métro	Los Angeles[19]

---

[14] For which a recipe is given in my *Shaping of America*.

[15] I am deathly allergic to these two items, for no known reason. "The whole creation groaneth and travaileth in pain together ..." (Romans 8:22).

[16] One can forgive what they did in World War II, but one cannot forget.

[17] In spite of its obnoxious CEO, since this low-fare company has stuck it to larger, overpriced carriers such as Air France.

[18] When we were in Hong Kong, tee-shirts were on sale with the inscription: "I survived China Air."

[19] Since it effectively doesn't have any.

Appendices

Note: This autobiography intentionally omits some sensitive material. Based on the author's interest in cryptography, he gives the following keys possibly capable of pointing a few readers in a direction to find and decode such material elsewhere among Montgomerian *trésors*:

Titanium
OS 9.1
Pascal 4.5
-19

2. LE COMTE DE ST GERMAIN DE MONTGOMMERY

Article on the title of Comte de St Germain de Montgommery and the family visit to a Montgomery castle in Normandy, together with a family photograph (*La Gazette de la Manche*, 19 September 2007)

20 septembre 2007

Ducey
Des descendants de Montgomery en visite

Ce week-end, Valérie Houlbert, ducéenne passionnée par l'histoire et hôtesse à l'office de tourisme, a accueilli, dans la demeure des Montgommery, John Warwick Montgomery et sa famille venus se ressourcer en la terre de leurs ancêtres. Cet avocat à la cour européenne, comte de Saint-Germain de Montgomery et baron de Kiltartan appartient à la branche anglaise de cette seigneurie.

Des descendants de Montgomery en visite.

Ducey

Journées du patrimoine

Retour en terre ancestrale

Un beau livre sur le château, des journées du patrimoine, une illustre visite, tout arrive à point en ce moment pour la ville des Montgommery.

L'opportunité du calendrier, quelques jours avant les journées du patrimoine a permis mercredi à un descendant des Montgommery, de se rendre sur la terre de ses ancêtres et d'y être fort bien accueilli à l'Office du tourisme d'abord, puis au château. John Warwick Montgomery (avec un seul «m», tout comme le célèbre maréchal, ainsi que toute la branche écossaise) comte de St-Germain-les-Montgommery (cette fois avec deux «m» comme la branche française) et baron de Kiltartan venait pour la première fois à Ducey.

■ Le comte John Warwick Montgomery accueilli par Valérie Houlbert.

Résidant tout à la fois à Strasbourg où il est avocat au conseil européen, et à Londres, professeur émérite de droit et de sciences humaines il a expliqué combien cette illustre famille était encore bien vivante «via une société qui représente 500 membres, certain étant même aux Etats-Unis». Il a confirmé les origines «normands fils de normands» de ses ancêtres, ajoutant avec humour que ces rudes guerriers collectionnaient «rapines et pillages» comme d'autres de nos jours les timbres ! Il a été accueilli à Ducey par Valérie Houlbert qui lui a servi ensuite de cicerone, connaissant parfaitement un sujet sur lequel elle vient d'écrire un livre. En conclusion de cette visite, a eu lieu la signature du livre d'or de l'Office du tourisme.

Le comte John Warwick Montgomery accueilli par Valérie Houlbert.

3. AUTOBIOGRAPHICAL LETTER BY JOHN WARWICK MONTGOMERY, THE AUTHOR'S GREAT GRANDFATHER

(Together with His Obituary, and Documents in the Hand of his Sister, Ann Jane Montgomery)

Appendices

For the information of those that come after me I was Born in the town land of Ballywoodack Parish of Donegore. Country Antrim. Ireland On May the 5th 1827 My Fathers name was James. Died at the age of 73 My Mothers Name was Elizabeth Warwick Montgomery died & 75 I had 6 Sisters. Mary. Margaret. Agness. Ann, Martha & Ester. And one Brother Andrew Grandfathers given name was William. Died at the age of 60 Grandfathers on Mothers Side. his name was John died at 80 Father was a Farmer. And I made myself useful untill I became Sixteen. then went to Learn the Shoemakers Trade. and Served Four and one half years. And all I got was my board. then I began Business for myself. In after three years. Aunt Martha was coming to America. and I got the fever to go along that was in 1849. but My good Mother felt so bad about me going. that I put it off a year. untill 1850 it was considered quite an undertaking in those early days to leave Father, Mother, Brother & Sisters

156

not knowing as you should ever see them again which proved too true. On April 4th we took a boat at Belfast, and Sailed down the Clyde to Greenock, Scotland where our Ship was that was to take us to New York. the name of the Ship was Brooksby, we Sailed next day, but after we had been out 24 Hours we had an Accident the Bowsprit broke and we had to return for repairs. had a very Stormy passage, Hatches nailed down part of the time. Bulworks all Swept off and many thought we would never reach Land. but after a Six weeks passage we landed in New York. and came out on a Street then called Dover it was paved with wooden blocks. and I was afraid I never would get my foot on a Stone again. After a little Stroll through N.Y. took the Boat for Troy. then Central to Attica. there was no R. Road nearer. Came on foot to Orangeville. Nex day came to Warsaw April 16th went to the House where Mr J.C. Burton now lives. his Father in law Mr Roswell Gould lived there then. there is where I Eat my first Meal and Stayed the first night then I began work with a Man by the name of Isaac C Bronson 14 Dollars for first 3 months 15 pr months for next 3 Month then I began to work By the Piece which I found was more profitable for I could make 15 a week I made Wellington Boots. But after I had been with him one Year and ten months. he moved away to Rockford. see then 3 of us for he kept 12 or 15 men all the time J. C. Hurlburt. Harry Tuttle and my Self went in Company but only remained One Year, and I Bought them Out. There was not much to buy, for we just made to Order, and I had lent them their part of the money So they went to work for me. Soon after that I Bought a wooden Building just about where Our Store is now for 1.200. from Jane P. Green a Sister of Mr Auguste Frank Turned out a watch valued at 50. Dollars for first Payment and ran in debt for the rest which I managed to pay after a while. Shoes were made to order principally in those days, I kept Six or Eight men working all to measure. The first Sale work that I remember being brought into town I bought in Rochester had on a Sleigh with

3. Autobiographical letter by John Warwick Montgomery …

One that it is a very Cold day without an Overcoat. the fact was I had not any. we put up at Bergen all night going and coming. I did not know a person in Rochester I had neither Money nor Credit. I wanted Misses and Childrens Shoes. there was a Man named Jessie Hatch, On Water Street, Mad Such Shoes I went there and told him what I wanted. That I wanted time that I had no money. he told me to go and get my dinner and he would talk with his Brother. and let me know when I got Back. he wanted to know if I knew any one in Rochester that would Bouch for me I told him not one. but he decided to let me have them about One Hundred Dollars worth of them I merely Speak of this incident to Show my first Starting Point. in the meantime my two Sisters Came Came that was a great Comfort to me Many a Heart to heart talk we had about Home Land after a while my Sisters Both got Married to two Brothers Malcom & Thomas Service, Amy Jane that married Thomas Service Died in about a year after She was married and left a little Boy who also Died at the age of 4 years he was Adopted be with Service his fathers Brother

I need not tell you who my Sister Agness married as you all know Malcom Servis and family I had now been in Warsaw about ten years I was comparitively alone. both my Sisters were married I had my eye on a little girl with Auburn hair She was quite young, but I had waited a good while and I could wait a little longer and in due time I put a very Serious question to her and after thoughtfull consideration I was rewarded by her Saying Yes. We were married Febr 9-1860 we have lived on Buffalo St. in the town of Wethersfield 3 Years, then on East Buffalo Street, then on Mechanic Street. but for the last 35 Years on East Court Street My Wife and I have been joined in one yoke we have Drawn Lovingly together God has Blessed us with a Large family of Children 2 Girls and 5 Boys but has taken the 2 Girls and one of the Boys to the better land. but has Still left us 4 Boys that live in our midst to See to us, and Comfort us in our Old Age

August 20-1912

John W. Montgomery

3. Autobiographical letter by John Warwick Montgomery ...

In the few lines that I have written, have said nothing about my Spiritual Life, which is by far the most important. I was brought up a Presbyterian as Father and Mother were, and Attended Church and Sabbath School in Childhood and Youth. when I was fourteen years old I united with the Church. when I left for America I brought my letter with me. which read thus This to Certify that John W. Montgomery is a Member of the Presbyterian Church, and in the full enjoyment of all its privelages, we would recommend him to the fellowship of the Church where ever it may please Devine Providence to order his Residence. when I came to Warsaw I presented my letter to the Session and was Cordially Received Rev A. J. Young was then Supplying the Pulpit

Two Documents in the Hand of Ann Jane Montgomery

> Know the Lord
> My son know though the Lord
> Thy fathers god obey
> Seek his protecting care by night
> His guardain hand by day
> James Montgomery Elisa Montgomery
> Mary E Thompson John Montgomery
> Margret Montgomery Agness Montgomery
> Ann Jane Montgomery Martha Montgomery
> Andrew Montgomery Esther Montgomery
> Ballgwodock Co of Antrim
> Parish of Donegore
> Ireland February 17, 1855
>
> Ann J Montgomery is my name Ireland
> was my Nation Ballgwodock was my
> dwelling place and heven my
> expatation when I am dead and
> in my grave and all my bones
> are rotten this little scrap will tell
> my name when I am quite forgotten
> Ann J. Montgomery

Hymn For an Infant Class.

A giddy lamb one afternoon
Had from the fold departed;
The tender shepherd missed it soon
And sought it broken hearted;
Not all the flock that shared his love
Could from the search delay him
Nor clouds of midnight darkness move
Nor fear of suffering stay him

But night and day he went his way
In sorrow till he found it;
And when he saw it fainting lie,
He clasped his arms around it.
Then, safely folded to his breast,
From every ill to save it,
He brought it to his home of rest,
And pitied and forgave it.

Ann J. Montgomery of Warsaw Feuy the 19 1855

In Memoriam

Mr. John W. Montgomery was born at Ballywoodock, Parish of Donegore, County Antrim, Ireland, May 4th, 1827. He was the son of James and Elizabeth Warwick Montgomery. Both his father and mother lived beyond the period of three score and ten years. Mr. Montgomery had one brother and six sisters, two of whom came to America. One sister was afterward united in marriage to Mr. Thomas Service; the other is Mrs. Malcolm Service who now lives at LeRoy, N. Y. Mr. and Mrs. James Montgomery were farmers and their son attended school at the village which was three miles distant. At the age of sixteen he was apprenticed to a shoe maker and spent four and a half years learning his trade, with no compensation except his board and the knowledge and experience which he gained. But his workmanship was skillful and thorough.

Three years after completing his apprenticeship Mr. Montgomery decided to come to America. It was a serious step for a young man to leave his parents and sisters and brother and cross the ocean in a sailing vessel probably never to return to his native land. But he embarked at Belfast, April 4th, 1850, and passed down the Clyde to Greenock, Scotland, from which place he secured passage on a sailing vessel to New York city. The sea was so rough that crew and passengers despaired of seeing port again. But at the end of six weeks they docked at the foot of Dover street in New York. The same day he took a Hudson river boat to Troy, and there changed to the New York Central railroad with a ticket for Attica, N. Y. From Attica he walked to Orangeville where he spent one night and the next day came to Warsaw, arriving here on May 16th, 1850, a few days after his twenty-third birthday. His first night in Warsaw was passed at the home of Mr. Roswell Gould in the house which is now the residence of Mr. and Mrs. Joseph C. Buxton.

Mr. Montgomery began his business life in Warsaw in the employ of Mr. Isaac C. Bronson. Twenty months later he formed a partnership in the making of shoes with Mr. J. C. Hurlburt and Mr. Harvey Tuttle. This partnership continued for one year when Mr. Montgomery purchased the total interest in the business and began the manufacture of shoes on his own account. He purchased from Mrs. Jennie Frank Greene, a sister of Mr. Augustus Frank, a wooden building on Main St., located about where the Montgomery shoe store now stands. A few months later he brought from Rochester a stock of ready made shoes for women and children and opened the first shoe store in Warsaw. These beginnings of his business career were almost entirely on credit, but his thrift, industry and honesty soon made him one of the substantial business men of the town. With the exception of three years spent on a farm in the town of Wethersfield, his business life in our community continued for sixty-six years. He was deeply interested in all public questions and generous whenever his assistance was needed. His reputation for honesty, integrity and steadfastness for his convictions extended throughout Wyoming county. He was one of the first excise commissioners in Warsaw, has been a trustee of the village, and was at the time of his death the President of the Cemetery Association.

Mr. Montgomery's marriage to Miss Anna Crawford took place on February 9th, 1860, Dr. Nassau performing the ceremony. Mrs. Montgomery also was a native of Ireland and about ten years younger than her husband. Their domestic life was in many respects ideal. As he himself said "We have lived under one yoke and we have always pulled together." Seven children were born to them: two daughters and five sons. Four sons survive, Mr. Edward T. Montgomery, Mr. J. Frank Montgomery, Mr. John A. Montgomery and Mr. Charles H. Montgomery. There are six surviving grand children and one great grand son. Theirs was the home preeminently of the daily Bible and daily prayer. Their interests were mutual and they co-operated perfectly. It was one of those homes of quiet dignity and religious devotion, standing far back from the noise of change and the perplexing turmoil of life, which furnish the stability and substantial character to our American citizenship.

Mr. Montgomery's spiritual life was in his own words," by far the most-important." His father and mother were Presbyterians. He united with the church when he was fourteen years of age and when he came to America brought a letter from his home pastor commending him to the Christian fellowship of the Presbyterian church, wherever Providence might direct his course. His first Sunday in Warsaw he went to church. There are a few people who remember him as a young man on that occasion. At the first communion he presented his letter to the Session and was received into the fellowship of the church. That was near the close of the pastorate of Rev. A. T. Young whose ministry here covered three years from 1847-1850. Mr. Montgomery has thus been a member of this church sixty-six years and at the time of his death had been in the church fellowship for a longer period than any other name on the records. In 1871 he was elected an elder and was the last surviving member of the strong session under the ministry of Dr. Joseph E. Nassau. Mr. Montgomery's spiritual life was nourished by the Bible and made strong and vital by daily prayer. He was physically strong by reason of good habits of living. His mind was clear and keen to the last. His faith was undimmed by any doubt or uncertainty regarding the future, and he often repeated, especially during the last year since the death of Mrs. Montgomery, the lines:

"But the city to which I am journeying
Will more than my trials repay.

All the toils of the road will seem
    nothing
When I get to the end of the way."

The funeral services were held from the late residence on East Court street Monday afternoon at two o'clock, Rev. George D. Miller, D. D., officiating. The four sons and the son-in-law, Mr. Frederick B. Keeney, acted as bearers. The burial was in the family lot in the Warsaw cemetery.

Appendices

JOHN W. MONTGOMERY
BORN MAY 4, 1827
DIED FEBRUARY 18, 1916

4. BIOGRAPHICAL ARTICLE ON MAURICE WARWICK MONTGOMERY, THE AUTHOR'S FATHER[1]

Maurice Warwick Montgomery

Member of a family long established in Northwestern New York, Maurice Warwick Montgomery is of the third generation to engage in business and industry at Warsaw and to contribute constructively to its life and affairs. He is one of the two brothers who make up the Montgomery Brothers, Inc., dealers in fuels and farm feeds, is prominent in civic circles and heartily cooperative in movements and projects that make for the best interests of the town.

The first of the American branch of this family was one John W. Montgomery, born at Ballywoodock, Parish of Donegore, County Antrim, Ireland, on May 4, 1827, the son of James and Elizabeth (Warwick) Montgomery, both of whom lived past seventy years. At the age of sixteen, John W. Montgomery was apprenticed to a shoemaker, and spent four and a half years learning his trade. He was a grown man when on April 4, 1850, he set sail for the New World from Belfast, and at the end of six weeks landed in New York City. He made his way to Warsaw on May 16, 1850, and was employed by Isaac C. Bronson. In 1852 he formed a partnership with J. C. Hurlburt and Harvey Tuttle, to make shoes. A year later he purchased the interests of his partners, and shortly after opened the first shoe store in Warsaw, where he continued in business for sixty-six years, except for three years spent on a Wethersfield farm. He was a most progressive Citizen; one of the first excise commissioners of Wyoming County; president of the Cemetery Association ; and for two-thirds of a Century a devout Presbyterian. On February 9, 1860, John W. Montgomery married Ann Crawford, also a native of Ireland, and they were the parents of two daughters and five sons. John W. Montgomery was called to his reward on February 18, 1916.

One of the above sons was James Franklin Montgomery, who was a founder of Montgomery Brothers in 1899, and who remained connected with the business until his passing on July 15, 1942. He and his wife, Bessie L. Montgomery, were the parents of Maurice Warwick Montgomery, of this account. The latter-named was born on November 9, 1901, in Warsaw, and was educated in the grade and high schools of his birthplacc and the Univcrsity of Buffalo. He joined the staff of Montgomery Brothers in 1923, and a decade later was admitted as a member of the firm. As mentioned, this concern engages in the coal and coke trade, the distribution of various types of agricultural feeds, and they are the manufacturers of the popular brand "Oatka" dairy and poultry rations, with headquarters and mill in Warsaw. In the division of management, James R. Montgomery looks after the fuel trade, while Maurice Warwick Montgomery is the mill Superintendent. The latter-named was town councilman in 1945 and 1946; affiliated with Warsaw Lodge, No. 549, Free and Accepted Masons, of which he is a past master; member of the Independent Order of Odd Fellows and Warsaw Grange, Patrons of Husbrandry. He is a member of the United Church of Warsaw.

On July 21, 1928, at Warsaw, New York, Maurice Warwick Montgomery married Harriette G. Smith, daughter of Fred R. and Flora W. Smith. Mr. and Mrs. Montgomery are the parents of two children: I. John Warwick, born October 18, 1931. 2. Mary Ann, born January 16, 1938.

5. JOHN WARWICK MONTGOMERY'S MATERNAL GRANDMOTHER, FLORA WELLMAN WATROUS,

teaching in a one-room school ca. 1899; also, her wedding photograph with her first husband, Fred Rodell Smith, and the news article reporting his accidental death; also a photograph of Flora with her daughter, Harriette Genevieve, John Warwick Montgomery's mother

Flora Wellman Watrous, teaching in a one-room school (ca. 1899).

Wedding photograph of Flora Wellman Watrous and her first husband, Fred Rodell.

Automobile Fatality[1]

Prominent Warsaw Citizen Loses Life As Result

Known all over County

Fred R. Smith, Insurance Man the Victim. Driver Not Blamed

During the past week Warsaw people have had it brought home to them with telling force the seriousness of the automobile situation in the heavy toll of lives that are being taken everyday in all parts of the country. At the funeral of the Fancher boy on Friday killed in the early part of the week, came the death from the same cause of Fred R. Smith, one of Warsaw's best known business men, in the full strength of his manhood and great usefulness.

    The funeral services of the Fancher boy were held in the chapel of the Presbyterian church, and Mr. Smith, with his usual helpfulness was there with his car to carry the officiating clergyman to the

---

[1] First published in: *Wyoming County Times,* vol. XLVIII, no. 31, August 4, 1921, p. 1.

cemetery. The hearse with several automobiles was standing at the curb in front of the church facing south and there were a number of cars parked in the center of the street leaving only a narrow roadway between. Mr. Smith had been to the west side of the street and started back to the east side evidently to say something to his wife who stood, at the curb Just as he stepped through the center line of cars, a car driven by Whitney Bradt of Castile came along and Mr. Smith did not see it in time to avoid being struck though the car was traveling very slowly. He was thrown to the pavement striking the back of his head with terrible force. The car made a quick stop so that it did not run over the prostrate form, but the front wheel crowded against him so that it had to be pushed back before he could be released. Mr. Smith was unconscious and was taken to the Warsaw Hospital, where it was found that two two ribs were broken and his skull [...] morning, when he passed away. More than eight hundred people gathered at the Baptist church Monday afternoon, August first to express their respect for the memory of Mr. Smith and their sympathy for his bereaved wife and daughter and father. Mr. Smith's personality and character and business relations had given him a large acquaintanceship in Wyoming County and had attached to him a host of friends who feel a personal loss at his sudden death, the circumstances too connected with the fatal accident touched the heart of the community. Mr. Smith was in the prime of life, was very active in business and at the time of the accident was assisting at the funeral services for a boy who had been a member of Mrs. Smith's school at South Warsaw. A tense feeling of sorrow pervaded the whole community.

Mr. Fred R. Smith was the son of Mr. Rodell Smith. His mother Mrs. Jennie Smith died January 16th, 1916. He was born in the Town of Attica September 16th, 1874. While he was still young the family moved to Wyoming where Fred attended the Academy until he was sixteen years of age. In the same year he came to Warsaw and entered the grocery of Mr. Eggleston as a clerk. Afterwards he was in the employ of Mr. Kendrick Luther in the grocery business and from there went to the Ballintine Hardware Company as a clerk. For one year he and his family lived in Attica. For the balance of his life he was engaged in the insurance business, first with the Prudential Company, then for several years he was associated with Mr. William

H. Mc-Connell as an agent for the State Mutual Insurance Company and during the last year he was engaged in business for himself as agent for the Penn Mutual Insurance Company under the Rochester District Office. Mr. Smith's agreeable personality, his genial nature his tireless energy, his knowledge of the business and the confidence he uniformly inspired gave him a remakable success as an insurance writer. He gave every promise of an exceptionally bright and successful future, had not his career been cut short by the sad fatality which ended his earthly life. In 1899 Mr. Smith was united in marriage to Miss Flora A. Wellman of LaGrange, who, with one daughter, Miss Harriette G. Smith, survives him. In the same year Mr. Smith united with the Baptist church of Warsaw and from that time became very active and earnest in religious work. He was the successful superintendent of the Sunday school for fourteen years. He was chairman of the Board of Ushers and was always at the door to welcome strangers. He was devout and spiritual in his Christian character, his earnestness and consistency were apparent to all, he bore daily witness to his faith and sought to win others, men, women and children, to the Christian life.

Warsaw has lost one of its best and most active citizens. He was a ready helper in all activities for community welfare and during the period of the war was a member of many of the war-work committees. We shall greatly miss his responsive personality and contagious enthusiasm.

The funeral services were held at the Baptist church of Warsaw Monday afternoon, August first at 2:30 o'clock. Rev. Morgan Millar of the Congregational church read the Scripture passages, Rev. George D. Miller of the Presbyterian church made the prayer, and the pastor, Rev. Archie D. Barker made the address. The bearers were Addison W. Fisher, William R. Crawford, Emery A. Ellinwood and Chauncey Stevens, J. Frank Montgomery and E. E. Rowe. The burial was in the Warsaw cemetery.

Flora with her daughter, Harriette Genevieve, John Warwick Montgomery's mother.

6. JOHN WARWICK MONTGOMERY AS A CALLOW YOUTH

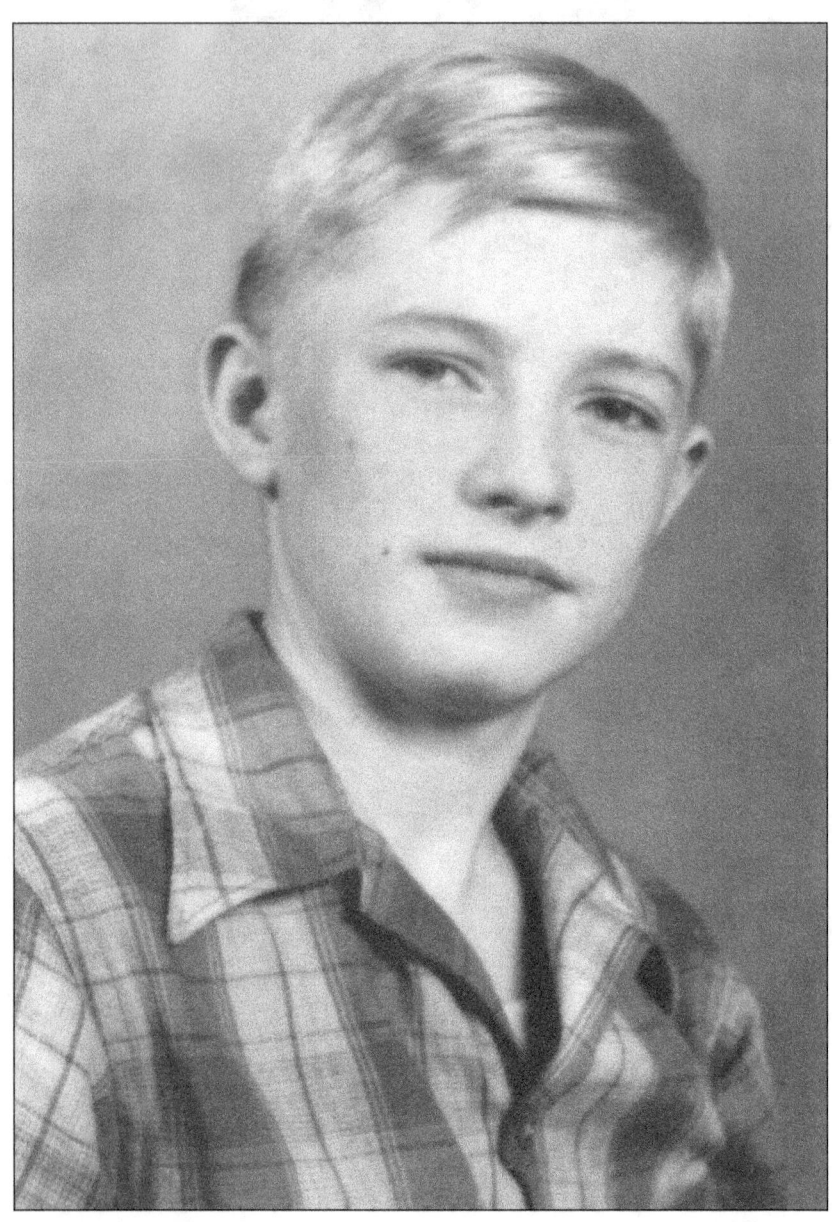

7. TEACHING NEW TESTAMENT GREEK AT THE REVD DR DON DEFFNER'S UNIVERSITY LUTHERAN CHAPEL, BERKELEY, CALIFORNIA (18 APRIL 1954)

8. PREACHING ASSIGNMENTS DURING A YEAR AT THE HAMMA DIVINITY SCHOOL

SUPPLY PREACHING APPOINTMENTS DURING 1958
(POINT OF DEPARTURE IN EACH CASE: SPRINGFIELD, OHIO)

DATE	PLACE	REMUNERATION	LODGING
JAN. 12	VAN WERT, O.	$35 – 16	
JAN. 19	VAN WERT, O.	35	
JAN. 26	LANCASTER, O.	25	LATIN TUTORING ($5/hr.)
FEB. 2	PAULDING + OAKWOOD, O.	50 – 18	
FEB. 9	HUNTSVILLE, O.	35 – 8	$45
FEB. 16	LOUISVILLE, KY.	40	
FEB. 23	MARKWARD + MONROEVILLE, IND.	40 – 16	
MAR. 2	N. BALTIMORE, O.	35 – 15	
MAR. 9	STOUTSVILLE + TARLTON, O.	27 – 10	
MAR. 16	MILAN, IND.	30 – 20	
MAR. 23	HUNTINGTON, W. VA.	35 – 26	
MAR. 30	HEBRON, KY.	25 – 16	
APR. 6	CROMWELL, IND.	35 – 27	
APR. 13	FINDLAY, O.	35 – 14	
APR. 20	COLD SPRING, KY.	30 – 16	
APR. 27	UNIONTOWN, O.	50 – 26	
MAY 4	NEW CUMERSTOWN, O.	35 – 21	
MAY 18	STOUTSVILLE + TARLTON, O.	27 – 10	
MAY 25	PAULDING + OAKWOOD, O.	50	
JUNE 1	GALION, O.	40	
JUNE 8	NEW HAVEN, W. VA.	55	
JUNE 15	HUNTSVILLE, O.	35	
SEPT 28	CROSSROADS + SATRNA, O.	55	
OCT 5	UNIONTOWN, O.	50	
OCT 12	MILLERSBERG, IND.	35	
OCT 19	INDIANAPOLIS, IND.	35	
OCT 26	MADISON, IND.	25	
NOV 2	LONDON, O.	25	
NOV 9	KETTERING, O.	15	
NOV 16	IRWIN, O.	15	
NOV 23	LORAIN, O.	35	
NOV 30	LOUISVILLE, KY.	40	
DEC 7	NILES, O.	50	

9. JAMES LUTZWEILER, ARCHIVIST, ON JOHN WARWICK MONTGOMERY

The Papers, Pulse, Person, Pictures, and Porpoise of John Warwick Montgomery (American Theological Library Association Special Collections Interest Group Presentation) by James Lutzweiler, Southeastern Baptist Theological Seminary[1]

"John Warwick Montgomery," I replied. John Warwick Montgomery constituted one-third of my answer to a question. John Warwick Montgomery (hereafter JWM), Paige Patterson and Terry Sanford, the late Duke University president and U.S. Senator from North Carolina, all together make up the complete answer to the same question. The question was this: "If you could have lunch today with any three people of your choice, who would they be?" It's a question I often ask others, and one that I am asked myself on occasion by those to whom I pose it.

On 29 March 2005 I placed this question before JWM over lunch at The Athenaeum, an exclusive club in London where the Lutheran scholar is a member. He had kindly invited me there after I had proposed a get-together. Originally scheduled to meet on April Fool's Day, we both adjusted our calendars to meet earlier, a seemingly insignificant chronological (and perhaps even superstitious) detail. But in the overall scheme of things, it was not an insignificant alteration. The end result was that I had and still have three more days of reflection on the delightful occasion than I would have had if we had met three days later. For those who don't care how long or intense their pleasures are, this will make no difference. Those who have sucked the marrow out of life will understand. William Wordsworth was one. In "Daffodils" sucked he:

---

[1] First published in: Sara Corkery (ed.), *Summary of Proceedings* (Chicago: American Theological Library Association, 2006), pp. 68-70.

> For oft when on my couch I lie
> In vacant or in pensive mood,
>
> They ["they" = daffodils] flash upon the inward eye
> Which is the bliss of solitude.
>
> And then my heart with pleasure fills
> And dances with the daffodils.

So, then, "Long live *Carpe diem!*" on the couch or on the divan, whether the flash upon the inward eye be daffodils or doctors of theology.

Before I put the question to JWM about whom he would like to dine with if he had three choices (sadly, I was not one of them, but the rules of the inquiry are that it cannot be anyone presently at your table), we had already been deep in pleasurable exchange. It began the moment the vibrant academic walked in the door. I had arrived ten minutes early, driven by faraway Vince Lombardi's Green Bay Packer maxim "If you aren't ten minutes early, you are fifteen minutes late" and yet another, to wit, "People count the faults of those who keep them waiting." Having as many faults as I do, I did not wish to leave any of my doors, windows, vents or even eyes of needles open wide enough for a penetrating mind like JWM's to drive a double-decker bus through, not to mention a caravan of camels.

Smiling and gripping my hand, JWM began instantly to show me around The Athenaeum. It was clearly a sanctuary of scholarship, one at which he himself had recently lectured on "Do Human Rights Need Religion?" to a group of distinguished members and guests that included the retired canon of St. Paul's Cathedral and author of the contemporary hymn "Christ Triumphant," the Rev. Canon Michael Saward, who also introduced him. Outside it was stately but reserved. Inside it was very quiet and a plush, architectural beauty. Before heading to the resplendent dining room, he led me up a grand staircase at the bottom of which, he later pointed out, Charles Dickens and William Makepeace Thackeray had reconciled after twelve years of alienation. Harmony happens.

In full view, as we ascended the stairs to the first landing, was a mural-sized, quasi-revealing painting of the Greek goddess Athena with a miniature leaf barely covering what Marvin Pope in the Anchor Bible calls her "rounded crater"—which for the genitally challenged is not her breasts. The deaf, mute Athena would later listen in on a toast to Adam and Eve offered up for JWM by his luncheon guest, a toast soon to be revealed. The toast followed shortly after JWM's description at the top of the stairs of a book that he said contained the names of fifty or so Nobel Prize winners who were either presently or previously members of The Athenaeum. Surely we were gamboling all about in tall cotton, as folks have never quite yet said just that way around my own Southern staircase or anywhere else for that matter. But we were.

The room at the top of the staircase was the library. And what a library it was. I think he said it contained 80,000 volumes, mostly leather-bound collector's editions. It also contained about eighty bottles of various spirits on a freestanding table, apparently there for consumption by anyone so inclined. There was no bartender in sight, and I assumed the literati sort of just helped themselves, as the spirit and spirits moved. But I was too intoxicated on books to have my sensitivities numbed artificially. I walked around in a trance with JWM, a PhD in theological bibliography with 18,000 books of his own, providing animated color commentary as my guide. I could have spent two weeks in this room right then and there. But lunch was waiting, and we wandered on toward it.

Walking back down the grand staircase—and for reasons still inexplicable to me—my eyes were automatically drawn to the aforesaid little leaf gilding the goddess. Anticipating that at the table we might soon be imbibing some biblical—but not Baptist—beverage, I suggested that we pause and right then and there lift at least an imaginary glass to our first parents, who were once also adorned a la Athena. JWM lifted his imaginary goblet in the air, as I did mine, and I proposed:

Here's to Eve, the mother of our race,
Who wore a fig leaf in just the right place.

Thinking I was through, JWM here broke the silence of the reserved Athenaeum with a howl of delight, while I joined in antiphonally. But I wasn't through. Like a balanced biblical bard, surrounded by the critical spirits of Britain's best men of letters, I toasted on:

And here's to Adam, the father of us all,
Who was Johnny-on-the-spot, when the leaves began to fall.

At this revelation we both laughed uproariously, and I wondered if this staid staircase had witnessed such collective hilarity since it was first established back in the 1820s. Were we a couple of seasoned scholars—he, anyway—or were we simply some schoolboys again like Saint Exupery's Little Prince? I suspect a blend of both.

We descended the staircase and entered the dining room, taking our seats at a small table by a window overlooking the ghosts of Titanic victims, who had purchased their tickets a block away, and the pigeon-plastered statues of King Edward VII, American Revolutionary War general John Burgoyne, Lord Curzon and Florence Nightingale that lined the street just outside. Seated at the table next to ours were a number of mucky-mucks whose professional appearance but unknown identity gave them a pleasant air of Sherlockian mystery. I did not want to discover otherwise and let my imagination run amok.

"Whosoever will may come" does not apply at The Atheneum. And even if it did, few would find the lunch tab of $128-plus that JWM picked up digestible. That tab included a bottle of Alsatian wine, which had quickly become a topic of discussion. Sensitive to my Southern Baptist associations, JWM, now a Frenchman, gingerly approached the question of quaffing a quart with him. With my own family's roots in Alsace-Lorraine and never having had a drop of this particular delicacy, I hastened to assure him quite piously and persuasively that the same Jesus who had once turned water into wine could certainly, upon request, convert this damnable stuff back into water—but hopefully not before passing it over my taste buds, and yet just before causing offense to one of my brothers. With that the order was placed, and with that the bottle was ultimately liquidated, though I confess here that I forgot to request the Redeemer to reverse the miracle.

[Here I am omitting the remaining paragraphs that may ultimately be found in the forthcoming Festschrift. Topics discussed in these paragraphs include Jerry Falwell, C. S. Lewis, Joseph Stalin, Robert Service, Maple Leaf Rag, J. Edgar Hoover, the Mafia, Svetlana Alliluyeva, Jimmy Carter, Bill Youngmark, Paul Tillich, Crater Lake, vulva, The Fundamentals, Harold Lindsell, lawyers, Chuck Colson, "The Yellow Rose of Texas," spotted owls, Ernest Shackelton and a bon vivant, to name just a few.] Thereafter the presentation concluded.

In preparation for this paper, the presenter once asked Dr. Montgomery if he ever planned to write an autobiography. He enthusiastically replied, "Yes. I have stirred up enough trouble in life that I might as well stir some up in death," or words to that effect. Indeed, John Warwick Montgomery has been controversial. But that is the very nature of his chosen field of endeavor: apologetics. Solomon said, "Where there are no oxen, the barn is clean." He did not say, but it is true nevertheless, that "where there are no oxen, there are also no steaks." Montgomery has given much high-protein food for thought to the Christian community, while engaged in some messy fights in which others sometimes did not wish to be engaged or were ill equipped to be engaged (like WA. Criswell's humiliating defeat at the hands of Madalyn Murray O'Hair). That he has been misunderstood from time to time should come as no surprise. When the esteemed church historian Martin Marty addressed the ATLA congregants in Chicago just before the Special Collections session under review, he characterized J. Frank Norris as a Baptist preacher who had killed a newspaperman "simply because the journalist had written something unfavorable about Norris." The fact is that Norris killed a common thug from an area in Ft. Worth called Hell's Half Acre, where a prostitute had once been nailed to an outhouse. The thug had come out to Norris's church for the express purpose of killing him, having already crucified him verbally. Other than that, Martin Marty was exactly right. An exact or, at least, an approximately exact take on the person and pulse of John Warwick Montgomery can be found in his marvelous collection of papers that he has taken great care to preserve and that are available for review by those interested in precision, not just French impressionism. They will find that, above all, the pulse of Montgomery was and still is the personal salvation of those who are biblically lost.

10. PROFESSOR DON MORGENSON ON JOHN WARWICK MONTGOMERY

Out of the west comes a knight all agleam,
Out of the west amid maidens screams.
His white steed is snorting
His lance all aquiver
Dispersing the lists, who cower and shiver.
The headpiece though snug is a very good fit,
The proboscis protrudes a bit through the slit.
The facepiece is raised, his jaws drip with flummery,
We hail thee, Sir John, Sir John Warwick of Gomery.

The story has it he arrived with a boom
No childhood, no youth, mature from the womb.
No marbles, no hopskotch, no jumprope and all
He foresook all of these for conquests in Gaul.
He rejected that old favourite, Mother Goose
To figure his lost diapers hypotenuse.

Over the lea our hero doth ride
With Squire Luther right at his side.
His fame spread throughout all of the nations
Through his scrolls and black Muslim publications.
Sir John and his steed, and Luther with a gavel
Had a card they handed you—Have Lance, Will Travel.
Into the desert, with Sir John on their tail
Sin and Ignorance flew, they must not prevail.

Armour untarnished, crusader supreme
He struck the last blow for the academic regime.
With ignorance staggering, and sin all undone
His accolades, olive-wreaths, and laurels are won.
The only thing left, alas and alack
Are those mediaeval libraries with their unpurged stacks
So upward and onward, we must all away
Come Luther, good steed, come hither I say.
To the top of the stacks, to Dewey Decimal Hall
Now dash away, dash away, dash away all!

10. Professor Don Morgenson on John Warwick Montgomery

The entourage left, like the wind was a'speeding,
Sir John leaving Bede, Spengler, Toynbee, all bleeding.
Fighting footnotes, slashing secondary sources,
Sir John dauntless, fearless, mustered his forces.
Then Sir John stopped, beating the forslugginger mass,
Approaching slowly was a beautiful lass.
What lady exists who could force such a choice?
Ah yes, obviously, 'tis the Lady Joyce.
They left together, but John vowed he'd return,
The torch in the stacks would continue to burn.

Sir John carries on in fine style it is said,
In bibliophile fashion he plows on ahead,
His basement is full, reprints galore,
His precious old volumes filling the floor.
His books have wandered out to the porch ...
And ah, Lady Joyce is there holding the torch.
Congratulations, Sir John, you're our favourite knight
Now a Ph.D. your are licensed to fight.

11. THE PARIS LATIN QUARTER DURING THE "DAYS OF MAY," 1968

12. FLYERS FOR THE "DEFENDING THE BIBLICAL GOSPEL" AND "PRACTICAL CHRISTIAN LIVING" SEMINARS

Greater Des Moines Area Seminar on
DEFENDING THE BIBLICAL GOSPEL

Lecturer: Dr. John Warwick Montgomery
Dynamic Theologian, Scholar, Author, Debater, Apologist

PRINCIPAL LECTURER IN LAW, LUTON COLLEGE OF HIGHER EDUCATION, ENGLAND,

Dr. Montgomery, ~~Dean of The Simon Greenleaf School of Law, Orange, Ca.,~~ is one of the most colorful figures of contemporary Protestantism. He holds two earned doctorate degrees (one from a European university), and seven other degrees besides; he is an English Barrister and the author of some 37 books and over 100 articles. He has debated such representatives of liberal religion as death-of-God theologian Thomas Altizer, the late bishop James Pike, and "new morality" advocate Joseph Fletcher. He has served as invitational visiting professor at Roman Catholic DePaul University, Concordia Seminary (Lutheran) in Ft. Wayne and St. Louis, the University of California at San Diego, the University of Maryland in Europe, and has taught in French at the Lutheran Study Center in Paris. For three years he served as chairman of the Department of History at Wilfred Laurier University, Ontario, Canada, and for ten years he taught apologetics at the Trinity Evangelical Divinity School. He has climbed to the top of Mt. Ararat in Turkey (17,000 ft.) in conjunction with searchers for vestiges of the Ark. Biographical studies of him appear in Who's Who in America, Who's Who in France, Who's Who in Europe, Who's Who in the World, and the Dictionary of International Biography.

Monday, Tuesday, Thursday and Friday evenings
February 29, March 1, 3, and 4 (7-10 p.m.) &
Saturday, March 5 (9:30 a.m. to noon)
Peace Evangelical Lutheran Church
5615 S.W. 14th St., Des Moines, IA 50315
(Corner of SW 14th and Porter — ½ mile north of Army Post Road
and ½ mile east of Fleur Drive at main entrance to airport)

*Co-sponsored by Peace Evangelical Lutheran Church and the Des Moines Conference,
The Lutheran Church — Missouri Synod*

Five comprehensive lecture & discussion sessions offering a new, intensely practical, and thoroughly contemporary technique for evangelistic outreach to today's unbeliever. Designed to prepare you to be "ready always to give and answer [Gk., apologetic] to every man who asks you a reason for the hope that is in you" (1 Peter 3:15).

This unique seminar, held in recent years under the sponsorship of such leading evangelical organizations as Park Street Church (Boston), 4th Presbyterian Church (Washington D.C.), Coral Ridge Presbyterian Church (Florida), Concordia Lutheran Church (San Antonio), The King's College, and Westmont College, is now available in your neighborhood! Sessions will cover

- The existence of God (How can we know God exists?)
- The problem of evil (How can a good God permit evil?)
- The miraculous (How can miracles be reconciled with modern science?)
- The total truth of Scripture (What about alleged errors and contradictions in Scripture?)
- Can "higher" (redaction) criticism of the Bible ever be justified?
- The dead-end of secularism (Why Christ is the only answer)
- The best approach for answering the questions of the seeker (How to win arguments without losing souls)
- The Holy Spirit and the defense of the faith
- Reading plan for becoming a complete apologist

Cost: $35 for the course; text material furnished.
Preregistration is strongly recommended — places are limited.
For registration information see reverse side of this sheet (⟶).

Appendices

Greater Orange County Area
Seminar on
PRACTICAL CHRISTIAN LIVING IN THE LIGHT OF THE BIBLE

Lecturer: Dr. John Warwick Montgomery
Dynamic Theologian, Lawyer, Scholar, Author, Apologist

WHO IS THE LECTURER?

Dr. Montgomery, Dean of The Simon Greenleaf School of Law, Orange, CA, is one of the most colorful figures of contemporary Protestantism. He holds two earned doctorate degrees (one from a European university), and seven other degrees besides; he is an English Barrister and the author of some 37 books and over 100 articles. He has debated such representatives of liberal religion as death-of-God theologian Thomas Altizer, the late bishop James Pike, and "new morality" advocate Joseph Fletcher. He has served as invitational visiting professor at Roman Catholic DePaul University, Concordia Seminary (Lutheran) in Ft. Wayne and St. Louis, the University of California at San Diego, the University of Maryland in Europe, and has taught in French at the Lutheran Study Center in Paris. For ten years he taught in apologetics at the Trinity Evangelical Divinity School. He has climbed to the top of Mt. Ararat in Turkey (17,000 ft.) in conjunction with searches for vestiges of the Ark. Biographical studies of him appear in *Who's Who in America*, *Who's Who in France*, *Who's Who in Europe*, *Who's Who in the World*, and the *Dictionary of International Biography*.

Friday evening, September 20 (7 to 9:30 P.M.) and
Saturday, September 21 (9:30 A.M. to Noon & 2 to 4:30 P.M.)
The Simon Greenleaf School of Law, 3855 E. La Palma Ave., Anaheim, CA 92807
(Take the Tustin exit off the 91 Freeway, go east to La Palma and turn right)

Six lecture & discussion sessions, conveniently arranged on a Friday night and a Saturday morning and afternoon, offering a new, intensely practical, and thoroughly scriptural approach to the problem-areas of contemporary Christian living. Learn how to make Christ the center and circumference of *all* your experience, guided by one of today's most exciting evangelical speakers. A unique opportunity for reflection on vital topics seldom treated at real depth in the evangelical community.

The sessions will cover

- Today's "Battle for the Bible": why it's worth getting excited about
  (Is higher criticism possible for Bible-believers?)
- How to become a Renaissance Christian—a "man (or woman) for all seasons"
  (including a LIFETIME READING PLAN)
- Transforming marriage & family relationships
  (are divorce & remarriage ever open to Christians, and if so, when?)
- The meaning of Christian citizenship—left, right, and Christ-centered
  (evangelicals as revolutionaries? "Sojourners" vs. Moral Majority")
- What we can learn from other churches & from today's transdenominational movements
  (dispensationalists, charismatics, etc.)
- How to approach World's end
  (Premills & Pretribs; are we on the edge of the last times?)

Cost: $35 for the course; text material furnished.
Preregistration is strongly recommended—places are limited.
For registration information, see the reverse side of this sheet (———➤)

OCTOBER 13-15, 1994
St. Louis Area Seminar

7:00 - 9:30 P.M. T & F
9:30 A.M. - 4:00 P.M. S

DEFENDING THE BIBLICAL GOSPEL
LECTURER: DR. JOHN WARWICK MONTGOMERY
Theologian, Scholar, Author, Debater, Apologist

Dr. Montgomery, Professor of Law & Humanities, University of Luton, England, is one of the most accomplished figures in contemporary Protestantism. He holds two earned doctorates (Ph.D., Chicago, Th.D., Strasbourg, France), and seven other degrees in the fields of law, philosophy, history, theology and the classics. Dr. Montgomery is an English Barrister and the author of 38 books and over 100 articles. He has debated such representatives of liberal religion as death-of-God theologian, Thomas Altizer, the late bishop James Pike, and "new morality" advocate Joseph Fletcher. He has served as invitational visiting professor at DePaul University, Concordia Seminary in Ft. Wayne and St. Louis, the University of California, San Diego, the University of Maryland in Europe, and has taught in French at the Lutheran Study Center in Paris. For three years he served as chairman of the History Department at Wilfred Laurier University, Ontario, for ten years he taught apologetics at Trinity Evangelical Divinity School, Deerfield, and for seven years he was Dean of the Simon Greenleaf School of Law, Anaheim, a school he founded. Biographical studies of him appear in Who's Who in America, Who's Who in France, Who's Who in Europe, Who's Who in the World, and the Dictionary of International Biography.

This unique seminar has been held in recent years under the sponsorship of such diverse Christian organizations as Park Street Congregational Church (Boston), 4th Presbyterian Church (Washington D.C.), C. S. Lewis Society of Princeton University, Coral Ridge Presbyterian Church (Florida), Concordia Lutheran Church (San Antonio), The King's College (New York), St. Mark's United Methodist Church (North Carolina), Westmont College (California), Truro Episcopal Church (Virginia), Moody Bible Institute (Chicago), and Trinity Theological Seminary, Southwest Campus (New Mexico).

AREAS TO BE COVERED IN THE ST. LOUIS SEMINAR

- The existence of God (How can we know God exists?)
- The problem of evil (How can a good God permit evil?)
- The miraculous (How can miracles be reconciled with modern science?)
- The inspiration of Scripture (What about alleged errors and contradictions in Scripture?)
- Can "higher" (redaction) criticism of the Bible ever be justified?
- The dead-end of secularism (Why Christ is the only answer.)
- The best approach for answering the questions of the seeker (How to win arguments without losing souls.)
- The Holy Spirit and the defense of the faith.
- Reading plan for becoming a complete apologist.

To Be Held in the Sanctuary of
Craig Road Baptist Church
1745 Craig Road, Creve Coeur, MO 63146
(Just South of Westport Plaza at Page & I-270)

For More Information Contact:
Trinity Seminars
314-731-4544

SEMINAR LEADER

DR. JOHN WARWICK MONTGOMERY

Dynamic Theologian, Lawyer, Author, Debater, Apologist

Dr. Montgomery has earned nine degrees, including two doctorates, written 42 books and over 100 articles, most of them in defense of the Christian faith. His seminar style is lively, easy to understand, and laced with wit.

WHEN AND WHERE?

March 25 and 26, 7:00 to 9:30 p.m.
and March 27, 9:30 a.m. to noon and 1:30 to 5:00 p.m.
Concordia College, 7128 Ada Blvd.
Edmonton, Alberta

How to become proficient at answering questions about your faith.

What about alleged errors and contradictions in the Bible?

How can we know God exists?

How can a good God permit evil?

Can miracles be reconciled with modern science?

Is Christ the only answer?

"...the seminar gives a chance to get your questions answered. You will leave convinced that the Faith is not a delusion."

13. TOUR BROCHURES

Eastern Europe has awakened from totalitarian sleep. When summer smiles on a new Europe this year, join **Dr. John Warwick Montgomery** *on an unforgettable lecture tour to*

The Birthplaces of the REFORMATION in a UNITED GERMANY

Including Amsterdam, a Rhine Cruise, and the Musical Heritage of Bach and Handel

June 10 - 24, 1991

The Great Reformation Monument at Worms. Luther holds the open Bible and is surrounded by other Reformers. Here you will relive Luther's heroic declaration, "Here I stand. I can do no other. God help me. Amen!"

Appendices

Join
DR. JOHN WARWICK MONTGOMERY
FOR THE
300th ANNIVERSARY
BACH AND LUTHER TOUR

A previous Tour Group, before the Bach Statue at the great Evangelical composer's birthplace in Eisenach. Our East German guide and bus driver are standing in front of Dr. Montgomery.

1985: A VERY SPECIAL YEAR
1985: A VERY SPECIAL TOUR

The year 1985 marks the 300th anniversary of the birth of the greatest musician in all history: Johann Sebastian Bach. Bach's orthodox Christian belief — his simple faith in the Gospel as restored by Luther's Reformation — infused everything he composed, so that he has been rightly called "the Fifth Evangelist." Bach lived in East Germany, in what today is territory behind the "iron curtain." This great anniversary of the composer has given Dr. Montgomery the unique opportunity to create a tour to experience Christian life and witness in a part of the world offering the greatest contemporary challenge to historic Christian faith.

You will visit the Poland of Chopin and Solidarity; the Germany of Bach and Luther; the Prague of John Hus; and the Vienna of the Strausses and The Sound of Music. Whether you are a musician or tone-deaf, you will be sensitized to the frontier between belief and unbelief and to the perennial testimony of those who have devoted their God-given talents to the production of the Gospel in words and in song.

UNIQUE FEATURES OF THE TOUR
Where else can you find a vacation tour like this?

- Guided visits to the key Christian and Reformation sites of Eastern Europe with a professor who has led study tours to those locations for over twenty years, and who is renowned for his effectiveness as a communicator, for his liveliness, and for his ability to inspire.

- Principal travel by first-class European trains. Everyone has heard of the romantic Orient Express! Train travel remains today in Europe what it once was in the United States: a civilized and exciting way of seeing the country on a reliable schedule.

- Concerts for the musical, and a wide variety of local and fun entertainment for those with other tastes. Coordinated lectures to put it all together on such topics as:

    "The Alchemists of Prague and Today's Occultism"
    "John Hus and the Pre-Reformers"
    "Luther and the Reformation"
    "Bach the Fifth Evangelist"
    "Music and the Gospel"
    "The Vienna Circle of Philosophers and
        The Defense of Christian Faith"
    "Polish Christianity and
        The Contemporary East-West Crisis"

- Incredible shopping bargains on tasteful East European craft items (for example: wood carvings, primitive paintings, dolls, embroidery), Luther momentos, Bach and other musical recordings, sheet music, antiques, rare books; etc. etc. **The dollar has never been stronger in exchange against the currencies of the countries you will be visiting.**

- Discovery of another world. What is it like to be a Christian in the Eastern-bloc countries. Opinions pro and con are expressed by many church leaders and "authorities" — most of whom have never been there themselves. In his brief visits behind the iron curtain has the Rev. Billy Graham gotten an accurate picture? Why not find out for yourself? Expand your spiritual horizons! Confront a world few ever see, and obtain new insight into the Gospel of Christ.

Total Tour Cost for participants June 1-15, 1985
    from Los Angeles $2,692
    from New York $2,484   ITSLH 13002

 Lufthansa

CHINA
& HONG KONG

Join

DR. JOHN WARWICK MONTGOMERY

For

A Truly Astounding Christian Tour Experience

Visiting

BEIJING • XIAN • NANJING • SHANGHAI
GUILIN • CANTON • HONG KONG

May 29 - June 15, 1989

Join
Dr. John Warwick Montgomery
for the historical glories of
The Holy Land
including Mediterranean Cyprus

June 15 - July 1, 1986

13. Tour brochures

WHO IS THE TOUR LEADER?

Dr. Montgomery, Dean of America's unique Christian law school, the Simon Greenleaf School of Law, is one of the most colorful figures of contemporary Protestantism. He holds two earned doctorate degrees (one from a European university) and eight other degrees besides; he is a theologian, English Barrister, and author of thirty-seven books and over a hundred articles. He has debated such representatives of liberal religion as death-of-God theologian Thomas Altizer, the late bishop James Pike, and "new morality" advocate Joseph Fletcher. He has served as invitational visiting professor at Roman Catholic DePaul University, Concordia Seminary (Lutheran) in Ft. Wayne and St. Louis, the University of California at San Diego, the University of Maryland in Europe, and has taught in French at the Lutheran Study Center in Paris. For seven years he

Dr. Montgomery with Prime Minister Begin of Israel in Jerusalem, April 1978.

conducted the European Graduate Program of the Trinity Evangelical Divinity School. He has climbed to the top of Mt. Ararat in Turkey (17,000 ft.) in conjuction with the recent searches for vestiges of the Ark. Biographical studies of him appear in *Who's Who in America*, *Who's Who in France*, *Who's Who in Europe*, *Who's Who in the World*, and the *Dictionary of International Biography*.

SOME REPRESENTATIVE COMMENTS ON DR. MONTGOMERY'S PREVIOUS TOURS

FROM A YOUNG SECRETARY—It was the most tremendous experience I've ever had.

FROM A COLLEGE VICE PRESIDENT AND HIS FAMILY—Two weeks have passed since we completed the most fantastic and fruitful one week experience of our lives. I can heartily recommend your tour to anyone and consider it a lifetime highlight.

FROM A CAREER WOMAN—The Holy Land tour [1981] was the best trip ever! Thank you so much for making it so. I am now enjoying immensely your lectures and comments on tape, along with the books, maps, and brochures I bought in Israel. Studying God's Word is more exciting than ever.

FROM A UNIVERSITY STUDENT—The trip to East Germany last December was an adventure I will not soon forget. People are still asking me questions about it. Many times I have used my experiences to get the undivided attention of a group of people, which opens the door to witness to them about the greatness and saving power of our Lord. Some of my greatest experiences of the trip were the opportunities I had to share Christ with the East German people (at the correct time and place, of course).

FROM A BUSINESS MAN WHO TOOK HIS WIFE AND FOUR SONS (ages 23, 20, 18, 14)—I wish to thank you for the single greatest family experience that our family has ever experienced. You made the trip. If at any time a family is wavering as to whether they should take such a trip as a whole family, feel free to use my name. I sincerely believe that the decision was one of the finest decisions of my life. Thank you for all that you did for us: the informal meal hour discussions with the boys, my wife and me. I appreciate the fact that our youngest boy could ask you a question and he was treated with the same thoughtfulness as if it had been the college president asking the question. Out of this trip, the Lord willing, one of our sons has decided to put his two years in the army, get it over and then go to Seminary and into the ministry. As for Don, he feels it was a great spiritual experience and that he will never be quite the same because of the trip. It convinced him that he should go into Christian work of some kind.

FROM A PASTOR & SEMINARY PROFESSOR—I have had the opportunity to share with our congregation for three consecutive Sunday nights. Many visitors have been here from out of town and from other churches in town. I also have had invitations to speak at the ministerial association and four other churches. Our students who went have been interviewed on a television talk show.

FROM A BIBLE COLLEGE STUDENT—Personally, I felt that your lectures were the best part of the tour. They were so good that I almost wish that I could enroll in some of your classes.

FROM THE PRESIDENT OF A CHRISTIAN COLLEGE—This was one of the greatest experiences of our life together as a family and as individuals.

FROM A LUTHERAN LAYMAN—I take this opportunity to convey to you my sincere thanks for including me in the recent tour of the Holy Land. It was truly an enlightening and enriching experience and I shall cherish it as being one of the richest blessings that I have received from our Lord.

FROM A SCHOOL TEACHER — Our two weeks in the Holy Land [1981] were like a year Bethel Bible course rolled into two weeks before our very eyes. Everything I've heard and read about in the Bible since about age four was there before my eyes to see and experience for myself. Dr. Montgomery made this tour a truly exciting and memorable one. Our accommodations were the finest and often in perfect locations for the walking we could do during free afternoons. He gave seven lectures in the course of our trip, including such themes as, "The Bible Confirmed by Archeology" and "The Historical Reliability of Jesus' Miraculous Ministry." As if this weren't enough, we had the privilege of having Halvor Roenning, an instructor from the American Institute of Holy Land Studies, with us for the entire trip. From him we got a detailed picture of the Holy Land, including geography, history, archeology, a little botany, and Bible references and studies on specific pertinent subjects and places as we traveled. This was not a typical tour for tourists but rather an exciting course for Bible students!

14. ISRAEL PHOTOS: ONE WITH HALVOR RONNING, THE OTHERS WITH A CAMEL

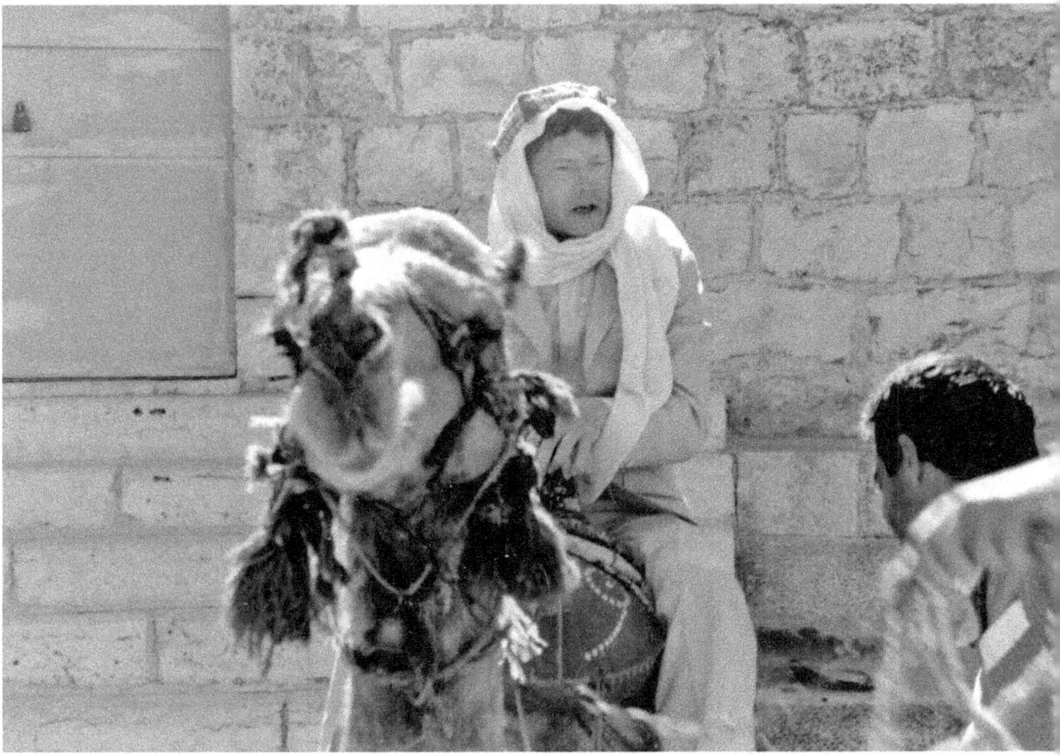

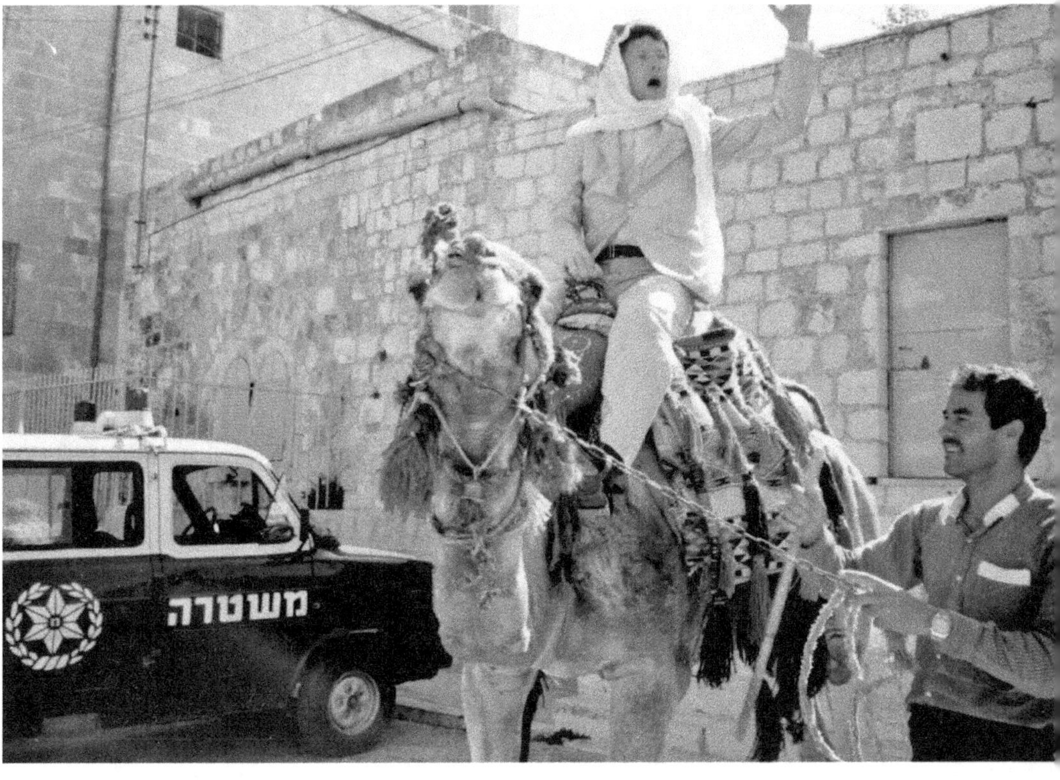
משטרה

15. TYPICAL ACTIVITIES AT THE SIMON GREENLEAF SCHOOL OF LAW

THE GREENBAG

A periodic update for friends of America's unique evangelical law school
THE SIMON GREENLEAF SCHOOL OF LAW

"The antiquity of the 'green bag', as the badge of a lawyer, is indisputable. It appears that barristers carried them in the reign of Queen Anne."

No. 11, March, 1986   Simon Greenleaf School of Law, Anaheim, California

SIMON GREENLEAF: WHERE THE FIRE BURNS BRIGHTLY

Some of the students who attend our school and many of the visitors who come to our campus are unaware of Simon Greenleaf's humble origins. In 1980 Dr. Montgomery, along with a small group of friends, launched out with a vision and determination on what many considered a quixotic quest: the founding of a law school unique among all the law schools in America because of its insistence on integrating the Bible with the law.

The first semester in the fall of 1980 began with a total of only 12 students enrolled in both the J.D. and M.A. programs. For the first two years of the school's existence classes were held in the educational building of Chuck Smith's Calvary Chapel, Costa Mesa.

The Simon Greenleaf School of Law
Facilities in Anaheim

In the fall of 1982, having outgrown the available space at Calvary Chapel, the school moved to larger facilities at Trinity Lutheran Church in Anaheim Hills. Over the next three years the enrollment steadily increased. Finally, in the summer of 1985, the Simon Greenleaf School of Law moved to a handsome building of its own in Anaheim.

Simon Greenleaf is now nearing the completion of its sixth year of existence. Throughout these years we have seen the hand of God blessing the school in many different ways.

God has touched people in numerous countries, calling them to study at Simon Greenleaf. We have had students from France, Norway, England, Zimbabwe, Iran, New Zealand, Australia and Canada. In addition, students have come to Simon Greenleaf from every part of the country.

The beautiful new Simon Greenleaf facilities are another evidence of the Lord's hand on the school. Simon Greenleaf is now housed in a 22,500 square-foot executive building with three floors of space, including classrooms and two impressive libraries for the law and apologetics programs.

Another area in which we have been blessed is in the continued increase in the school's enrollment. From 12 students in 1980, we have grown to nearly 100 students. This semester we have set a new Simon Greenleaf record for the number of students signed up for spring classes. The number of students registered in our J.D. program is up 19% from the spring of '85 and the number of students registered in our M.A. program is up 62% from the spring of '85.

Continued on Page 2

THE GREENBAG is published monthly by the Simon Greenleaf School of Law, 3855 E. La Palma, Anaheim, CA 92807. All rights reserved. The Simon Greenleaf School of Law, with its International Seminar in Theology & Law (held each summer in conjunction with the International Institute of Human Rights in Strasbourg, France) operate as a non-profit, degree granting institution of higher learning, organized and incorporated under the laws of the State of California and supervised by the Superintendent of Public Instruction of the California State Department of Education and the California Committee of Bar Examiners.

15. Typical activities at the Simon Greenleaf School of Law

THE GREENBAG

Simon Greenleaf on the radio:

The following is a list of all radio broadcasts by Simon Greenleaf faculty members.

Christianity on Trial with Dr. John Warwick Montgomery
Southern California KYMS - FM 106.3, Sunday
9:30 to 11:30 pm

The Bible Answer Man with Walter Martin
Satellite Radio Network, Monday - Friday, 2:00 - 4:00 pm
Call 1-800-438-6311 for listing in your area.

Let's Talk About The Bible with John Stewart
Southern California KBRT - AM 730, Sunday 2:00-5:45 pm

However, numbers and statistics do not necessarily accurately gauge the impact an institution has made or is making. God is much more concerned with quality than with quantity. The acid test for any academic institution is the quality of its graduates.

In looking at Simon Greenleaf's alumni we see that already they are having a tremendous impact on the society for Christ. The types of ministries that they are engaged in are quite diverse. Some graduates are practicing attorneys, ministering God's love to hurting people. Several alumni are engaged in the arena of defending human rights. Some have set up apologetic ministries and are proclaiming the Gospel in a milieu increasingly hostile to Christianity. Others have had writings published by major evangelical publishers and institutions. A number of Simon Greenleaf alumni have been accepted for doctoral studies at distinguished institutions such as Fordham University, Marquette University, Notre Dame University, the University of Essex, England, the University of Strasbourg, France, Tuebingen University, West Germany, etc.

We could continue to recount the things God has done here: the various ways He is using our faculty, students and alumni across the globe, and how the lives of many people have been touched and changed by this ministry. In a word, it appears that Simon Greenleaf is at this moment the evangelical graduate school where gospel excitement is at its peak – where, as it were, fire from heaven is touching earth!

If you would like more information on how you can help in this dynamic and unique ministry, or if you want information on how to become a part of this community of students, please write, call – or simply check and mail the coupon on the back page.

EVEN SMALL ESTATES REQUIRE A WILL

Sometimes people think they don't need a Will if they don't have much money or property. That can be a serious (and costly) mistake. In fact, many people have a larger estate than they think when such things as life insurance, pension plans and the family home are taken into consideration.

Without a Will the state determines who shall be the Guardian of your minor children.

Without a Will the state appoints a Personal Representative (Administrator) to distribute your assets according to state law.

Without a Will, and without heirs, your assets will be distributed to the *state* regardless of your special interests in family, friends or Christian causes.

For more information on preparing a Christ-honoring Will, contact America's Unique Christian Law School:

The Simon Greenleaf School of Law
3855 East La Palma Avenue
Anaheim, CA 92807

Name _____
Address _____
City _____ State _____ Zip _____
Phone (   ) _____
Date of Birth _____

197

Appendices

No. 11, March, 1986 — **THE GREENBAG**

NEW SIMON GREENLEAF LAW REVIEW ADDRESSES THE ABORTION ISSUE

The *Simon Greenleaf Law Review*, Volume V, is hot off the press, and it centers on what is very likely the most important moral issue of our day: abortion and the right to life. Essays featured in this issue are "Abortion and Human Life: A Christian Perspective," by Herbert T. Krimmel, professor of law at the Southwestern University School of Law, Los Angeles, California, and Martin J. Foley; "Lex Talionis and the Human Fetus," by Meredith G. Kline, professor of Old Testament at Westminster Theological Seminary in California and Gordon-Conwell Theological Seminary; and "An Evaluation of the Quality of Life Argument for Infanticide," by Dr. David K. Clark, professor of philosophy at Toccoa Falls College, Georgia.

Also included in the new issue of the *Law Review* is an essay entitled, "The Rights of Unborn Children," by Simon Greenleaf's Dean, Dr. John Warwick Montgomery. Last summer Dr. Montgomery was invited by Prof. Malcolm Jeeves of St. Andrews University, Scotland, to read this essay at the international conference on "Christian Faith and Science in Society," held at St. Catherine's College, Oxford, England. The three-day conference was jointly sponsored by the Research Scientists' Christian Fellowship (England) and the American Scientific Affiliation (U.S.). Nearly 300 physical and social scientists, theologians and other scholars from 15 different nations attended the conference. Included among the many renowned speakers were Donald M. MacKay (of Keele University, England), Walter R. Thorson (of the University of Alberta, Canada) and Edwin Yamauchi (of Miami University, Oxford, Ohio).

Dr. Montgomery's essay examines the abortion issue by showing what the current state of the law is in the United States and the United Kingdom and then introduces the perspective of non-common-law countries (such as West Germany and Spain) and that of the international and comparative law of human rights.

Contrary to the United States Supreme Court's *Roe v. Wade* decision of 1973, Dr. Montgomery concludes that we must squarely face the issue of when life begins.

In point of fact, a satisfactory legal understanding as to the beginning point of human life will necessitate reliance upon empirical, scientific evidence of human personhood. One must not create a legal definition of personhood which flies in the face of National Socialist law, the Jew – regardless of genetic evidence of his humanity – was deprived of his legal personhood and destroyed like worthless offal. Prior to the American Civil War and the anti-slavery Amendments to the U.S. Constitution, such judicial decisions as *Dred Scott* relegated slaves to the status of legal nonpersons in spite of clear biological evidence of their humanity. Wherever legal personhood has been defined without reference to objective genetic criteria, the door has been opened to the most frightful consequences.

What in fact does contemporary genetic research tell us? Geneticists have shown us that the fertilized egg is already an autonomous living being, genetically complete at conception. Any view which does not accept the fetus as a living being does so on philosophically and sociologically functional grounds, not on scientific evidence.

When reading for the English Bar in 1984, Dr. Montgomery received the Sudarshan Kapila Memorial Prize for his essay from the prestigious Council of Legal Education's Inns of Court School of Law (London). He also presented it by invitation as the 1985 Dwight Lecture in Christian Thought at the University of Pennsylvania, and at the Faculty of Law, University of Essex, England. The essay is published in its entirety in the new *Simon Greenleaf Law Review*.

In addition to the essays already mentioned, Volume V of the *Law Review* also features a number of stimulating and controversial book reviews. Among these is a detailed critique of Australian philosopher Michael Tooley's influential book *Abortion and Infanticide* (Oxford: Clarendon Press, 1983), in which the author argues that "neither abortion, nor infanticide, at least during the first few weeks after birth is morally wrong."

Order your copy of the new *Simon Greenleaf Law Review* today by using the coupon on the last page of *The Greenbag!*

15. Typical activities at the Simon Greenleaf School of Law

DATES TO REMEMBER

The following is a listing of upcoming times and locations of special events at Simon Greenleaf and speaking engagements of Simon Greenleaf faculty members. We invite you to attend where possible and ask that you remember these dates in your prayers.

> May 5 — 1986 Commencement activities for Simon Greenleaf School of Law graduates held at Trinity Lutheran Church, 4101 Nohl Ranch Road, Orange, California at 3:00 p.m. For details call (714) 998-2888.
> Commencement Speaker: Mayor of Anaheim, Mr. Don Roth

JOSEPH P. GUDEL

Apr. 5	Grace Graduate School, Long Beach, CA

JAN LARUE

Mar. 13	San Bernardino Christian Women's Club, San Bernardino, CA – (714) 893-3910
Mar. 18	Glendale Christian Women's Club, Glendale, CA – (714) 998-2888
Apr. 3	Irvine Christian Women's Club, Irvine, CA – (714) 998-2888
Apr. 9	Pasadena Christian Women's Club, Pasadena, CA – (818) 952-1528
May 13	Covina Christian Women's Club, Covina, CA – (714) 599-0139

HAROLD LINDSELL

Mar. 30	El Toro Baptist Church, El Toro, CA – (714) 830-7473

JOHN T. MOEN

Apr. 5	Grace Graduate School, Long Beach, CA

WALTER MARTIN

Apr. 4-5	Jesus Festival, Orlando, Altamonte Springs, FL – (305) 788-3450
Apr. 6-9	First Baptist Church, Fountain Valley, CA – (714) 847-3573
Apr. 11-13	First Assembly of God, Fort Myers, FL – (813) 936-6277
Apr. 20-23	Christian Research Institute-Canada, Edmonton, Canada – (403) 277-7702
May 4-7	Expo 86, Vancouver, Canada – (403) 277-7702

JOHN WARWICK MONTGOMERY

Mar. 21-22	Southern District of the Evangelical Theological Society, Meeting at Free Will Baptist Bible College, Nashville, TN – (615) 383-1340
Mar. 27	Cerritos College, Cerritos, CA

JOHN STEWART

Mar. 20	Cerritos College, Cerritos, CA

To: Simon Greenleaf School of Law
3855 E. La Palma
Anaheim, CA 92807

Dear GREENBAG:
The unique Simon Greenleaf ministry touches my heart! Enclosed are the tax-deductible contributions indicated. Send me postpaid the gift items I've checked.

Name _____

Address _____

_____
(include Zip Code)

Telephone ( ) _____

Amount Enclosed $ _____

☐ $50 I'd like Dr. Montgomery's book, *The Shaping of America*, offering a biblical perspective on our national history and pointing the way to Christian reconquest of politics, law, and society.

☐ $2 Send me the new (1986-88) catalog of the Simon Greenleaf School of Law.

☐ $10 Send me the second number of the Simon Greenleaf Law Review, featuring Dr. Francis Schaeffer's original essay on Christian faith and human rights.

☐ $10 Send me the third issue of the Simon Greenleaf Law Review, containing Dr. Montgomery's book-length analysis and critique of the Marxist approach to human rights.

☐ $10 Send me the fourth issue of the Simon Greenleaf Law Review, featuring Lord Chancellor Hailsham's spiritual autobiography.

☐ $12 Send me the fifth issue of the Simon Greenleaf Law Review featuring Dr. Montgomery's prize-winning essay on the rights of the unborn.

the Simon Greenleaf School of Law

In Conjunction With
FOCAL POINT
of THE EVANGELICAL FREE CHURCH, FULLERTON

Presents

"DEMONSTRATING THE RELIABILITY OF SCRIPTURE THROUGH FULFILLED BIBLICAL PROPHECY"

A Public Lecture By
Dr. Gleason L. Archer, Jr.

Before joining the faculty of Trinity Evangelical Divinity School, in 1965, Gleason L. Archer, Jr. was professor of biblical languages at Fuller Theological Seminary where he also served as acting dean. Presently, Dr. Archer is professor of Old Testament and semitic languages at Trinity and in alternate years serves as chairman of the division of Old Testament.

Dr. Archer holds the B.A. in classics from Harvard College, the A.M. and Ph.D. in comparative literature from Harvard Graduate School. In addition, he holds the LL.B. from Suffolk University Law School and B.D. from Princeton Theological Seminary. Dr. Archer has done post-graduate study at Chicago's Oriental Institute. He was ordained as a Presbyterian minister and served churches in New Jersey and Boston, Massachusetts. He now serves as a minister of the Evangelical Free Church of America.

Author of several books, including *Encyclopedia of Bible Difficulties* and *A Survey of Old Testament Introduction*, Dr. Archer has also contributed to a number of books such as *Wycliffe Bible Commentary*, *The Pictorial Bible Dictionary*, and *The Bible Expositor*. He is also a contributor to such periodicals as *Christianity Today*, *Westminster Journal*, and *Decision*.

| The Time |

Monday Evening, May 1, (7:00 p.m.)

15. Typical activities at the Simon Greenleaf School of Law

the Simon Greenleaf School of Law

3855 East La Palma Avenue
Anaheim, CA 92807
(714) 998-2888

THE SIMON GREENLEAF SCHOOL OF LAW

presents

THE FIFTH ANNUAL MOOT COURT BANQUET

In the past 20 years, the Christian community has seen the legalization of abortion, the use of sex education as a tool for teaching relativistic values, and the emergence of sex clinics on high schools campuses. Now more than ever, Christians need to be informed on these issues and to know their constitutional rights, such an opportunity is available through the Moot Court banquet.

At this years banquet, Simon Greenleaf students will argue a hypothetical case involving parental rights and those of school districts with respect to sex education, the operation of school-based health clinics, and abortions for minors without parental notification.

```
Date:  Friday, May 5, 1989
Place: Griswold's Hotel
       1500 S. Raymond
       Fullerton, CA 92631
Time:  7:00 p.m.
Cost:  $12.00 student
       $16.00 others
```

16. LETTER OF THE REVD POMEROY MOORE ON THE SIMON GREENLEAF CRISIS

ATTACHMENT 2

TRINITY LUTHERAN CHURCH
and Christian School
4101 E. Nohl Ranch Rd., Anaheim, CA 92807 (714) 637-8370

POMEROY J. MOORE
PASTOR

JAMES A. ELMORE
PASTOR

EVELYN N. BRADLEY
PRINCIPAL

November 4, 1988

David Berglund, Esq.
15650 Devonshire Street, #310
Granada Hills, CA 91344-7241

Dear Dave,

    I am in receipt of a copy of a letter to John Montgomery from John Wanvig as chairman of a committee to further investigate Montgomery, whereby the Simon Greenleaf Board is attempting to exercise spiritual jurisdiction over his actions and personal matters of his life. I am further informed that an "official hearing" has been scheduled with the demand that John Warwick Montgomery appear before the "committee." I am appalled at this action by members of the board.

    The statement, "Based upon our Biblical duty to exercise spiritual oversight in the Simon Greenleaf community, we will proceed with our due process hearing procedure," is most disturbing in this matter. The oversight inferred by this statement does not rest with the board, but with the Church according to proper ecclesiastical and pastoral procedure. If this were not done, then the board could possibly justify itself; but the fact of the matter is it has been, and continues to be, done in the most Scriptural and proper manner.

    As a member of the church and the pastoral staff at Trinity Lutheran, "spiritual oversight" is being exercised over John Montgomery by his church body. And for your information, this has not been conducted singly but in full consultation with the District President of the Lutheran Church Missouri Synod to which John's clergy status is certified and the President of the World Confessional Lutheran Association to which Trinity is a member. The matters regarding John's personal life, his divorce and his remarriage have all been subjected to our oversight procedures. This fully meets Jesus' prescription regarding inquiry into John's spiritual condition and the pursuance of the board can only be considered an hostile or unthinkable attack by an organization which is not a church.

    It is further known to us that John has submitted this entire case to Christian Conciliation before the calling of the board's committee hearing. Failure of the board to allow the conciliation proceedings to be un-hindered by its own actions can only further disqualify the board's intent in these matters.

    Dave, I again appeal to you to accept the spiritual jurisdiction of the Lutheran Church to properly and adequately deal with concerns regarding John's spirituality and integrity as a Christian and a clergyman of the church. I also strongly support the efforts at conciliation to which John has pledged himself, and urge you to be committed to these same ends.

Sincerely for the sake of the proclamation of the Gospel,

Pomeroy J. Moore

cc: John Wanvig, Ray Bouquet, Frank Diegmann, and

17. CROSS-EXAMINATIONS IN THE CENTRAL LUTHERAN CHURCH CASE

CERTIFICATE

STATE OF WASHINGTON) ss
COUNTY OF PIERCE)

I, CAROL A. TALBOTT, do hereby certify: That I am a certified shorthand reporter of the State of Washington; that the foregoing proceedings of December 16, 1978 were reported by me stenographically and later reduced to typewriting under my direction; that the foregoing is a true and accurate transcription of my machine shorthand notes.

CAROL A. TALBOTT

ELMER F. GROSHONG & ASSOCIATES
945 TACOMA AVE. SO.
TACOMA, WASHINGTON

Appendices

```
ATTENDING:   Kenneth Myklebust, Chairman  )
             LaVerne Nelsen                )
             John Anderson                 )
             Marvin Fisher                 ) Committee Members
             Harold Hauge                  )
             Harlow Jacobson               )
             Dr. Robert Mortvedt           )
```

The North Pacific District Executive Committee was represented by: DONALD L. THORESON, ESQ.

The Central Lutheran Church was represented by: JOHN WARWICK MONTGOMERY, ESQ.

17. Cross-examinations in the Central Lutheran Church case

PASTOR NELSEN: Ladies and Gentlemen, the Appeals and Adjudication Committee of the North Pacific District of the American Lutheran Church has called this meeting. We are here to hear the appeal of the Central Lutheran Church on the suspension from membership from the American Lutheran Church by the Executive Committee of the North Pacific District. I declare this hearing to be open in the name of the Father and of the Son and of the Holy Spirit, Amen.

We will call on Harold Hauge, a member of the Appeals Committee, to lead us in the morning devotions.

(Pastor Hauge gave readings from First Corinthians, Chapter 12, Verse 12, et seq. and led the assembly in prayer.)

PASTOR NELSEN: It is now 9:30, and Mr. Kenneth Myklebust will preside throughout the rest of this hearing.

CHAIRMAN MYKLEBUST: Ladies and Gentlemen, before we proceed, the District Committee on Appeals and Adjudication would like to open the proceeding with a statement of the procedure which will govern, and an outline of the issues and of the history of this matter.

I should state for the record that this hearing is being held at Central Lutheran Church in Tacoma, Washington, and we appreciate Pastor Redal and his congregation hosting us.

Before proceeding, I must also state that this is not a public hearing; if there are persons present who are not

```
 1  Q   Since no official interpretation or expression of special
 2      circumstances exists, by your own admission, would it be
 3      fair to say that when you limit that expression to geographic
 4      factors where it is not possible for a congregation to be
 5      served by an ALC pastor, that is your own personal judgment.
 6  A   No, sir. In the first place, I said "usually" with geographic
 7      factors involved. Secondly, it's the judgment and the
 8      practice over the nine years in which I have been in this
 9      office and the ten years that I served in the American
10      District in working with district presidents. It's not
11      purely my own thinking.
12  Q   All right. You'd say, then, that this was universal prac-
13      tice, or very widespread practice within the American
14      Lutheran Church?
15  A   No, sir; it is done in a very limited way.
16  Q   No, I mean that you would say that your interpretation here
17      that geographical factors comprise the limitation where
18      it is not possible for a congregation to be served by an
19      ALC pastor, that that is, as a matter of fact, the practice
20      of the American Lutheran Church.
21  A   "Usually" with geographic factors involved; with many other
22      factors involved as well, yes, it is the practice of the
23      American Lutheran Church.
24  Q   We determined at the outset, did we not, that you were the
25      district president of the North Pacific District of the
```

76

ELMER F. GROSHONG & ASSOCIATES
745 TACOMA AVE. SO.
TACOMA, WASHINGTON

```
 1              American Lutheran Church in 1974?
 2    A    Right.
 3    Q    Are you aware that the official 1974 handbook of the ALC
 4         lists, among some twenty non-ALC pastors serving ALC
 5         churches at that time, one Paul Felver, a clergyman of the
 6         United Methodist Church who then served as pastor of Good
 7         Hope Lutheran Church in Lind, Washington?
 8    A    Yes.
 9    Q    You approved him, did you not?
10    A    Yes, sir.
11    Q    You approved him under the special circumstances rubric?
12    A    Yes, sir.
13    Q    How far is Lind, Washington, from closest ALC church
14         served by an ALC pastor?
15    A    Seventeen miles.
16    Q    Seventeen miles. You're acquainted with article (D)2.10
17         of the district constitution where it is stated, "the
18         district dedicates itself to bear witness to the Christian
19         faith in fullness and purity, and to preserve and extend
20         the unity of that faith"?
21    A    Right.
22    Q    And to section (D)3 where that faith is defined as that of
23         the ALC, "as contained in chapter 3 of its constitution,"
24         to wit, to believe in the Bible as, "the inerrant word
25         of God and acceptance of the Book of Concord of 1580,
```

ELMER F. GROSHONG & ASSOCIATES
745 TACOMA AVE. SO.
TACOMA, WASHINGTON

```
1      not insofar as but because they are the presentation
2      and explanation of the pure doctrine of the Word
3      of God,"
4      Which is virtually what you were quoting yourself earlier,
5      I believe. Do clergy of the United Methodist Church
6      subscribe to the inerrant scripture or to the Book of
7      Concord, in order to be ordained or licensed?
8   A  No, sir. Not so far as I know.
9   Q  Did you examine Mr. Felver to determine his views of
10     biblical authority for approving the service at Good Hope?
11  A  I spent some three and a half hours with Pastor Felver, or
12     there abouts, and with Pastor Carlew (phonetic) for execu-
13     tive assistance to myself, in determining his theology.
14     It's one of those cases that I remember very well because
15     I was so pleasantly surprised to discover that he, with
16     some Lutheran background, and training as a Methodist, is
17     a Lutheran theologian.
18  Q  So you did determine that his views and biblical authority
19     were in conformity with chapter 3 of the constitution of
20     the ALC, to wit, "belief in the inerrent Word of God"?
21  A  I believe the things that I was concerned about most was
22     his doctrine of the way of salvation, his attitude on the
23     sacraments. Those were the things that I'd say in particular
24  Q  Oh, so you didn't actually deal with his views of biblical
25     authority, but you did approve him under the special
```

78

ELMER F. GROSHONG & ASSOCIATES
745 TACOMA AVE. SO.
TACOMA, WASHINGTON

1		circumstances rubric, to serve seventeen miles from an ALC
2		church served by an ALC pastor?
3	A	Yes; we had a large congregation unable to move --
4	Q	That is, to drive the seventeen miles?
5	A	To drive the seventeen miles, in addition to his own
6		responsibilities in that parish, and we had a congregation
7		there which was unable to function alone, and the Methodists
8		needed help as well, so the superintendent and I put a docu-
9		ment together following my consultation with Pastor Felver,
10		and then the congregations approved that and I officially
11		approved his serving.
12	Q	You're aware that article 5.13 of the ALC constitution
13		expressly limits the jurisdiction of the ALC in disciplin-
14		ary matters over its congregations two cases in which,
15		"disloyalty to the church's doctrinal position is evident"?
16		Maybe you'd like to take a look at that? That's article
17		5.13 that speaks of the jurisdiction of the American
18		Lutheran Church and the term of "discipline" is employed
19		with reference to disloyalty to the church's doctrinal
20		position. Are you acquainted with that?
21	A	I see it.
22	Q	All right, and we've established that article 3 which sets
23		forth the inerrency in scripture is required doctrinally
24		of those serving ALC congregations as pastors?
25	A	As ALC pastors, yes, sir.

1   MR. MONTGOMERY: No further questions.
2   CHAIRMAN MYKLEBUST: Is there any objection to
3   Father Campbell being excused, if he desires to leave?
4   MR. MONTGOMERY: Oh, not at all, but there would
5   be no reason for his having to.
6   CHAIRMAN MYKLEBUST: No, just in the event that he
7   found it necessary, you don't anticipate recalling him?
8   MR. MONTGOMERY: No.
9   CHAIRMAN MYKLEBUST: All right. You may call
10 your next witness.
11 MR. MONTGOMERY: I call Pastor Paul Felver. I
12 might state and as a preface to the questioning of
13 this witness, that poor Pastor Felver is an example
14 of what happens when one tries to travel by plane in
15 the Northwest in the wintertime, and I am delighted
16 to see that he is here in such good shape.
17 DR. PAUL FELVER,   Called as a witness for Central
                                    Lutheran, testified as follows:
18   EXAMINATION
19 BY MR. MONTGOMERY:
20 Q Pastor Felver, would you state your name for the record?
21 A Paul Felver.
22 Q Of what congregation are you a clergyman?
23 A The Laytah (phonetic)-Elmore Parish United Methodist
24   Church.
25 Q You are an ordained clergyman of the United Methodist

17. Cross-examinations in the Central Lutheran Church case

1		Church?
2	A	I am.
3	Q	Pastor Felver, where did you receive your seminary
4		training?
5	A	At the Methodist Theological School in Delaware, Ohio.
6	Q	Did you take any degree at a Lutheran Theological
7		seminary?
8	A	No degree.
9	Q	Did you serve for a time on contract as pastor of the
10		ALC church in Lind, Washington?
11	A	Yes, the Good Hope Lutheran ALC Church in Lind.
12	Q	For how long did you serve there?
13	A	For approximately two-and-a-half years.
14	Q	Who was the Northpacific District President at that
15		time?
16	A	Clarence Solberg.
17	Q	A survey, Pastor Felver, has recently been made of non
18		ALC pastors currently serving ALC churches. Because
19		you were not currently serving an ALC church you were
20		not sent this questionnaire, nor have you seen the
21		questionnaire. I want to ask you several of the questions
22		on that questionnaire now, orally.
23		What is the approximate distance between the ALC
24		church in Lind, Washington, and the nearest ALC church
25		served by an ALC pastor?

1	A	The nearest one would be of Ritzville, about 17 miles.
2	Q	17 miles; all right. Did you obtain approval from
3		the ALC district president to serve that congregation?
4	A	Yes, I did.
5	Q	All right. Were you given a list of special circum-
6		stances under which it was possible for you to serve
7		that parish?
8	A	Yes, these were things that we discussed. Bishop
9		Solberg and I did discuss these.
10	Q	All right. What, for example?
11	A	Well, the fact that the initial request had been from
12		the local congregation, from the Good Hope Congregation,
13		that I be allowed to serve, first in a preaching
14		capacity and then, later as a minister in a yoked
15		situation. I think the fact that the churches were a
16		block apart, the fact that both churches were in
17		economic difficulties at the time, and to share a
18		minister would be helpful to both congregations.
19	Q	You say you were asked by that parish to serve?
20	A	Yes, the beginning was that Pastor Kromeroth (phonetic)
21		from Odessa, which was about 30 miles away, would serve
22		communion on the first Sunday of each month, and I
23		would preach the other three. And then this developed
24		into the possibilities of a yoked ministry.
25	Q	I believe you mentioned to me when I asked you about

122

ELMER F. GROSHONG & ASSOCIATES
145 TACOMA AVE. SO
TACOMA, WASHINGTON

your theology, that you would consider yourself in
the tradition of Karl Barth?

A   Uh-huh.

Q   Barthian theology; is that correct?

A   Yes.

Q   All right. Pastor Felver, I have here a quotation or
two from one of our favorite theologians, Karl Barth,
in regard to the approach to scripture that Karl Barth
held —

MR. THORESON: Once again, I would like to ask
what point counsel is driving at before the question
is asked or before the answer is given.

MR. MONTGOMERY: Yes; I want to show how ecumenical and broad Bishop Solberg was in making it possible
for Pastor Felver to serve that congregation. That
there were no special restrictions placed upon him in
regard to this matter.

MR. THORESON: I don't think there's been any
suggestion of special circumstances placed on him.

MR. MONTGOMERY: We are concerned to determine
whether or not Bishop Solberg is exceedingly rigid in
his application of the requirements for non ALC clergy
serving in ALC parishes, and this is a question that
can help us along the way to that answer, because as
we have already seen, there is a practice in the ALC

against which we can view this.

CHAIRMAN MYKLEBUST: Well, from what Dr. Solberg has indicated when he testified, a substitute pastor, if we can call him that, his theology was one of the facts that he took into account and, as a consequence of that being one factor, you should be able to explore the theology of one of the substitutes that Dr. Solberg approved. And on that basis the objection would be overruled.

MR. MONTGOMERY: Yes.

Q I have here a statement from Barth's Church Dogmatics, from Volume I of the Church Dogmatics. This is the T.N.T. Clark Edition of the Dogmatics, English translation, Volume I, part 2, pages 529 to 30. Karl Barth says: "The biblical writers can be at fault in every word and have been at fault in every word and yet, according to the same scriptural witness being justified and sanctified by grace alone, they have still spoken the Word of God in their fallible and very human word." Would you agree with that?

A I think the way that I would interpret that, at least understanding Karl Barth to believe in the truth -- possible you might even use the word unerringness of God, and in the power of the edification of scripture. And in that sense, understanding Barth in

1   that way, I would agree with what he is saying.
2 Q You would agree then that God unerringly can provide
3   his Word of Grace, even though the human words are
4   erring and fallible that the writers provide?
5 A The power of God is made known through the weakness
6   of men, if that's what you're saying.
7 Q All right. Were you asked specifically to subscribe
8   to the ALC constitution in order to serve the church
9   in Lind?
10 A The words which were stated in the yoked ministry
11   document was that I was to be under the discipline of
12   the United Methodist Church, in my case, and subject
13   to the discipline of the American Lutheran Church. If
14   an American Lutheran pastor were to serve the same
15   yoke, that situation would have been reversed; he would
16   have been under the discipline of the American Lutheran
17   Church and subject to the discipline of the United
18   Methodist Church.
19 Q All right. In contrast to the position taken by Karl
20   Barth, here, there's a very strict article in the ALC
21   constitution, Article 3, which states that one must
22   regard the Bible as the inerrant Word of God. Were
23   you asked to subscribe to that expressly?
24 A Inerrancy is a word that was never discussed with me.
25   That's a new word to me, but it's something that I'm

1		not exactly -- I don't feel comfortable with that word,
2		so I don't know. No, it was not discussed.
3	Q	Bishop Solberg didn't bring it up, then?
4	A	No, not as I recall.
5	Q	All right.
6		MR. MONTGOMERY: Thank you very much, Pastor
7		Felver. Your witness.
8		MR. THORESON: I have no questions.
9		CHAIRMAN MYKLEBUST: Do any members of the com-
10		mittee have any questions? (no response.) Thank you,
11		Pastor Felver; we are sorry that you had the difficulty
12		you did in getting here.
13		(Discussion held off the record
14		regarding duration of testimony.)
15		MR. MONTGOMERY: I call Pastor Hellman to the
16		stand.
17		PASTOR WALTER HELLMAN, having been called as a witness
18		on behalf of Central Lutheran, testified as follows:
19		EXAMINATION
20		BY MR. MONTGOMERY:
21	Q	Would you state your name for the record?
22	A	Pastor Walter Hellman.
23	Q	Would you tell us briefly of your pastoral service in
24		the ALC?
25	A	I was ordained into the ministerium of the American

126

ELMER F. GROSHONG & ASSOCIATES
TACOMA AVE SO
TACOMA, WASHINGTON

17. Cross-examinations in the Central Lutheran Church case

Lutheran Church in 1921. I have served parishes in Washington, Oregon and California, and in addition, have held various positions other than the parish ministry within the church.

Q I understand that you were once a district president; is that right?

A That is correct.

Q Of what district was that?

A That was in the California district of the antecedent ALC, and later as executive vice president in the South Pacific district of the present ALC.

Q You will recall from other testimony, no doubt, that Article 5.13 of the ALC Constitution was referred to, in which discipline is associated only with disloyalty to the church's doctrinal position. In your opinion, as a former district president, can the ALC discipline a congregation for reasons other than doctrinal?

A No.

Q Paul Wiekert's letter of call, which has been introduced in evidence, sets forth his duties as a full time lay theological worker at Central Lutheran Church. These duties are three in number: youth work, visitation of the churched and unchurched, and evangelism. Along with this, Pastor Wiekert has preached in Central Lutheran Church; he has administered the sacraments

18. THE OLD SCHOOL HOUSE, LIDLINGTON, BEDFORDSHIRE

19. THE BESSARABIAN CHURCH CASE AT THE EUROPEAN COURT OF HUMAN RIGHTS

III. Applicants' Oral Argument (Part One)
Application No. 45701/99

Mitropolia Basarabiei Si Exarhatul
Plaiurilor and others v. Moldova

Mme la Présidente and Members of the Court, our remarks in the instant case will differ considerably from those we made in the case of *Larissis et al.* v *Greece*. There, the facts were in dispute and considerable time had to be devoted to establishing the legal basis for vindicating Applicants' religious activity. Here, there is no essential divergence of opinion on the facts: the Moldovan government has refused, and continues to refuse, the lawful registration of the Bessarabian Orthodox Church, and the Applicants claim that such refusal constitutes an egregious violation of the European Convention of Human Rights, Arts. 6(1) and 9 (these articles taken alone and in conjunction with Art. 14), together with Arts. 11 and 13. Therefore, unlike our oral presentation in *Larissis,* we shall ease the Court's task by speaking considerably slower and by taking less of the allotted time than we are allowed.

We begin by speaking to the questions received yesterday from the Court. We are asked, first of all, to specify any acts of intimidation against the Bessarabian Orthodox Church and/or its members after 12 September 1997 (the date when Moldova ratified the ECHR). In our Brief submitted to this Court 16 March 2000, we supplied as documentation an egregious instance among many of such intimidation (Appendixes C[4] and C[6]): the police having locked believers out of their own church in Cucioaia during the month of August 1998. We also refer the Court to several communications previously addressed to this Court, for example, a Helsinki Human Rights Commission report documenting acts of vandalism and persecution exerted upon the Bessarabian Orthodox Church and its members since 1997 (letters of 14 and 16 January 1999); and communications from by the Metropolitanate of Bessarabia documenting insults and threats recently directed to the Church and its members (letters of

9, 12, 15 and 19 January 1999). The Moldovan Government and its agents have done nothing concrete to protect Bessarabian Church interests in these and other similar instances.

As to the Court's second question of yesterday, namely, what internal legal protections exist in such areas as property rights from which the Applicant can benefit, and in regard to the violation of which it can complain under Article 6, we respond in terms of Appendix A of our submitted Brief of 16 March 2000 (the sections «Le manque de personnalite juridique» and «La transgression du droit de propriete» (para. 6-9): Without legal personality, the Bessarabian Church cannot employ the national court system to enforce its rights in regard to property ownership or in any other respect. As a result of the Government's intransigence in refusing to recognise and register it, it has no legal status whatsoever. Were that not the case, it would be able to rely on property and other civil statutes and remedies available, for example, to the Metropolitanate of Moldova owing to the latter's registered status.

In its written submission, the Moldovan government has provided a number of convoluted arguments to support its claim that the Applicants did not exhaust domestic remedies. These have properly been rejected by the Court in granting admissibility to the present Application, and require no further discussion here. On the single, central substantive issue—the Government's refusal to register the Bessarabian Orthodox Church as a religious organisation—what does the Government say to justify its actions?

The Government's claims reduce to three. First, we are told that the Bessarabian Church is not really a separate ecclesiastical entity at all: it is a mere schismatic group, and its members, being Eastern Orthodox in belief, do not suffer in the least from non-recognition, since they can happily worship in the Metropolitanate of Moldova—the chief Orthodox body recognised by the state and in communion with the Moscow Patriarchate. Second, the Government maintains that since, after 1940, there has been no Moldovan administrative unit called "Bessarabia," the use of such terminology can only produce bad cultural and national effects. Thirdly, the Government claims that the Bessarabian Orthodox Church is but superficially a religious entity: in reality, it is a political movement, insisting on relating itself to the Romanian (Bucharest) rather than the Russian (Moscow) Patriarchate because its true objective is to destabilise—indeed, destroy—the Moldovan Republic.

Such claims are almost too far-fetched to warrant serious response. On the first point, need it be pointed out that it is not the function of government to establish by fiat the defining boundaries of a religious body? If religious believers do not consider themselves members of Church A and wish instead to establish Church B, it is for *them,* not for the political authorities, to make such a decision. In the 19th century, Bismarck engaged in just such totalitarian decision making when he forced German Lutherans and Calvinists to unite in the so-called Prussian Union (after all, said the government, the two beliefs are *really* the same!); the result was the emigration of thousands of Lutherans from Germany who insisted on maintaining their own independent church body. Suppose, in the United States, the government were to assert that Southern Baptists could not function as a recognised church body, since their beliefs are really no different from those of the Northern Baptists—and that Southern Baptists should be satisfied to worship in Northern Baptist churches? Would anyone today in a civilised nation benefiting from the common or civil law traditions regard this as a legitimate governmental act?

The argument that the Bessarabian Orthodox Church does not deserve recognition because no "Bessarabian" administrative unit currently exists appears to confuse *semantics* on the one hand with law, religious freedom, and human rights on the other. Should the British government refuse to allow Imperial Oil to incorporate because the sun has now set on the British empire? Should the French government refuse to allow a church with the name *Eglise de la Gaule,* on the ground that "Gaul" as an administrative entity has not existed for centuries? To quote Humpty Dumpty in Lewis Carroll's *Through the Looking-Glass:*

> "When *I* use a word ... it means just what I choose it to mean—neither more nor less."

> "The question is," said Alice, "whether you *can* make words mean so many different things."

"The question is," said Humpty Dumpty, "which is to be master—that's all."

Here, the issue is simply whether a government can legitimately be the master of religious vocabulary, arrogating to itself the right to recognise only those groups with whose terminology it feels comfortable.

Thirdly, the Moldovan government claims that the Bessarabian Church is nothing more than an underground Romanian political movement. What evidence does it offer for this extraordinary claim? Nothing beyond the fact that individuals connected with the Church (such as Mr Cubreacov, member of the Parliamentary Assembly of the Council of Europe, who sits beside me as one of the Applicants in this case) has systematically criticised in the media and before international bodies the Moldovan government's refusal to recognise his Church! Last we heard, the expression of dissent in a state which has ratified the European Convention on Human Rights does not constitute illegal revolutionary activity.

What legal principles should be brought to bear on this issue? Why is the Moldovan's government's refusal to register the Bessarabian Church in violation of the European Convention?

International human rights law recognises the right of a state to set forth procedures for the registration of religious bodies—*as long as registration does not become a cloak for the denial of fundamental rights to religious believers and their churches*. Thus, the Dutch Advisory Council on International Affairs, in its report (No. 21, June 2001) titled, *Registration of Communities Based on Religion or Belief,* after having analysed the existing law, concludes:

> "Governments have a positive duty to make freedom of thought, conscience and religion or belief possible. They must not interfere with the development of new communities centred around a new belief or adhering to a different interpretation of an existing belief. If such new communities do not wish to be part of an existing community, they should not be denied registration on the grounds that either the number of institutions based on religion or belief must be kept within reasonable limits or that such institutions must remain unified. In

this regard, it should also be noted that although the idea of an established or official religion or belief is not in itself a violation of international law, such a system should be non-discriminatory: this means that the state may not withhold registration from religious and belief communities because it wants to protect an established or official religion or belief. Nor may a state withhold registration because it does not approve of the religion or belief concerned. Such communities should be able to obtain legal status according to the same criteria as other associations."

This is precisely the position reached by this Honourable Court in recent cases which have come before it. Besides those cited in our submitted brief, we refer the Court to the reasoning and the decisions reached in *Serif* v *Greece* (No. 38178/97; ECHR 1999-) and *Hasan and Chaush* v *Bulgaria* (No. 30985/96; ECHR 26 Oct. 2000); cf. *Stankovitnd the United Macedonian Organisation Ilinden* v *Bulgaria* (No. 29221/95 and 29225/95; deliberation in private 17 October 2000).

In *Serif (para.* 51-54), this Court refused to justify the criminal conviction of a Moslim religious leader because he conducted religious activities outside of the framework of a recognised Moslem body:

> 51. ... The domestic courts convicted the applicant on the following established facts: issuing a message about the religious significance of a feast, delivering a speech at a religious gathering, issuing another message on the occasion of a religious holiday and appearing in the clothes of a religious leader. Moreover, it has not been disputed that the applicant had the support of at least a part of the Moslem community in Rodopi. However, in the Court's view, punishing a person for the mere fact that he acted as the religious leader of a group that willingly followed him can hardly be considered compatible with the demands of religious pluralism in a democratic society.

52. The Court is not oblivious of the fact that in Rodopi there existed, in addition to the applicant, an officially appointed Mufti. Moreover, the Government argued that the applicant's conviction was necessary in a democratic society because his actions undermined the system put in place by the State for the organisation of the religious life of the Moslem community in the region. However, the Court recalls that there is no indication that the applicant attempted at any time to exercise the judicial and administrative functions for which the legislation on the Muftis and other ministers of "known religions" makes provision. As for the rest, the Court does not consider that, in democratic societies, the State needs to take measures to ensure that religious communities remain or are brought under a unified leadership.

53. It is true that the Government argued that, in the particular circumstances of the case, the authorities had to intervene in order to avoid the creation of tension among the Moslems in Rodopi and between the Moslems and the Christians of the area as well as Greece and Turkey. Although the Court recognises that it is possible that tension is created in situations where a religious or any other community becomes divided, it considers that this is one of the unavoidable consequences of pluralism. The role of the authorities in such circumstances is not to remove the cause of tension by eliminating pluralism, but to ensure that the competing groups tolerate each other (see, mutatis mutandis, Eur. Court HR, Plattform "Ärzte für das Leben" v. Austria judgment of 21 June 1988, Series A no. 139, p. 13, § 32). In this connection, the Court notes that, apart from a general reference to the creation of tension, the Government did not make any allusion to disturbances among the Moslems in Rodopi that had actually been or could have been caused by the existence of two religious leaders. Moreover, the Court considers that nothing was adduced that could warrant qualifying the risk of tension between the Moslems and Christians or between Greece and Turkey as anything more than a very remote possibility.

54. In the light of all the above, the Court considers that it has not been shown that the applicant's conviction under Articles 175 and 176 of the Criminal Code was justified in the circumstances of the case by „a pressing social need". As a result, the interference with the applicant's right, in community with others and in public, to manifest his religion in worship and teaching was not „necessary in a democratic society for the protection of public order" under Article 9 § 2 of the Convention. There has, therefore, been a violation of Article 9 of the Convention.

In the *Hasan* case, this Court reached precisely the same conclusions as to the illegitimacy of state interference in the religious activities of believers. The Bulgarian government, which had substituted another Muslim leader for a leader validly elected by the faithful, was found to have violated the rights of the Muslim community to choose its own leadership. In paras. 67, 78, 81, and 82 of its Judgment this Court declared:

67. The applicants further maintained that State interference with the internal affairs of the religious community had not been based on clear legal rules. They considered that the law in Bulgaria in matters concerning religious communities did not provide clarity and guarantees against abuse of administrative discretion. In their view the relations between the State and religious communities in Bulgaria were governed not by law, but by politics. Indeed, the replacement of the leadership of the Muslim religion had curiously coincided with the change of government in Bulgaria.

78. Nevertheless, the Court considers, like the Commission, that facts demonstrating a failure by the authorities to remain neutral in the exercise of their powers in this domain must lead to the conclusion that the State interfered with the believers' freedom to manifest their religion within the meaning of Article 9 of the Convention. It recalls that, but for very exceptional cases, the right to freedom of religion as guaranteed under the Convention excludes any discretion on the part of the State

to determine whether religious beliefs or the means used to express such beliefs are legitimate. State action favouring one leader of a divided religious community or undertaken with the purpose of forcing the community to come together under a single leadership against its own wishes would likewise constitute an interference with freedom of religion. In democratic societies the State does not need to take measures to ensure that religious communities are brought under a unified leadership (*Serif v. Greece,* no. 38178/97, § 52, ECHR 1999-).

81. The Government's argument that nothing prevented the first applicant and those supporting him from organising meetings is not an answer to the applicants' grievances. It cannot be seriously maintained that any State action short of restricting the freedom of assembly could not amount to an interference with the rights protected by Article 9 of the Convention even though it adversely affected the internal life of the religious community.

82. The Court therefore finds, like the Commission, that Decree R-12, the decision of the Directorate of Religious Denominations of 23 February 1995, and the subsequent refusal of the Council of Ministers to recognise the existence of the organisation led by Mr Hasan were more than acts of routine registration or of correcting past irregularities. Their effect was to favour one faction of the Muslim community, granting it the status of the single official leadership, to the complete exclusion of the hitherto recognised leadership. The acts of the authorities operated, in law and in practice, to deprive the excluded leadership of any possibility of continuing to represent at least part of the Muslim community and of managing its affairs according to the will of that part of the community. There was therefore an interference with the internal organisation of the Muslim religious community and with the applicants' right to freedom of religion as protected by Article 9 of the Convention.

One would be hard put to find cases more on all fours with the instant case: here, the Moldovan government, operating with a religious registration procedure open to great abuse through political influence, decides what constitutes and what does not constitute legitimate religious connections and endeavours to force believers, against their will, into a denominational arrangement (the Metropolitinate of Moldova) when they wish to worship within the framework of Bessarabian Orthodoxy.

Granted, there are limitations on Article 9 freedoms of religious activity and on Article 11 freedoms of association: governments may indeed legitimately limit such freedoms in the interests of public safety, public order, health, morals, and the protection of the rights and freedoms of others; national security may also legitimate restrictions on assembly and association. However, these limitations are allowable *only* where "necessary in a democratic society." What kind of restrictions on religious activity are therefore permissible, and can the Moldovan government justify its treatment of the Bessarabian Orthodox Church along those lines?

The very recent decision of this Court upholding Turkey's banning of the fundamentalist Prosperity Party (*Refah Partisi and others* v *Turkey* [Nos. 41340/98, 41342-41344/98, decision of 31 July 2001]) indicates clearly that a religious position which is inherently anti-democratic and anti-pluralistic can be banned from the political arena in the interests of preserving the open societies which the European Convention on Human Rights endeavours to guarantee. At para. 50 of that decision, a further illustration is provided:

> La Cour a également estimé que le fait d'empecher un opposant islamique algérien de se livrer à des activités de propagande sur le territoire suisse était nécessaire, dans une société démocratique à la protection de la sécurité nationale et de la sûreté publique (*Zaoui c.Suisse* (déc.), no. 41615/98, 18 janvier 2001, non publiée).

One can easily imagine other examples: an Aztec Church advocating and engaging in human sacrifice, or an Anthropophagous Church (not "loving your neighbour" but "digesting your neighbour") being legitimately denied religious recognition and registration in Member States of the European human rights system.

But to suggest that the Bessarabian Orthodox Church is an affront to national security or public morals is an utter absurdity. The Moldovan government has in no way demonstrated such, and the burden to do so—a heavy legal and human rights burden indeed—rests squarely with the state.

As fully demonstrated in our written, documented submissions, the Bessarabian Church has suffered much from lack of recognition by the Moldovan government. Its clergy and laity have been subjected to physical abuse and persecution either directly from government agents or indirectly through lack of police protection. Its pastors have been denied social insurance benefits such as pensions on the ground that they have not served a recognised religious body. The Church cannot own property. And, in the most general terms, it cannot benefit from the legal system, since it has no juridical personality whatsoever.

Adding insult to injury, on 19 September 2001—whilst the instant case was in the bosom of this Honourable Court—the Moldovan Cabinet of Ministers, chaired by Premier Vasile Tarlev, approved a decision declaring the state-registered Metropolitanate of Moldova, under the Moscow Patriarchate, to be the successor in legal interest of the unregistered Bessarabian Metropolitanate! Such a decision, if implemented, would short-circuit this Court's judgment by eliminating, by state action, Applicant's right to exist as a separate, registrable, ecclesiastical entity. How many times must we reiterate that Article 9 of the ECHR vests in believers, not in government, the determination of their religious commitment, and that Article 11 definitively guarantees religious believers the right to choose their organisational associations?

Simultaneously with the above-described Cabinet decision, President Vladimir Voronin addressed a letter to this Honourable Court in an effort politically to influence its judgment in the instant case. He incredibly argues that since the state has recognised the Metropolitanate of Moldova, to recognise the Bessarabian Metropolitanate would be "l'intervention de l'état dans les affaires intérieures de l'Eglise, ce que constituterait une violation flagrante de la Constitution de la République de Moldova (art. 31)"! The convoluted logic here seems to be that once the state recognises one church, to allow another to operate legally is state interference with religious affairs.

The President needs to rethink what interference in religious matters *actually* means: it occurs, as here, where the state substitutes itself for believers in deciding which churches deserve recognition and which deserve only to be cast into outer legal darkness.

The latest act in this unfortunate drama consists of the intervention of the state-registered Metropolitanate of Moldova in the instant case. Its nine-page, self-serving argument by undated letter (accepted by this Court 25 September 2001 for submission by the Government in the name of the church) consists of (1) the claim that the Bessarabian Orthodox Church is schismatic and represents, at most, but 10% of the practising Orthodox believers in the country; (2) the assertion that to recognise and register it is to encourage "destabilisation of Moldovan religious life" and the deterioration of the country's "social-political" framework; (3) an attempt to discount as "disinformation" the independently demonstrated instances of persecution suffered by clergy and members of the Bessarabian Church at the hands of the dominant church body and with the concurrence of the Government; and (4) the argument that a single Orthodox church body is the only thing left which can hold all Moldovans together.

To these arguments, we can only point out the obvious. In the open, democratic societies of Europe, sustained by the legal machinery of the ECHR, even "schismatics" have the right to exist and be recognised by the state. (Would this Court tolerate for a moment a State Party's refusal to recognise and register the Methodist Church because the Anglican Church could well argue historically that Methodists are schismatic Anglicans?) And numbers of adherents have nothing at all to do with the matter. (Does a church deserve the protections of the ECHR only when its numbers reach a certain percentage?) Article 9 gives those with religious convictions the right to believe, practice, and associate with other likeminded believers—and specifically opposes state interference in such matters. A state has no business making religious decisions for its people—by registering a single church so as to "stabilise" the country. If there are religious conflicts, even with political overtones, they must be resolved on a level playing field where all churches and religious organisations are afforded the same rights as guaranteed by the ECHR. The issue before this Honourable Court is neither schism nor stabilisation: it is *religious freedom*—freedom for the Bessarabian Orthodox Church no longer to suffer as a second-class organisation persecuted by those irrationally fearful of it.

Surely, the current situation must not be allowed to continue. We respectfully call upon this Honourable Court to rectify this sad state of affairs by finding for the Applicants on all counts.

IV. Applicants' Oral Argument
(Part Two: Rebuttal)

This Honourable Court will have noted that the Government's arguments just presented do little more than reiterate what they have said in their written submission. To this we can only repeat with even greater emphasis what we have said as to the fallaciousness of such argumentation.

Rather than wasting the Court's valuable time with further repetitions, we shall conclude with three related considerations which we believe should influence the final judgment and the need for its serious implementation.

First, *the root argument of the Moldovan government.* In its unsuccessful attempt to postpone this hearing *sine die,* the Government offered a two-year old "Communiqué" (15 January 1999) to show that it was making serious efforts to obtain better relations between the Applicant (the unrecognised Bessarabian Metropolitanate) and the Government-recognised Metropolitanate of Moldova. Needless to say, this Honourable Court did not regard such diplomatic activity on the part of the State as providing a friendly settlement within the terms of Convention jurisprudence or as advancing the legal situation in any way. But the very fact that the Government would present such an argument points to the underlying fallacy in its entire reasoning. To quote the Government's letter of request for a postponement (1 September 2001): the instant case "est un conflit purement intraconfessionel et non un litige entre l'Etat et la religion."

The Government continues to hold that no violation of the ECHR occurs if a State chooses to recognise one religious body whilst refusing to register another—as long as the object is to reduce disagreements between the two churches! It should be painfully obvious that the State is, at best, taking sides in a religious controversy and, at worst, interfering with the religious practices of its citizenry. Article 9 makes such government interference an egregious human rights violation—pure and simple. The state is obliged by the Convention to take a *neutral and non-discriminatory position vis-a-vis religions desiring recognition*. If it does not, it must justify its interference by discharging the heavy evidential burden of showing that the rejected religion is the source of serious social ills, as defined in Article 9, para. 2. The Government engages in nothing more than a feeble rationalisation when it characterises its foray into church affairs as a mere attempt to arbitrate and mitigate "a purely interconfessional conflict." Interference is interference. Pigs is pigs. The inter-church relations of two Orthodox bodies and their patriarchs has *no bearing whatsoever* on the issue in this case; that issue is the *Moldovan government's* refusal to recognise and register one of these church bodies but not the other.

Secondly, *the root motivation on the part of the Moldovan Government.* Why is the Government reduced to such patently illogical arguments? The reason, sad to say, lies in its underlying value-system. The Government, doubtless from its double heritage of Caesaropapism and Marxist totalitarianism, hates the idea of too much religious diversity. The 17th century aphorism of *Cuius regio, eius religio* again rears its ugly head. An open marketplace of ideas, where religions not necessarily agreeing with each other coexist, seems incomprehensible to the Moldovan authorities—even though their official commitment to the ECHR compels such.

One thinks of the attitude of Roman imperial government towards the early Christians. Legal philosopher Adam Gearey has recently described it thus: "Roman disdain for Christianity is hostility towards a belief in personal salvation that can put the individual in opposition to the political community. The violence with which the Romans persecuted the early Christians is thus the physical reflex of a system of ideas and beliefs that felt challenged by something that seemed to move beyond it. ... A new interpretation performs a kind of violence on any opposed view" (*Law and Aesthetics* [Oxford: Hart, 2001], p. 62). For the *Roman state,* read the *Moldovan state;* for the *early Christians,* read the *Bessarabian Orthodox believers.*

Thirdly and finally, *the strength of the Government's conviction.* As we have seen, the Moldovan government operates with an underlying philosophy of paternalism—of benevolent despotism—whereby it must keep its citizenry from hurting themselves by joining churches which are bad for them. The state sees the marginalisation, and, indeed, the elimination of the Bessarabian Orthodox Church as a positive duty. To achieve this is vital to the country and to its people: the existence of a single, dominant Orthodox body (the Metropolitanate of Moldova) makes political and cultural life immensely easier for everyone.

This Honourable Court must not overlook the strength of this conviction. In an interview of 8 February 2000 with Ion Rabacu, a chief counsellor in the Moldovan government and an official of the Directorate for Social Affairs which oversees the State Service for the Affairs of Cults, the distinguished Keston Institute asked Rabacu whether his Government would register the Bessarabian Metropolitanate if Moldova lost the instant case in Strasbourg. "He responded categorically: 'No, it will not register it.'" On 19 September 2001—less than two weeks ago—the Moldovan Premier Vasile Tarlev declared to the press: "The Government will not fulfill the decision of the European Court of Human Rights with its eyes closed, because the Republic of Moldova is an independent country and has its own national interests. We will fulfill the ECHR decision in case it is a well thought and balanced decision on the international level."

Now, we appreciate that only the Council of Ministers can enforce the judgments of this Honourable Court. However, the intransigence of the Government—as fully demonstrated throughout the long history of this matter both in Moldova and in Strasbourg—warrants, we submit, a resounding judgment in favour of the Applicants and the full damages prayed for. A clear message needs to be sent that, within the ambit of the European human rights system, governments have no legal choice but to treat all religious convictions and religious organisations with equal respect.

19. The Bessarabian Church case at the European Court ...

European Court of Human Rights—JWM with fellow barrister and 2d chair Alex Dos Santos following oral argument in the successful Bessarabian Church case

In Bucharest with representatives of the Romanian and Bessarabian Orthodox Churches and the University of Bucharest

233

Appendices

With Vlad Cubreacov of the Moldovan Parliament after our victory in the Bessarabian Church case before the European Court of Human Rights

With one of the Bishops following JWM's receiving the Patriarch's Medal (the highest ecclesiastical decoration of the Romanian Orthodox Church)

20. APPOINTMENT AS EMERITUS PROFESSOR, UNIVERSITY OF BEDFORDSHIRE

from the office of the
Vice Chancellor

Park Square
Luton
Bedfordshire
LU1 3JU
England

Telephone:
01582 489226

Facsimile:
01582 489362

Email:
tony.wood
@luton.ac.uk

5 November 1996

RWH5078.2530

Professor John Warwick Montgomery
Faculty of Business

Dear John

I am pleased to confer on you the title of Emeritus Professor of the University of Luton, in acknowledgement of the contribution to scholarship you have made during your period of appointment as Professor, and of the ambassadorial role you have played both nationally and internationally on behalf of the University.

The appointment will take effect immediately upon your retirement from the permanent staff of the University.

The professorial scrutiny panel suggested that you should meet the Director of Research to discuss your proposals for continuing your association with the University as an Emeritus Professor, and I accept that advice. Once you and he have agreed a plan, I will arrange to meet you to discuss the description attached to your title.

My congratulations on the distinction of being the first individual to attain this honour from the University.

Yours sincerely

Tony Wood

Dr A J Wood
Vice Chancellor

University of Luton Registered Office
Park Square Luton Bedfordshire LU1 3JU England
Telephone: 01582 34111 Facsimile: 01582 743400
Vice Chancellor Dr Tony Wood

21. INTERNATIONAL ACADEMY OF APOLOGETICS, EVANGELISM AND HUMAN RIGHTS, STRASBOURG, FRANCE

The International Academy of Apologetics, Evangelism & Human Rights

The International Academy of Apologetics, Evangelism & Human Rights is affiliated with Concordia University, Mequon, WI., U.S.A.*

Founded as Concordia College in 1881, CUW is a Christian higher education university located a few miles north of Milwaukee, on Interstate 43. The CUW campus was once a convent and is situated on the breathtaking bluffs of Lake Michigan. Concordia University Wisconsin is known nationally and internationally as a premier Lutheran Christian university and is widely recognized for a meaningful integration of faith and learning. CUW alumni assume significant servant leadership responsibilities in the Church and communities across the nation and around the world.

Concordia University Wisconsin is a Lutheran higher education community committed to helping students develop in mind, body, and spirit for service to Christ in the Church and the World.

For further information contact:

Dr. Gaylund K. Stone,
Dean of The School of Arts and Sciences
Concordia University Wisconsin
12800 North Lake Shore Drive
Mequon, WI.
53097 USA
262-243-4242 (within the U.S. only)
262-243-4351 (fax)
www.cuw.edu (web site)

* U. S. undergraduate academic credit for participation in the program of the International Academy of Apologetics, Evangelism and Human Rights may be arranged through Concordia University Wisconsin. Concordia University Wisconsin is accredited by The Higher Learning Commission of the North Central Association of Colleges and Schools. Participants desiring graduate credit for Academy attendance should contact the Academy directly.

Patrons
- Robert Meyer, Ph.D.
- Steve Bryant, Esq.
- Kurt and Debra Winrich

Faculty & Advisory
- John Ankerberg, M.A., M.Div., D.Min., Chattanooga, TN, U.S.A.
- John A. Bloom, M. Div., Ph.D., Biola University, La Mirada, CA, U.S.A.
- Ross Clifford, M.A., D.Th., Morling College, New South Wales, Australia
- William A. Dembski, Ph.D., Southwestern Baptist Theol. Seminary, Fort Worth, TX, U.S.A.
- Gary Habermas, M.A., Ph.D., Liberty University, Lynchburg, VA, U.S.A.
- Craig Hazen, Ph.D., Biola University, La Mirada, CA, U.S.A.
- John Heininger, M.A., Sutherland, Australia
- Michael Horton, Ph.D., President, CURE
- Willy Humbert, Sc.D., National Center for Scientific Research, Strasbourg, France
- Philip Johnson, B.D., Sydney, Australia
- Gregory Koukl, M.A., Stand to Reason, Los Angeles, CA, U.S.A.
- Steve Kumar, Ph.D., Auckland, New Zealand
- Charles Manske, Ph.D., Concordia University, Irvine, CA, U.S.A.
- Josh McDowell, M. Div, Richardson, TX, U.S.A.
- Angus Menuge, Ph.D., Concordia University Wisconsin, U.S.A.
- Chad Meister, Ph.D., Bethel College, IN, U.S.A.
- Mr. Justice Dallas K. Miller, Lethbridge, Alberta, Canada
- John Warwick Montgomery, Ph.D., D.Théol., LL.D., London, England & Strasbourg, France (Academy Director)
- Will Moore, B.A., B.Ed., Edmonton, Canada
- J.P. Moreland, Ph.D., Biola University, La Mirada, CA, U.S.A.
- Craig Parton, M.A., J.D., Santa Barbara, CA, U.S.A. (United States Director)
- Rod Rosenbladt, M.A., Th.D., Concordia University, Irvine, CA, U.S.A.
- Michael Saward, London, England
- Thomas Schirrmacher, Th.D., Bonn, Germany
- M. Tapolyai, M.D., D.Min., University of Cluj, Romania
- James Wakefield, LL.B., Nottingham University School of Law, England
- Oliver Wilder-Smith, M.B., M.D., Ph.D., D.Sc., University of Nijmegen, Netherlands

Ninteenth Annual European Summer Study Session of the

International Academy of Apologetics, Evangelism & Human Rights

Strasbourg, France
July 7-18, 2015
www.apologeticsacademy.eu

A UNIQUE OPPORTUNITY
to learn to defend historic biblical faith in an increasingly secular age, devoid of a solid basis for human rights.

21. International Academy of Apologetics, Evangelism and Human Rights ...

Professors in Residence (2015)

John Warwick Montgomery, Ph.D. (Chicago), LL.D. (Cardiff), D.Théol. (Strasbourg); Barrister-at-law; Visiting Professor, Patrick Henry College, Purcellville, Virginia; author of more than fifty books, including *Christianity for the Tough Minded* and *Human Rights & Human Dignity*.

Craig Parton, M.A. (Simon Greenleaf), J.D. (Hastings College of Law); member of the California Bar; partner in the oldest and most prestigious law firm in Santa Barbara; trial lawyer and specialist in civil liberties and legal defense of the biblical gospel.

Rod Rosenbladt, M.A., M.Div., Th.D. (Strasbourg); Professor of Apologetics, Concordia University-Irvine; Co-Host, *The White Horse Inn*.

Oliver H.G. Wilder-Smith, M.D. (Frankfurt), Ph.D. (Nijmegen), D.Sc. (Aalborg University); University Medical Centre, Nijmegen, Netherlands; Adjunct Professor, Aalborg University, Denmark; author of more than sixty scholarly papers; organiser of the Millstatt Forum Christian conferences; son and apologetics successor of the late Dr. A.E. Wilder-Smith.

The Location

Strasbourg, enchanting capital city of the Alsace, on the Rhine River dividing France and Germany; at once ancient (with its still inhabited medieval quarter and its university founded by John Calvin) and modern (the seat of the Council of Europe and the European Court of Human Rights); only one-half hour from the Black Forest, one hour from Heidelberg, two hours from the Swiss Alps, three hours from Luxembourg, and 2 hours and 20 minutes (on the TGV) from Paris.

The Program

In 2015, the International Academy will offer the following lecture and seminar program, taught in English by the Professors in Residence:
- The Apologetic Task Today
- Philosophical Apologetics
- Scientific Apologetics
- Historical Apologetics
- Legal Apologetics
- Apologetics and Human Rights
- Apologetics and Medical Issues
- Cults, Sects, and the World's Religions
- Biblical Authority Today
- Open Discussion

Each of these ten subjects will be treated by one or more of the Professors in Residence for a minimum of 4 hours (total class instruction: 45 hours). A reading list will be provided on initial registration so as to permit background study prior to the summer session.

All participants attending at least 90% (40 hours) of scheduled class sessions will receive a Certificate of Completion/Certificat d'Assuidité from the Academy. Those registrants wishing to receive U.S. academic credit will sit for a written examination on the final day of the program. Successful completion of this culminating examination qualifies a student for 3 semester hours of academic credit; additional credit up to a total of 9 semester hours may be earned by arrangement with Concordia University Wisconsin (undergraduate credit) or with the Academy itself (graduate credit). On attending a second Academy program in Strasbourg (not necessarily in consecutive years), and after completing the written examination at the end of that session, one may sit for an oral examination which, if successfully completed, leads to designation as a Fellow of the Academy (F.C.A.). Also, on attending a second Academy session in Strasbourg, one may defend a thesis on an approved apologetics topic, thereby obtaining the Academy's Diploma in Christian Apologetics (DipLC.A.) or Human Rights (DipLH.R.).

Sponsors

- Bucer Seminar, Bonn, Germany
- Canadian Institute for Law, Theology and Public Policy, Edmonton, Canada
- Christian Apologetics Program, Biola University, La Mirada, CA, USA.
- Christians United for Reformation (CURE), U.S.A.
- Cranach Institute, Fort Wayne, IN, U.S.A.
- Evangelical Apologetics Societies of New Zealand and Australia
- Concordia University Wisconsin, Mequon WI, U.S.A.
- Rockford Institute for Religion & Society, Rockford, IL, U.S.A.

The Costs

Only $2,995, exclusive of transportation to/from Strasbourg. This amount covers registration, lodging throughout the session, and most meals. It also covers all tuition and instructional fees for the Academy and a minimum of 3 semester hours of U.S. academic credit for those who qualify. (Supplemental undergraduate academic credit in connection with the Academy's program may be earned by arrangement with Concordia University Wisconsin; additional fees may apply.) A full day's bus excursion to the Vosges mountains and the medieval villages of the Alsace on Bastille Day (July 14) is also included. This amazingly low price is possible because the French government subsidises bona fide foreign students as well as students who are French nationals.

The Scholarship Fund provides 10 scholarships of $1,000 each to needy students to attend the 2015 International Academy Summer Study Session.

An additional scholarship of $1,500 for a science educator or a student majoring in science or in science education is generously provided by Drs. Don and Mary Korte, Fellows of the Academy.

Criteria: (1) financial need; and (2) intended benefit from participation.

Deadline for all scholarship applications (by personal letter): March 1, 2015.

Who May Participate?

University, college and seminary students; clergy; laity; lawyers; lecturers and researchers; student workers; and members of human rights organizations. Only 20 registrants will be accepted in toto for the summer of 2015, so register as soon as possible!

How to Register

Send $300 non-refundable deposit; remainder ($2,695, also non-refundable) is due in two equal payments on April 1 and May 1, 2015. (Make cheques payable to "M. le Pr. J.W. Montgomery" and mail them to the Strasbourg address below using ordinary airmail; *not* a commercial mailing service such as UPS or FedEx or any service requiring a signature.) Your deposit holds your place. You will receive, by return mail, a full packet of materials, including the official registration form to be filed with proof of status, in accord with French university practice. Registrants should plan to arrive during the business day on Monday, July 6, 2015.

Registration deadline: April 1, 2015

INTERNATIONAL ACADEMY OF
APOLOGETICS, EVANGELISM
& HUMAN RIGHTS
Prof. J. W. Montgomery
2, rue de Rome
67000 Strasbourg
France

Tel. & Fax: +33-3-88610882
E-mail: 106612.1066@CompuServe.com

For further information in the U.S.A. contact:

Craig A. Parton, Esq.
United States Director
33 Langlo Terrace
Santa Barbara, CA 93105

Tel: (805) 617-3020
E-mail: cap@ppplaw.com

237

22. JEAN-MARIE MONTGOMERY'S FATHERS' DAY POEM, 2009

CHER PAPA …

Il te ressemble

Comment tu trouves mon lapin ?

Mon père à moi, aimé avec tant de foi,
Tu es mon tout à moi, car je crois en toi,
Avec ta fidélité, je me sens protégé,
Ta bonté, ma émerveillé,
Dieu ta conduit à moi, pour me donner la foi,
Chaque année nous fêtons la fête des pères,
Et je le reconnais, j'en suis fier,
Le rôle de papa est très important,
Pour moi le fils, et vous, parents,
Profitons des moments ensembles,
Car ils nous rassemblent,
Tu sais, tu devras me supporter encore très longtemps,
Car j'ai besoin de toi très souvent,
Les moments passé ensemble reste gravé à jamais
Et je le pense, pour l'éternité,
Laurence, Sarah et, moi, te souhaitons
Une vie sans peine, car on t'aime !
Que Dieu vous protège, mami et papi
Car nous avons besoin de vous, toute notre vie.

Laurence, Sarah et J-Marie

21 juin 2009

23. SO YOU THINK BECOMING A BARRISTER IS DIFFICULT?

Try the French Bar![1]

It is a commonplace that the French legal system is code based, in contrast with the case-law approach of the Anglo-American common law. True, common law jurisdictions depend more and more on codifications, and there are important areas of French law (for example, administrative law) in which case law—*jurisprudence* is the French term—predominates. But overall the generalisation holds. This is true for the rules of admission as an *avocat*: they are expressly set forth in a series of laws and decrees collected in the *Nouveau Code de Procédure Civile*—the Law of 31 December 1971, art. 11 ff.; the Decree of 27 November 1991, art. 42 ff., 99 and 100; and the "RIN" (the *Décision* of the National Council of the Bars of France, 2005, which has normative legal force). Since there is no single national French bar (the bars are regional, half of all French lawyers belonging to the Paris bar), the individual bars can and do supplement the RIN regulations with their own *réglements intérieurs*—permitted as long as these do not conflict with the national rules.

So how does one become an *avocat*? The answer is a bit like the answer to the question, "How do nudists dance?": *Carefully, very carefully*. In point of fact, there are several answers to the question, depending on one's particular status. If one is a French citizen or a foreigner wanting to obtain his or her legal training in France, the standard route consists of obtaining a master's degree in law (the former *licence en droit*), followed by an 18-month programme at a regional centre of professional training; the latter has both an entrance and a final examination, and the programme consists of courses, a major project, and an apprenticeship. Successful completion leads to the "CAPA"—the aptitude certificate allowing one to apply to become a member of a French bar. It is noteworthy that exceptions of various kinds to these requirements exist for members of related professions; thus, a law professor at a French university will automatically be admitted to the bar simply by virtue of his professorial rank.

239

But if one is a foreign lawyer—i. e., not a French citizen but a legal practitioner in another country—all will depend on whether one is or is not a citizen of one of the EU countries or of a member state of the European Economic Community (Switzerland being expressly included as well).

For the non-EU lawyer wishing to become a French *avocat*, the key issue is whether his or her country has bar admissions rules reciprocal to those of France; if so, those rules will of course apply. If not—which is the usual situation—an examination (the celebrated "Article 100" test) is the only route available. This examination consists of two 3-hour written papers, one in civil law, the other—at the candidate's choice—in administrative law, commercial law, employment law, or criminal law. These are followed by two oral examinations: one chosen by lot among two subjects—(1) civil, criminal or administrative procedure and (2) the French judicial system and its organisation—and the other, *déontologie,* i. e., the nature, professional standards, and ethics of French legal practice. One must obtain an overall passing average (10 out of 20 points) and the examination can be taken only three times. If one passes, one has the right to be enrolled in any of the French regional bars as an *avocat* in full standing.

For the non-French EU lawyer, the regime is different. If, say, a German or a U.K. lawyer simply wishes to plead a single case, he will be allowed to do so with the aid of a French practitioner (much like the *pro hac vice* rule in American jurisdictions, though that rule applies to a lawyer from one American State wishing to plead a single case in an American State where he/she is not a member of the Bar). Should the non-French EU lawyer wish to set up an office (primary or secondary) in France, this is possible—but only if he or she joins a French bar under one's legal title of origin; practice will be limited to that lawyer's foreign law and will not extend to giving advice on French law or to pleading in French tribunals.

Interestingly, this EU-directed arrangement was fought tooth and nail by French bars, which did not want competition from other EU lawyers. And even more restrictive jurisdictions—Luxembourg being the archetypal example—tried all sorts of underhanded ruses to prevent foreign EU lawyers from even this limited bar membership. When the Luxembourg bar tried to augment the European directive with a local language requirement (French, German, and Luxembourgish!), the European Court of Justice ruled that this was contrary to the spirit of the free establishment of European workers and against the clear intent of the directive (decision of 19 September 2006).

But a non-French EU lawyer, even when he or she successfully enters into such an arrangement, is very obviously a second-class citizen. He or she must pay the full fees to the bar that a French *avocat* pays and must fulfil the same annual continuing legal education requirements that apply to the French *avocat*—but one's name appears in small letters in a separate section of the *Tableau des Avocats* (the official regional listing) or in minuscule type in the Paris Bar directory.

And if the non-French lawyer wishes to become a full-fledged *avocat*? Here, two paths exist. The one appears simple and non-threatening: three years of practice in France, and no examinations! This possibility, to be sure, came about not through any French efforts (quite to the contrary) but by way of a European directive of 16 February 1998—which did not get transposed into French law until 11 February 2004! (It now comprises Articles 89 and 90 of the revised Law of 31 December 1971.) The problem with this alternative is that the three years of required full-time practice need to be in "French law." But, being a foreign attorney, the non-French lawyer is not supposed to be practicing French law! The text goes on to say that if there is insufficient evidence of such practice, the bar to which he or she applies has the right to "evaluate the regular and effective character of the activity exercised, as well as the capacity of the candidate to pursue such." This, of course, leaves open a wide area of discretion to the local bar—even though, technically, the burden of proof in rejecting the candidate falls on the bar, not on the applicant.

The second route for the non-French EU lawyer to become an *avocat* is to pass "Article 99" examinations. These are set individually for each applicant, and can consist of up to four tests, depending on how closely the candidate's legal education and experience parallel the French model. One examination is always on the practice and ethics of the profession (*déontologie*). The others are specified from a list derived from the CAPA requirements; civil law is a standard—plus commercial law, administrative law, criminal law, and employment law. If four subjects are assigned, one of them (chosen by the National Council of the Bar, which sets the list for each candidate) must consist of a four-hour written examination. The other subjects are tested by oral examination before juries. Two examination periods maximum are now set each year, one in Paris, the other in Versailles; in Paris, the jury consists of three examiners (a law professor who is a specialist in the given subject, a former member of the Bar Council, and a practitioner), whereas Versailles employs five-member juries.

If the European lawyer comes from a Napoleonic Code jurisdiction (say, Italy) or from a strongly French-speaking area (say, Belgium), he/she may be required only to do an oral in one or two subjects (*déontologie* is always mandatory). But all U.K. lawyers (solicitors, barristers, Scottish advocates), being from common-law backgrounds—after all, even the civil-law Scots end up before the common-law Supreme Court of the United Kingdom—are required to do the maximum of four subjects, and this means at least the one 4-hour written examination plus three oral examinations. The style of these examinations is not the "practical, problem-solving" style of the Art. 100 examinations, but the academic, essay style of the French university curriculum, where, for example, in the legal area, one always divides one's answer into two major subsections! To pass, one must average 10 out of 20 *in toto,* and one can only sit for the examination three times.

And now, a personal word. After two years as a member of the Strasbourg bar and three years a member of the Paris bar—both under my foreign practicing title of barrister-at-law (England and Wales)—I applied to take the oath as a French *avocat*. My dossier was replete with evidence of my legal activity in France, chiefly in the area of my specialty, religious liberty litigation before the European Court of Human Rights in Strasbourg. I was informed that this was inadequate. Why? Because I could not show that my income derived principally from this practice. *Of course it did not:* I am a university professor and my legal work has been largely *pro bono*. I pointed out, using an article on the Paris bar's own website, that historically the French bar has valued unremunerated service in behalf of the poor and downtrodden. Indeed, the French bar grew out of eleemosynary service by lawyers who were clergy. "Would a physician be less good a doctor if he treated patients for free?" I asked. I also reminded the powers-that-be that one of the differences between French lawyers and Anglo-American lawyers is that the French *avocat* must *not* engage in any form of commercial activity. Indeed, an *avocat* cannot simultaneously be a member of any other profession (medicine, accountancy, etc.)—with the exception of university teaching or a religious ministry. (A few years ago, in 2003, a young *avocate* was suspended for having played an accordion for money on a public street—though this was reversed on appeal.) My arguments were to no avail. I withdrew my application and determined to take the tougher route.

I was therefore left with the Article 99 examinations. In spite of my possessing four earned law degrees, including the LLD—the higher doctorate in law—from Cardiff University, the National Council of French Bars required me to pass the maximum of four examinations. Their only concession, on the basis of my practice in France, was to substitute criminal law for civil law as the four-hour written examination. The oral examinations required of me were in commercial law (with its independent *Code de Commerce* and separate commercial courts), administrative law (again, independent of the *Code Civil,* and having its own "supreme court," the Conseil d'Etat), plus, of course, *déontologie.* The subject of my four-hour paper in criminal law turned out not to be any of the traditional, classical areas (crimes against the person, against property, against the state or against humanity), but "the criminal liability risks of corporations"!

I passed. Then, in completing the paper work for admission as an *avocat à la cour* (Paris), I was told that my *contrat de collaboration* with my colleagues in chambers had to be revised to state a minimum monthly salary! (This may be justified to prevent young associates from falling into slavery, but it again smacked of an unrecognized commercialism in a profession officially opposing filthy lucre as having anything to do with its nature.) But, all of this having been finally resolved, I took the oath to become an *avocat* in an impressive ceremony in the First Chamber of the Palais de Justice's Court of Appeal—where the trial of Pétain had been held following the liberation of Paris and the defeat of the Nazis.

Was it worth it? Of course. But never think that lawyers are lacking in old fashioned territorialism—even when it goes against there own principles. The oath of the *avocat* pledges him or her not only to "dignity," "conscientiousness," "independence," and "honesty"—but also to "humanity." Surely "humanity" should embrace greater appreciation of the high legal standards of our European states in general, as well as (why not?) the recognition that a lawyer can be a fine practitioner even if he is not well remunerated for it.

24. PREACHING AT THE CHRISTMAS SERVICE, 2010, AT THE MARSEILLES CATHEDRAL

25. CONGRATULATIONS: JOHN WARWICK MONTGOMERY'S CONTRIBUTIONS TO RELIGIOUS FREEDOM ADVOCACY

The directors and board members of IIRF congratulate the chair of its academic board on the occasion of his 80th birthday[1]

On 18 October of this year, Professor Dr Dr Dr John Warwick Montgomery will celebrate his 80th birthday. This seems incredible not only to him but also to all who know him, since he continues to carry on his academic and legal activities unabated. Just take as an example the annual International Academy of Apologetics, Evangelism and Human Rights, in Strasbourg, France, of which he serves as director and teaches at least two courses (www.apologeticsacademy.eu).

For those unacquainted with Professor Montgomery's work or for those who have not seen his website (www.jwm.christendom.co.uk), here is a brief account of his past and present involvements, followed by a summary of his important contributions in the field of religious liberty. Dr Montgomery, though a naturalised English subject and a European resident, holds the position of Distinguished Research Professor of Philosophy and Christian Thought at Patrick Henry College in Virginia, where, one semester each academic year he teaches apologetics (the defense of the Christian faith), philosophy of law, and international human rights. Previous positions include Professor of Law and Humanities, University of Bedfordshire, England (he retains Emeritus status there) and member of the Federated Theological Faculty of the University of Chicago. He holds twelve earned degrees, including three doctorates (Ph.D., Chicago; D.Théol., Strasbourg; LL.D., Cardiff, Wales), and an honorary doctorate from the Institute for Religion and Law, Moscow.

Professor Montgomery is an American lawyer (California, District of Columbia, Virginia, Washington State bars, and the bar of the U.S. Supreme Court), an English barrister, and an avocat à la Cour, barreau de Paris. He is author or editor of more than 60 books in the fields of Christian theology, apologetics, law, and literature (www.ciltpp.com) and over one hundred scholarly journal articles. Studies of his work include Dr Ross Clifford's book-length *John Warwick Montgomery's legal apologetic: An apologetic for all seasons* (Bonn, Germany: VKW); a massive Festschrift honouring him was published a year ago: William Dembski and Thomas Schirrmacher (eds.), *Toughminded Christianity: The legacy of John Warwick Montgomery* (Nashville, TN: B&H).

Dr Montgomery's legal specialty is the defense of religious freedoms, particularly Christian evangelism. He has been involved in landmark cases, such as the case of the "Athens Three," obtaining acquittals at the Athens court of appeal of YWAM missionaries and a Greek evangelical pastor for alleged "proselytism." Professor Montgomery's advocacy produced positive results in a series of Greek cases *(Larissis et al.)* before the European Court of Human Rights in Strasbourg; Greek military officers were vindicated in their evangelistic presentations of the gospel to laymen—though the Court, sadly, refused to upset the Greek anti-proselytism statute or to allow the officers to evangelise military personnel below their rank. (On these Greek cases, see Montgomery, *The Repression of Evangelism in Greece* [Lanham, MD: University Press of America].)

Recently, Dr Montgomery won a religious liberties case before the European Court of Human Rights of such importance that Sir Nicolas Bratza, one of the judges of the Court, in a public lecture at Lincoln's Inn, London, referred to it as the most important Article 9 (religious freedom) case to come before the Court since the new procedures under Protocol 11 came into force in 1998. *Bessarabian Orthodox Church v Moldova* vindicated the right of a small Orthodox church body, under the aegis of the Patriarch of Bucharest (Romania), to be registered in Moldova; the government (consisting largely of ancient U.S.S.R. Marxists) had insisted on just one Orthodox Church—one aligned with the Moscow Patriarchate. This case established the clear precedent that governments cannot exclude church bodies on theological or political grounds: believers must be allowed to form their own churches, to own property, and to engage in evangelistic and other ecclesiastical activities without interference from the state. As a result of this legal victory, Professor Montgomery was invited to Bucharest and received the coveted Patriarch's Medal of the Romanian Orthodox Church. (On the Moldovan case, see Montgomery, "Life can be difficult if you are Bessarabian Orthodox," in his forthcoming book, *Christ as centre and circumference* [Bonn, Germany: VKW].)

We thank God for the grace and talents he has bestowed on Dr Montgomery and we wish him many more years of service to the wider community—particularly in his role as Honorary Chairman of the Academic Board of the International Institute for Religious Freedom.

Angus Menuge, Ph.D., Professor of Philosophy,
Concordia University Wisconsin

26. POETICAL CONTRIBUTION TO *ENCHANTONS LA VIE*

Je voudrais trouver les mots

Je voudrais trouver les mots
pour dire tous les maux révoltants
de notre temps. Et çe mal intérieur,
en nos cœurs secs, déroutants,
qui errent dans l'indifférence,
se vautrent dans une pauvreté de sentiments.
Pauvreté de vie, destruction, fanatisme,
famine. Les portes de l'enfer
et leurs relents nucléaires
apportent une désespérance amère.
Chacun de nous, dans une belle discordance
Avidement cherche sa meilleure pitance
pendant que l'homme qui se dit de finance
bannit sans vergogne le mot «repentance».

Et pourtait. Pourtant, encore j'espère!
Je rêve de villes propres et prospères
sans tyran délirant. De retrouver enfin le chemin
des églises et des presbytères de mon enfance
où les hommes laissent à la porte
leurs folles illusions trompeuses, leurs violence
là où le volubilis grimpe sur les toits.
Je rêve d'un monde dont Ie centre est du Christ la croix:
un monde de repentance, de foi et de tolérance.

If only I could find the words

If only I could find the words
to describe all the revolting evils
of our time—and that inner evil
of our desiccated hearts,
wandering from the true path in a land of indifference,
vaunting themselves in cheap sentiment:
cheapness of life, destruction, fanaticism,
famine. The gates of hell
with nuclear stench
convey nothing but bitter despair.
Each of us in confusion and discord,
avidly seeks trivial advantage
whilst those who have made money their god
shamelessly ban even the word "repentance".

And yet! And yet—I continue to hope.
I dream of clean and prosperous cities,
free from the madness of tyranny.
I yearn to find yet again
the churches and chapels of my childhood,
where believers leave at the door
their silly and deceptive illusions, their violence—
there where the morning glory clings to the steeple.
I dream of a world centred on the cross of Christ:
a world of repentance, faith, and tolerance.

John Warwick Montgomery

27. PHOTO ALBUM

John Warwick Montgomery at Trinity Evangelical Divinity School

Appendices

27. Photo album

The author on the peak: 1:30 P.M., Monday, August 17, 1970

The author and one of his Kurdish companions on the summit; Navarra's tattered tricolor is visible

Dr. Montgomery removing his crampons just below the ice cap on the descent

John Warwick Montgomery on a Ararat Exploration

Lecture Tours in Europe

27. Photo album

Prof. Halvor Ronning & Dr. Montgomery during the 1981 (Holy Land Tour)

Dr. Montgomery at Jacob's well (Israel)

Graduation M.Phil. in Law, University of Essex, England, 1983

27. Photo album

Dr Laird Harris at Covenant Theological Seminary

With Prime Minister Begin in Jerusalem

Clowning in China

27. Photo album

*Lany and JWM in costume on a Sherlock Holmes
Society of London pilgrimage*

JWM with Dr Ross Clifford at a teaching session of the International Academy of Apologetics, Evangelism and Human Rights, Strasbourg, France

JWM lecturing at the castle ruins of the Nideck, Alsace, in one of his summer academic programmes

27. Photo album

With students in the Montgomery flat, 2 Rue de Rome, Strasbourg (July 1996)

*At the bust of Albert Schweitzer, Kaysersberg, Alsace (July 2004).
Far left: Craig Parton; far right: Rod Rosenbladt*

Lanalee de Kant Montgomery at the harp

Lany Montgomery

The Montgomery clan at a Cretan Fountain

Lany, Son Jean-Marie, Daughter-in-Law Laurence

27. Photo album

Alex Dos Santos and JWM in the Montgomery Citroën C3 (vintage 1925)

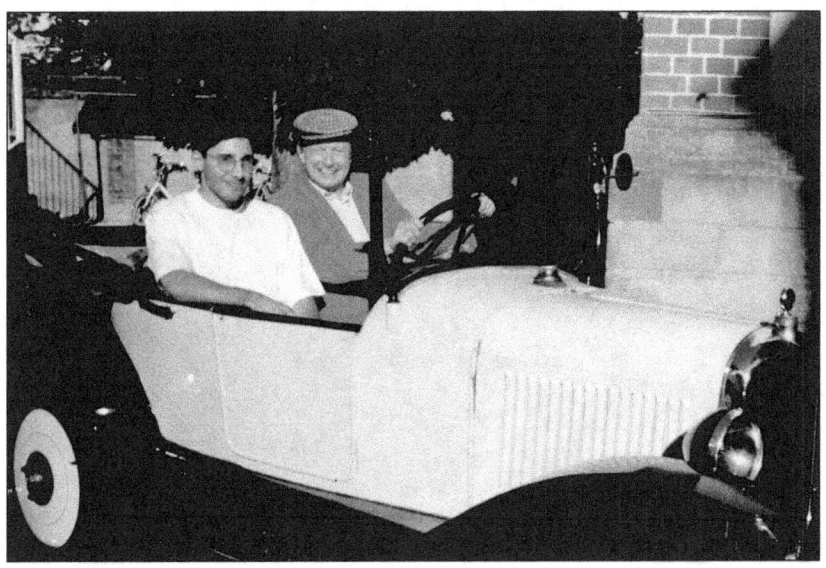

Ibid.

The Montgomerys' senior bear Winston (chief of a collection of some 50 teddy bears)

ALF likes Citroën

27. Photo album

Another eminent JWM bear

Traction Avant (1954)

JWM and Dr. Charles Manske in Strasbourg, France

27. Photo album

JWM in ancestral territory

Le Comte de St Germain de Montgommery & son Fils en Normandie

Appendices

Clan Montgomery Society International

BREVET D'ARMOIRIES

LE CONSEIL FRANÇAIS D'HÉRALDIQUE

s'étant réuni en Assemblée le

01.06.2002 à Sceaux (92)

a homologué les armoiries de

Monsieur John Warwick MONTGOMERY

dans ses registres sous la forme:

> d'or au bras armé d'une lance brisée en chevron, la pointe à senestre, le tout d'argent; mantelé d'azur chargé en chef d'un écusson d'argent chargé d'un feu de 3 flammes de gueules, mouvant de la pointe de l'écu, et accosté vers la pointe de 2 fleurs de lys d'or.

et qu'elles sont conformes aux lois et règles de la science héraldique, et ont été officiellement enregistrées sous le numéro

2002 / 528

En conséquence de quoi
le présent Brevet a été délivré pour servir et valoir ce que de droit

Jean-Jacques LARTIGUE
Président du C.F.H.

The official French registration of the family's coat-of-arms

Appendices

JWM is receiving the Freedom of the City of London

In the Montgomery clan garb (note the tartan—and the knees!)

27. Photo album

JWM receiving the higher doctorate in law (LL.D.) from Cardiff University, Wales, July, 2003, based on the totality of his legal publications

JWM being received into the Ordre des Avocats at the Palais de Justice, Paris, having passed the French bar examinations and taken the oath as a French avocat (8 July 2009)

In English barrister's legal dress

In French legal dress for those holding a doctor's degree in law (note the three bands)

Appendices

JWM at podium, Imam Shabir Ally seated: the London Christian-Muslim debate

To be continued—by God's grace ...

Index of Names and Places

Names

Ali, Shabir	105	Barker, Archie D.	172
Allbeck, W. D.	39	Barnhouse, Donald Grey	32
Allen, Fred	25	Baron, Raymond	94
Allen, Gracie	25	Barta, James	123
Alliluyeva, Svetlana	180	Barth, Karl	57, 63
Ally, Imam Shabir	278	Bartlett, Robert	17
Alnor, William	92, 93	Beckwith, Frank	86
Altizer, Thomas	63, 64, 65, 75, 138	Beckwith, Paul	31
		Begin, Menachem	77, 259
Anderson, Sir Norman	83, 84	Belmondo, Jean-Paul	125
Andreae, Johann Valentin	47, 48	Benny, Jack	25
		Bergen, Edgar	25
Ankerberg, John	58, 115, 236	Berger, Vincent	109
Anthony, Richard	149	Berglund, David	89, 91, 92
Aquinas, Thomas	86	Bingham, Joseph Walter	72
Archer, Gleason	59, 87	Black, Max	33
Atatürk, Kemal	111, 139	Blackstone, Sir William	121
Augustine	144	Blackwood, William	17
Aznavour, Charles	149	Blair, Cherie	85
Bach, J. S.	66, 117, 148	Blair, Tony	85
Bacon, Francis	20	Blake, William	19
Bacon, Nicholas	20	Bloom, John	115, 236
Bahnsen, Greg	13	Bornkamm, Günther	50
Baker, David W.	75	Bornkamm, Heinrich	50
Ball, Louise	28	Brabner-Smith, John W.	73, 74, 79
Barber, Cyril J.	91, 124		

281

Index of Names

Bradt, Whitney	171	Clinton, Bill	148
Bratza, Nicolas	109, 247	Cole, Nat	149
Braun, Wernher von	27	Colson, Chuck	181
Bronson, Isaac C.	167	Como, Perry	149
Broughton, William P.	71	Cook, Walter Wheeler	72
Brown, Harold O. J.	68, 144	Cooper, Lane	29
Brown, Joe	69	Craig, David	43
Bucer, Martin	50	Craig, William Lane	58
Burgoyne, John	180	Crawford, Ann(a)	18, 168
Burkee, James	55	Crawford, William R.	172
Burns, George	25	Crosby, Bing	149
Burtt, Edwin A.	33, 34	Crouch, Jan	80
Butler, Samuel	33	Cruise, Tom	150
Byrnes, Steve	130	Cubreacov, Vlad	222, 234
Calvin, John	47, 49, 50, 89, 237	Cullen, David	49
		Culver, Robert	59
Campbell, Robert	56	Curzon, Lord	180
Caplan, Harry	33, 34	Darwin, Charles	58
Carey, George	140	Davy, Sir Humphry	141
Cario, William	127, 128, 129	Day, James	96
Carnell, E. J.	30, 64	Deffner, Don	38
Carnell, John	87	De Gaulle, President Charles	48
Carter, Jimmy	180	DeLoach, Andrew	93
Cassin, René	81	DeLorean, John	143, 151
Charles, Prince of Wales	85, 148	Dembski, William	13, 17, 42, 52, 62, 115, 141, 145, 247
Charles the Simple	20	Denning, Lord	82, 83
Christ, Jim	35	Départdieu, Gérard	117, 118
Churchill, Winston	148	Diamond, Aubrey L.	84
Clark, Gordon	13	Diana, Princess of Wales	85
Clifford, Ross	71, 115, 236, 246, 262	Dibon, Paul	48

Index of Names

Dickens, Charles	141, 178
Diegmann, Frank	94, 98
Dietz, Beth and Jim	32
Diplock, Lord	83
Doherty, Ashton	107
Donoghue, Laurence	90
Dony, John G.	103
Doran, Neal	123
Dos Santos, Alex	107, 233, 267
Douglass, Harry S.	22, 167
Dumpty, Humpty	221, 222
Duval, Nicolas	137
Dyer, James	103
Eckelmann, Herman John	30, 144
Edmond, Thierry	137
Edward VII, King	180
Eggleston, Mr. (grocer)	171
Ehlke, Roland	120
Einaudi, Mario	33
Elchinger, Marc	117
Eliade, Mircea	64
Ellinwood, Emery A.	172
Evans, Harry	59
Fabricius, Johann Albert	142
Fairweather, Paul	88
Falwell, Jerry	76, 77, 180
Faraday, Michael	141
Farnholtz, Jimmy	26
Feinberg, Paul and John	59
Ferry, Patrick	128, 129
Fibber McGee & Molly	25
Fisher, Addison W.	172
Flack, E. E.	39, 40
Fletcher, Joseph	65, 85
Forell, George	45
Fosdick, Harry Emerson	31
Francineau, Robert and Patricia	97
Francisco, Adam S.	140
French, Francis Arthur John	20
Fuller, Charles	57
Fuller, Daniel	57
Fullhard, Marthe and Willy	117
Gaebelein, Frank E.	56
Geisler, Norman	59, 86
Geissert, Fritz	117
Genghis Khan	54, 123
Gerstner, John H.	57
Gewirth, Alan	17
Gildersleeve, The Great	25
Godber, Joyce	103
Goddard, Robert	27
Golden, Jack	79, 92
Gordon, David Stott	52
Grafton, Anthony	14
Grant, Hugh	117
Greenleaf, Simon	81, 82, 85–94
Griffith-Jones, Robin	84

283

Grounds, Vernon	64	Horton, John Theodore	22, 169
Guégan, Bertrand	142	Horton, Michael	115
Habermas, Gary	13, 115	Houlbert, Valérie	153, 154
Haden-Taylor, Susan	114	Howard, Jay	78
Hailsham, Lord	83	Howe, John	62
Hall, James Parker	72	Hubbard, David Allan	56
Halverson, Richard	61	Huber, Donald L.	52
Hamilton, William	56	Hughes, Lisa	94, 95
Händel, Georg Friedrich	148	Humbert, Willy	118
Hanegraaff, Hank	90	Hunter, Howard	118
Harris, Laird	259	Hurlburt, J. C.	169
Hassan, Prince of Jordan	77	Ibsen, Henrik	150
Hazen, Craig	115	Jaki, Stanley	87
Hein, Steven	124	Janssen, F. A.	48
Heitzig, Skip	62	Jenkins, David	104
Hemingway, Ernest	82, 149	Johnson, John F.	54
Henry, Carl F. H.	51, 56, 62, 80	Johnson, J. W.	137
		Johnson, Samuel	144
Herbert, George	11	Jones, Bob Jr.	56
Higgins, Jack	114, 115	Jones, Robert	137
Hodeir, André	18	Jordan, Neal	32
Hoffman, Irving	32	Joyce, James	22, 33
Hoffman, W. Howard	114, 145	Juergensen, Art	73
Hogg, Edward	99, 114, 118, 119	Jung, Carl Gustav	64
		Kaiser, Walter	59
Hollande, François	133, 139	Kantonen, T. A.	39
Holmes, Arthur F.	65	Kant, Ronald de	97
Holmes, Sherlock	80, 104, 105, 261	Kantzer, Kenneth	52, 59, 62
		Kedington, Ambrose	21
Hooker, Richard	92	Kedington, Roger	21
Hooper, Walter	44	Keillor, Garrison	36, 99
Hoover, J. Edgar	180		

Index of Names

Keith, Scott	130, 136
Kennedy, Howard	107
Kennedy, James	61
King, Anne	34
Kloha, Jeffrey	128
Klug, Eugene	98
Kohl, Helmut	117
Korte, Don and Mary	126, 127
Koukl, Gregory	115
Krueger, Harold	57
Kucks, Mike	123
Lancaster, Burt	118
Langdell, Christopher Columbus	72
LeFoe, Dominic	149
Leonard, Graham	87
Levis-Baudin, L.	147
Lewis, C. S.	30, 44, 61, 144, 180
Lewis, Sinclair	37
Ley, Willy	27
Lienhard, Marc	49, 50
Lincoln, Abraham	79, 148
Lindbeck, George	45
Lindsell, Harold	13, 62, 86, 87, 146, 181
Litz, Letetia	98
Litz, Stanton	99
Liviu, Damian	110
Loetscher, L. A.	40
Lombardi, Vince	178
Loo, Beverly	94
Lund, Jacky	25
Lund, Soren	25
Luther, Kendrick	171
Luther, Martin	14, 30, 39, 40, 46, 59, 66, 68, 71, 76, 89, 117, 125, 139, 144, 146, 182
Lutzer, Erwin	58, 61, 87
Lutzweiler, James	14, 42, 142, 177
Maas, Korey D.	140
Mackay, Lord	82, 83
Macron, Emmanuel	133, 139
Mahler, Gustav	148
Maier, Paul	90
Maier, Walter A.	137
Malcolm, Norman	34
Manske, Charles	80, 115, 270
Marshall, Catherine	121, 122
Marshall, Peter	121
Martin, Edward	120
Martin, Walter	75, 77, 79, 80, 86, 90, 144
Marty, Martin	181
Masinelli, Tony	61
Maugham, W. Somerset	133, 139
Mayer, Johann Friedrich	71
McCarthy, Charlie	25
McCollum, Laura	123
McCollum, Steve	123
Mc-Connell, William H.	171
McDowell, Josh	92, 115

Index of Names

Mcilroy, David H.	84
McWilliams, Albin	26
Mendelssohn, Felix Bartholdy	148
Menuge, Angus	115, 126, 136, 248
Menzing, Pastor	74
Meyer, Robert	91
Milkon, Harvey	90
Millar, Morgan	172
Miller, Dallas	79, 115
Miller, George D.	172
Milton, John	149
Moeckel, Ed	38
Moen, John	79
Monteux, Pierre	96
Montgomery, Ann Jane	155, 162
Montgomery, Bernard of Alamein	18
Montgomery, Bessie L.	28, 168
Montgomery, B. G. de	17
Montgomery, Catherine	111
Montgomery, Elizabeth Warwick	167
Montgomery, Francis J.	19
Montgomery, Harriette G.	19, 22, 168, 169, 172, 173
Montgomery, James Franklin	19, 168, 172
Montgomery, James R.	168
Montgomery, Jean-Marie	21, 22, 115–117, 145, 238, 266, 271
Montgomery, John Warwick (Great Grandfather)	18, 19, 144, 155, 168
Montgomery, Joyce Ann Bailer	37, 38, 88, 94–96, 116, 183
Montgomery, Lany	18, 88, 96–101, 103, 110, 112, 115–118, 124–126, 138, 142, 145, 261, 264–266
Montgomery, Mary Ann	23, 28, 88, 121, 126, 168
Montgomery, Maurice Warwick	19, 29, 167, 168
Montgomery, May	19
Montgomery, Roger de	17, 20, 21
Moore, James	58
Moore, Pomeroy	81, 91, 92, 98
Moore, Russell D.	116
Moore, Will	17, 61, 62, 115, 145
Moreland, J. P.	115
Morgenson, Don	45, 182
Morgenson, Donald	46
Morris, John	104
Mueller, Marlène and Alphonse	117
Muller, Kurt Oscar	116
Murray, William	63
Newman, John Henry	33, 136
Newman, Paul	150

286

Index of Names

Nicholi, Armand	32, 87	Preus, Robert	55, 75, 98
Nietzsche, Friedrich	139	Proust, Marcel	149
Nightingale, Florence	180	Puccini, Giacomo	149
Nixon, Bryan	62	Rabacu, Ion	232
Noll, Mark	58	Raugust, Ramon	91
Norris, J. Frank	181	Reagan, Ronald	148
North, Helen	34	Redal, Reuben H.	98–101
Noual, Eric	137	Rice, John R.	
Obama, Barack	117	and Mrs. John R.	34
Ockenga, Harold John	56, 61	Rider, Barry A. K.	84
O'Hair, Madalyn Murray	62, 63, 181	Robbins, John	86
		Robertson, Arthur Henry	81, 87
Osborne, Oz	130	Robertson, Pat	108
Otten, Herman	54	Robinson, James M.	31
Ove, Bob	38	Robinson, Joseph	84
Parton, Craig	86, 115, 130, 236, 263	Rodgers, Thomas	118, 119
		Rohr Sauer, Alfred von	53
Parton, Ellen	130, 136	Romberg, Sigmund	144
Pascal	135, 144, 152	Ronning, Halvor	80, 194, 257
Patterson, Paige	177	Rook, Ron	88
Patton, Thomas	119	Roosevelt, Teddy	148
Paul, Leroy	54, 103	Rosenbladt, Rod	55, 88, 96, 103, 115, 130, 136, 145, 263
Paxson, Ruth	31		
Pelikan, Jaroslav	41	Rosenbladt, Ted	145
Pierard, Richard	64	Rostopovich, Mstislav	148
Pike, James	56, 65	Routley, Erik	45
Pope, Marvin	178	Rowe, E. E.	172
Popkin, Richard H.	43	Sadat, Anwar el-	76, 77
Potzern, Benjamin	71	Saint Exupery, Antoine	180
Poulos, George	61	Sanford, Terry	177
Pound, Roscoe	72	Sarkozy, Nicolas	117, 148
Preus, Jacob	53, 55, 74		

Index of Names

Saward, Michael 141, 178
Scaer, David 75
Schaeffer, Francis 65
Schirrmacher, Christine 110
Schirrmacher, Thomas 13, 17, 42, 52, 62, 110, 115, 138, 141, 145, 247
Schumacher, Robert 88
Schwarz, Jeff 137
Schweitzer, Albert 263
Sekulow, Jay 108, 111
Service, Robert 180
Shackelton, Ernest 181
Shakespeare, William 41, 82, 145
Sherlock, Thomas 84
Sherlock, William 84
Shestack, Jerome 93
Sider, Ronald 42
Sittler, Lucien 117
Smith, Alexander McCall 149
Smith, Chuck 81
Smith, Fred R. 22, 168–172
Smith, Jacob A. 88
Smith, Jennie 171
Smith, Rodell 169, 171
Smith, Wilbur 30, 59, 87
Sproul, R. C. 86
Stainer, John 148
Stalin, Joseph 180
Steadman, Melvin Lee 74
Steiner, William A. 84
Stephenson, Carl 33
Stevens, Chauncey 172
Stewart, Don 92
Stewart, John 92
Strindberg, August 150
Stroll, Avrum 43, 44
Strombeck, J. F. 31
Taft, William Howard 71
Tarlev, Vasile 228, 232
Thackeray, William Makepeace 141, 178
Thatcher, Margaret 148
Thompson, Wesley Scott 110
Thornwell, J. H. 86
Tillich, Paul 180
Tischer, Herr, of East German Tourist Bureau 67
Todd, Richard 121
Toepel, Friedrich 138
Tollefsen, John 135
Trembath, Harry 101
Tuttle, Harvey 168
Tyrrell, Alan 106
Ungerer, Toni 18
Vahanian, Gabriel 49
Veith, Gene Edward 115, 120, 125, 127, 140
Vigness, Paul G. 98, 99
Voeltzel, René 69
Voronin, Vladimir 228
Voss, Kevin 126
Wagner, Richard 149

Index of Names

Walker, Graham	121, 125	Williams, Vaughan	93, 96
Wallach, Luitpold	34	Winchell, C M.	37
Wallis, Jim	58	Winrich, Debra and Kurt	130, 145
Wanvig, John	89		
Warwick (family)	18	Wittgenstein, Ludwig	135
Watrous, Guy	23	Woodbridge, John	58
Webber, Lloyd	150	Woodward, Bob	92
Weil, Simone	28	Wordsworth, William	177
Wellman Watrous, Flora	22, 23, 24, 144, 168–170, 172, 173	Wren, Christopher	148
		Wyrtzen, Jack	33, 62
Wendel, François	47, 49	Wythe, George	121
Wetterlé, E.	116	Yamauchi, Edwin	64
Wilde, Oscar	11	Young, Andrew W.	18
Wilder-Smith, Oliver	115	Youngmark, Bill	180
Wilder, Thornton	149	Zacharias, Craig	59
Wilken, Todd	137, 138	Zacharias, Ravi	58, 59
Wilkerson, Ralph	78	Zuidema, Jason	43
Williams, Edward T.	22, 167		

Places

Africa	31, 110, 115
Albuquerque	62
Alexandria	74
Alsace	49, 51, 116, 151, 180, 262, 263
Ankara	139
Antrim, County	18, 19, 167
Ashwan	77
Australia	66, 88, 115, 138
Baden-Baden	116
Ballymena	18
Bedfordshire	127, 218
Beijing	66, 136, 138, 150
Berkeley	37, 39
Berlin	42
Bischwiller	69
Bonn	110
Bucharest	109, 221, 233, 247
Buffalo	18, 19, 168
Bulgaria	223, 225
California	37, 38, 62, 71, 72, 75, 80, 89, 91–96, 101, 103, 121, 130 (Southern), 136, 175, 246
Canada	31, 37, 42, 43, 53, 79
Castile	26
Chicago	41, 42, 52, 56, 60, 61, 63–65, 71, 87, 128, 177, 181, 246
China	66, 136, 138, 151, 260
Cologne	50
Crater Lake	180
Down, County	18
Dublin	136
Eisenach	66
Eisleben	66
England	17, 20, 21, 50, 58, 61, 72, 81–85, 87, 95, 98, 100, 101, 103, 104, 106, 112, 115, 121, 134, 135, 136, 137, 141, 242, 246, 258
Erfurt	66
Fiji	66, 88, 138
Florida	24, 25
France	14, 17, 20, 21, 39, 45, 48, 51, 53, 68, 70, 73, 76, 78, 81, 91, 94, 118, 123, 130–133, 137, 138, 141, 151, 239–243, 246, 262, 270
Germany	45, 48, 50, 51, 66, 67, 68, 71, 80, 109, 110, 116, 128
Glasgow	18
Greece	87, 134, 219, 223, 224, 226
Hawaii	112, 138
Heidelberg	50
Hong Kong	151
Illinois	45, 52, 68, 74, 79, 114
Indiana	38, 39, 55, 74, 98, 99, 114
Ireland	18, 19, 20, 130, 167, 168

290

Index of Places

Israel	76, 77, 80	Moscow	107, 134, 220, 221, 228, 246
Istanbul	68, 139	Nantes	132, 133
Ithaca	32, 34, 35	Nevada	114
Izmir	111, 139	Newburgh	99, 114, 118, 119
Jamaica	115	New York	18, 22, 27, 32, 38, 42, 61, 74, 88, 118, 131, 167, 168
Jamestown	121		
Jerusalem	19, 80, 259		
Kentucky	39	New York City	32, 38, 42, 88, 167
Keuka Lake	27		
Kiltartan	20, 153	New Zealand	66, 88, 115, 138
Kitchener	42, 43	Niederroedern	117
Kracow	138	Ohio	38, 39, 52, 55
Las Vegas	114	Oxbridge	102
Lidlington	103, 104, 140, 218	Oxford	102, 103, 106
London	17, 18, 44, 80, 81, 94, 100–105, 111–113, 121, 140, 141, 148–150, 177, 247, 261, 274	Paris	45, 48, 96, 108, 109, 116, 117, 131 (Lassere), 132, 136, 137, 141, 142, 150, 151, 184, 242, 243, 246, 275
Los Angeles	90, 99	Philadelphia	92, 137
Lucerne	97	Poland	138
Luton	102, 103, 113	Rochester	19
Mainz	50	Romania	107, 109, 115, 247
Marseilles	139	San Diego	43
Mequon	126	Scandinavia	115
Mexico City	98	Scotland	18, 50
Milan	149	Singapore	112
Milwaukee	56, 126	Soufflenheim	117, 144
Missouri	38, 53, 54, 55–58, 75, 89, 101, 103, 126, 137, 138	Springfield	38, 40, 55, 56, 74
		Ste Foi de Montgommery	21
Moldova	107, 108, 219, 220, 227–230, 232	St Germain de Montgommery	21, 147, 271

Index of Places

St Louis 53, 54, 101, 103, 128, 137, 138
St Petersburg 25
Strasbourg 39, 45, 47–51, 55 68–70, 73, 75, 81, 88, 91, 93–96, 100, 101, 108, 110, 115–117, 120, 123, 124, 126, 130, 133, 134, 135, 137, 138, 143, 150, 232, 236, 242, 246, 247, 262
Switzerland 43, 50, 57, 76, 97, 240
Tacoma 98, 99, 100, 101, 112
Tonga 138
Toronto 42, 43, 45, 105
Turkey 68, 111, 139, 224, 227
United Kingdom 19, 20, 83, 87, 114, 117, 131, 242
Vancouver 96
Versailles 242
Virginia 61, 74, 79, 120, 121, 148, 246
Wales 17, 82, 85, 120, 134, 242, 246, 275
Warsaw 18, 19, 22–24, 26, 29, 31, 38, 132, 133, 167, 168, 170–172
Washington 27, 61, 71, 73, 74, 98, 100, 120, 246
Waterloo 42, 43, 44, 45, 51, 99
Williamsburg 121, 148
Wisconsin 127
Wittenberg 39, 45, 52, 66, 71
Wyoming, County 19, 24, 26, 131, 168, 171
Yorktown 121

www.ingramcontent.com/pod-product-compliance
Lightning Source LLC
Chambersburg PA
CBHW050339230426
43663CB00010B/1920